W9-CBE-646

Green Mountain
BOYS *of* SUMMER

Green Mountain Boys *of* SUMMER

Vermonters in the Major Leagues
1882-1993

Edited by Tom Simon

The New England Press, Inc.
Shelburne, Vermont

In Memory of
Guy Waterman
May 1, 1932 - February 6, 2000

Publishers: Al and Maggie Rosa
Editor: Mark Wanner
Text Design: Mark Wanner
Cover Design: Andrea Gray
Marketing Associate: Megan Berman

© 2000 by Tom Simon

All rights reserved. No part of this book may be reproduced or transmitted in any form or by any means, electronic or mechanical, including photocopying, recording, or by any information storage and retrieval system, without permission in writing from the publisher, except by a reviewer, who may quote brief passages in a review.

Manufactured in the United States of America
First edition
Cover Painting "Gardner Safe at Third" by Lance Richbourg

For additional copies of this book or for a catalog of our other titles, please write:

The New England Press
P.O. Box 575
Shelburne, VT 05482

or e-mail: nep@together.net

Visit us on the Web at www. nepress.com

Photographs on pp. 50, 98, 133, 151, 157 courtesy of the National Baseball Hall of Fame Library, Cooperstown, New York
Photograph on p. 15 courtesy of Transcendental Graphics

Library in Congress Cataloging in Publication Data

Green Mountain boys of summer: Vermonters in the Major Leagues, 1882-1993 / edited by Tom Simon.-- 1st ed.
    p. cm.
  Includes index.
  ISBN 1-881535-35-5 (cloth) -- ISBN 1-881535-36-3 (paper)
  1. Baseball players--Vermont--Biography. I. Simon, Tom (Thomas P.), 1965-

 GV865.A1 G72 2000
 796.357'092'2743--dc21

                                          00-023545

Contents

Vermont is a small state and the players she has contributed
to the big show are few in comparison with such other states
as California or Pennsylvania. But when Vermont produces a
player, she produces a good one.

John J. Ward
Baseball Magazine
November 1920

Foreword

To the uninitiated, Vermont may be closer to the last than the first state one associates with baseball. Even a native Vermonter who threw baseballs fast enough to reach the major leagues remembers throwing more snowballs. But as Vermonters know—and this wonderful history conveys—we have green diamonds as well as green mountains, summers as well as winters.

For more than a century, from the Worcester Ruby Legs to the Boston Red Sox, Vermonters have played in the major leagues. It is a rare achievement, to be sure, but the rarity reveals a hundred years of dreams. Recounted here are the lives of thirty-four Vermonters who "made the majors," reflecting what is changed and changeless—in baseball as well as in Vermont.

In the middle of this century, a Vermont summer—at least for a boy freed from chores—was spent playing ball. So familiar was the ritual that my dog bounded for the field as soon as I reached for my bat and glove. I can still see him pacing the pasture's diamond, impatient for the game to begin. If the baseball of my Vermont boyhood had more in common with the century's beginning than its end, these vignettes reflect how deeply the game's pastoral roots have been planted.

But the big leagues meant big cities. Vermont readers in particular will be fascinated by the stories of country boys in the city. Rutland may have been larger than Los Angeles in 1882, when the first Vermonter made his major league debut, but it wasn't as urban as New York, or even Boston. From hard-drinking brawlers to college graduates for whom major league baseball was a footnote to an accomplished professional life, the boys from the Green Mountains were exposed to a very different world. When one reads that a Vermonter handed tips directly to African-American porters instead of joining teammates in the practice of humiliating them by throwing the change on the floor, one learns something about the country, baseball, and Vermont.

Vermont had already produced two presidents by 1882. There have been none from Vermont since. Of the thirty-four Vermonters who have played major league baseball, only four have played within the last two decades. Shelby Foote has said that for every southern boy reliving the Civil War, time stops on July 3, 1863, when Pickett began his charge at Gettysburg. It may be that for every Vermont boy reliving a World Series, it will never be later than 12:33 a.m., October 22, 1975.

Then again, if future major leaguers sprout from beginnings as improbable as these, one spring morning when the sun is warming and the snow is melting, a young Vermonter will pack snow into a ball and let it fly. And, if he is very good and very lucky, there will be another major league baseball player from Vermont—where the summers make the game and the winters make the memories.

JEFF AMESTOY
WATERBURY CENTER, VT.
JUNE 29, 1999

Acknowledgments

First of all, I'm deeply indebted to the membership of the Larry Gardner (Vermont) Chapter of the Society for American Baseball Research ("SABR"), without whom this book never would have been written. In particular, I'd like to thank Lance Richbourg for his spectacular cover painting and Guy Waterman for his editorial advice and general wisdom.

We are fortunate to have as fine a publisher as New England Press, which does a beautiful job publishing books of regional interest. My thanks to Al and Maggie Rosa for taking a chance on our project and to our editor, Mark Wanner, who is hereby made an honorary member of the Larry Gardner Chapter—even if he prefers tennis to baseball.

We caught another break when the Vermont Historical Society decided to put up a two-year gallery exhibit entitled "Baseball in Vermont: An Enduring Love of the Game." My thanks to Jackie Calder, Gainor Davis, and Martha Nye of V.H.S. for their enthusiasm for our project.

My special thanks to Chief Justice Jeffrey Amestoy of the Vermont Supreme Court for writing the Foreword. Thanks also to John Dumville of the Vermont Division for Historic Preservation for his support of baseball-related roadside historical markers.

We made extensive use of three special collections in our research. The clippings files at the National Baseball Library were invaluable, and I'd like to thank Jim Gates, Tim Wiles, Cory Seeman, and Scot Mondore for their help and hospitality during the Gardner Chapter's three roadtrips to Cooperstown. The University of Vermont's archives and the Wilbur Collection at the Bailey-Howe Library were rich sources of material on UVM alumni in particular and Vermont history in general. We were also fortunate to have access to the Tom Shea Collection, which is currently under the stewardship of Dick Thompson. Without Mr. Shea, one of SABR's greatest biographical researchers, we would know next to nothing about several of the more obscure early players presented in this book.

The best thing about this project was meeting the players and their families, many of whom have become great friends. My thanks to the following: Margaret Cusick; Paul Abbey; Betty Abbey Royce; Katie Quinn; Arlington Pond; Frederick Dupee; John Gardner; Larry Gardner, Jr.; Vadis Gardner Rhodes; Ray Collins, Jr.; John Leidy; Georges Leclair III; Harriet Stafford Mitiguy; John Durkee; Bill Keefe; David Keefe; Gary Keefe; Gordon Keefe; Margaret Keefe Rooney; Mary FitzSimonds Rini; Donna Marzouk; any other Keefes I accidentally omitted; Oscar Maki; Robert Murray, Jr.; David Slayton; Crip Polli; Margaret Polli Caccavo; Birdie Tebbetts; Steve Lanfranconi; Carol Ann Lanfranconi Lapham; Dave Lapointe; Kit Lapointe; Ernie Johnson; Calvin Fisk; Leona Fisk; Cecil Fisk; Pat Putnam; Marguerite Burrell; Len Whitehouse; Mark Brown; Tony Lupien; Bill Lee; Bill Rochford; and Chris Rochford.

Finally, the contributors and I thank the following who assisted our project in many ways: Allen Beebe; Alban Berthiaume; Jim Bready; Marty Brownsey; Bruce Butterfield; Scott Cahoon; Craig Carter; Chuck Clarino of the *Rutland Herald*; Bill Corcoran; Tracy Daw; Mary Densmore; Jeanne and Dennis DeValeria; Richard Edmunds of the Bethel Historical Society; Elsa; Kim Ehritt of Middlebury College Alumni Records; Cappy Gagnon;

Janice Geraw of the Enosburgh Historical Society; Pauline Giamola and Rick Leggett of the St. Michael's College Archives; Dario Giannelli; Josh Goyette; Maggie Hale and Nancy Dean of the Cornell University Division of Rare and Manuscript Collections; Carolyn Hanson; Roger Harris; Harry Hayden; Sylvia Holden; William Horn of the F. W. Olin Foundation, Inc.; Judy Hoyt of Orleans' Jones Memorial Library; Robert C. Jones; Jeff Kaufman of "The Talk of Vermont"; Kensey; Barbara Krieger of the Dartmouth College Archives; Karen Lane of Barre's Aldrich Library; Jeffrey LaValley of Dean College Alumni Programs; S. Patrick Mahar; Mark McGuire; Steve McNeil; Joane Mechalak of the Tufts University Archives; Dave Moore; David Nemec; Ray Nemec; Ann Oakman of the Proctor Free Library; Joe Overfield; Guy Page of the *Colchester Chronicle*; Jean Peterson of the Vermont Marble Company; David Pietrusza; Bob Ratti; Joseph Reaves; Bob Richardson; Charlie Ross; Russell Ross; Tim Ryan; Ralph Silva; Gwenda Smith of the Strafford Historical Society; Frederica Templeton of the Burr & Burton Seminary Archives; Hank Thompson; Bill Twomey; Dale Walter of the Olin Corporation; Laura Waterman; and Mylinda Woodward of the University of New Hampshire Archives.

TOM SIMON

Introduction

Shivering in a windswept barn in Essex Center as the drizzle outside turned to flurries, three grown men—baseball archaeologists—rummaged through a pile of old cast-iron farm gadgets, half-expecting to pull a bat or a ball from among the rusted pulleys and horseshoes. Thousands of teetering old barns grace the Vermont landscape. What made this one special is that it once belonged to Bert Abbey.

Who is Bert Abbey? He's one of a select group of Vermont ballplayers to reach the major leagues. Don't feel ignorant if you didn't know that. We didn't either until we started doing research for this book. In fact, as little as three years ago we felt we had a securely secret code if we left messages on each other's answering machines: "Hey, Bert Abbey, this is Heinie Stafford. Give me a call."

Now Abbey, Stafford, and their ilk are heroes, practically household names—that is, in the few-dozen households that include active members of the Larry Gardner (Vermont) Chapter of the Society for American Baseball Research ("SABR"). A network of more than 6,000 baseball fanatics, SABR has more than forty members in the Green Mountains, giving Vermont the distinction of having more SABR members per capita than any other state.

The Larry Gardner Chapter was founded in a Shelburne living room during Game One of the 1993 World Series. Since then we've held meetings all over the state with special guest speakers like former major leaguers and award-winning authors; helped establish an annual Larry Gardner Day celebration in his hometown of Enosburg Falls; persuaded the legislature to fund historic site markers for Burlington's Centennial Field and the birthplaces

of Gardner and Ray Collins; made several annual pilgrimages to the National Baseball Hall of Fame and Library in Cooperstown; played Town Ball (an early version of baseball) at the Calvin Coolidge Homestead; and thrown a party on the 100th anniversary of Babe Ruth's birth, complete with videotapes of two Babe Ruth movies and Ruthian servings of barbecued ribs and beer. Along the way we've had a lot of fun and made many new friends.

But the "R" in SABR stands for Research, and while a few of us had published an article or two on baseball, most had done nothing of the sort. So approximately two years ago we decided as a group to research and write a book with a chapter on each of the Vermont-born players listed in the Fourth Edition of *Total Baseball*, the official encyclopedia of Major League Baseball.

We decided to limit the book to only those players listed in *Total Baseball* as having been born in Vermont. Thus, Carlton Fisk and Mark Brown are included even though they returned to their New Hampshire homes as soon as they were released from the hospital in Bellows Falls, Vermont, where both were born. Mike Rochford is not, even though he moved to South Burlington from Massachusetts as an infant. Several "Flatlanders of Summer"—adopted Vermonters like Rochford, Tony Lupien, and Bill Lee—have such strong ties to the state that they merited mention in a separate section.

In the early innings of our research, one of the things we learned is that the birthplaces listed in *Total Baseball* are not written in stone (though the book is so heavy that it almost feels that way). SABR's national biographical committee finds dozens of errors every year, and we turned up a few ourselves. According to fairly conclusive evidence, three of the "Vermont" players—Sun Daly, Arlington Pond, and Crip Polli—weren't born in Vermont at all. Each, however, is listed as a Vermonter in *Total Baseball*, and after some discussion we decided to leave Pond and Polli in the lineup because of their significant contributions to Vermont baseball. Daly has been omitted, because his only connection to the state was the one summer he played for a Rutland town team.

Those born in the Green Mountains hailed from every corner of Vermont, from St. Albans and St. Johnsbury in the north to North Pownal and Brattleboro in the south. Eleven of the state's fourteen counties are represented. The players also comprise a fair sampling of the ethnic groups that make up the state's population: Yankee farmers like Bert Abbey, Ray Collins, and Ray Fisher; French-Canadians like Lee Viau, Jean Dubuc, and Ralph Lapointe; Irishmen like Ed Doheny, Amby McConnell, and Dave Keefe; Italians like Crip Polli and Walt Lanfranconi; and Scandinavians like Elmer Bowman and Ernie Johnson.

The biggest surprise was the colorful variety of their lives, both in and out of baseball. Here are a few of the Green Mountain Boys in capsule form:

• an engineer who played major league baseball as a summer job during college, then got serious and launched a business career that made him a multi-millionaire and founder of a Fortune 500 company;

• a psychotic lefthander who turned violent and was locked up in an insane asylum, even as his teammates participated in the first-ever World Series;

• a physician who left the Baltimore Orioles in midseason to enlist in the Spanish-American War and became a national hero in the Philippines for his inspirational labors to control leprosy, yellow fever, malaria, and cholera;

• a schoolteacher and masterful pitcher who was unjustly banished from baseball in 1921, became a legendary college baseball coach for four decades, then was triumphantly reinstated as a player in good standing just short of his ninety-fifth birthday;

• and a man who made the last out of the 1916 season in his only at-bat in the majors, but went on to invent a process that revolutionized the manufacture of women's stockings and who later served in the Vermont legislature.

For more than half of the thirty-four included players we managed to track down relatives, which often led to scrapbooks, photo albums, family legends, and treasured memorabilia. One of the six to whom we spoke directly was Mark Brown, a pitcher of recent vintage who won a single game in his entire major league career. Researcher Jeremy Rosenberg described the experience:

He sat with me in the break room at Milt & Ron's Transmission Shop, still wearing a uniform (powder blue with a patch over each breast), hands still dirty like a ballplayer's. I watched him interact with customers, employees seeking counsel, his brother-in-law and father-in-law regarding prices, and all the while dealing with a newcomer inquiring into events from a part of life long since past. A couple weeks later he sent me a thank you note. Imagine him, the ballplayer, thanking me, the historian!

To those of us who worked on this book, these Green Mountain Boys are more than just baseball players. We became obsessed with finding every last detail about their lives—even going so far as to poke around in an old barn looking for who-knows-what.

TOM SIMON
BURLINGTON, VT.
JANUARY 18, 2000

NOTE: *Anyone interested in joining the Larry Gardner Chapter of SABR may request a membership application by writing to Tom Simon, 118 Spruce Street, Burlington, VT 05401.*

Early Vermonters

(1882-1903)

The National League was beginning its seventh season on May 1, 1882, when twenty-four-year-old Fred Mann took the field in the top of the first inning at the Worcester Driving Park Grounds. In an auspicious debut, Mann went three-for-five that day and handled six chances flawlessly at third base, leading the Worcester Ruby Legs to a 6-5 win over their arch-rivals, the Boston Red Caps. What nobody noticed at the time was that Mann had thus become the first Vermonter to play in a major league baseball game.

Though early baseball was primarily an urban pastime, the Green Mountain State supplied a healthy share of major leaguers before the turn of the century. In addition to Mann, four more played during the 1880s, including Henry Porter of Vergennes, who won thirty-three games for the 1885 Brooklyn Grays, and Lee Viau of Corinth, who notched twenty-two wins as a Cincinnati Reds rookie in 1888. Other pitchers came along in the 1890s: Harry Burrell of Bethel in 1891; Essex farmer Bert Abbey the following year; and Northfield's Ed Doheny and Rutland's Arlington Pond in 1895. Of that group only Doheny remained in the majors when the game entered the twentieth century.

A couple of short-timers—Frank Dupee of Monkton and Doc Hazelton of Strafford—had come and gone by the summer of 1903, when Doheny was en route to his second consecutive sixteen-win season for the National League champion Pittsburgh Pirates. While his teammates were playing in the first-ever World Series that fall, however, Doheny was shut away in a Massachusetts asylum—for life, as it turned out. That bizarre and tragic note sounded a somber requiem to an otherwise successful twenty-two-year first act in the history of the Green Mountain Boys of Summer.

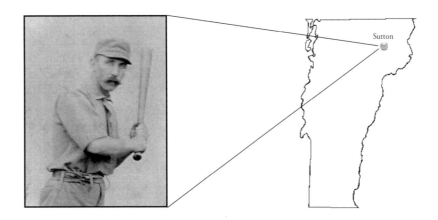

Fred Mann

The First Vermonter

On July 8, 1777, thirty-four delegates gathered at the Windsor Tavern and adopted the first Constitution of the Free and Independent State of Vermont. Fittingly, less than a century later, Windsor was also the place where the first Green Mountain Boy of Summer learned to play baseball. Though Fred Mann was born on April 1, 1858, in the Northeast Kingdom village of Sutton, his family moved to the thriving town of Windsor in the Connecticut River Valley sometime in the 1860s.

The Manns lived on Ascutney Street, just down the street from Windsor State Prison. Fred and his sister, Hattie, attended Windsor High School, where Fred was one of thirteen students who graduated in 1876. A few weeks later he marched with the volunteer firemen in the annual Independence Day parade, which took on special importance as a celebration of the nation's centennial. Of course, Fred was a member of the "Windsor boys" baseball team that was to play a game as part of that celebration, but it was one of many events washed out by rain.

Amateur Base Ball in Fred Mann's Day

Windsor calls itself the "Birthplace of Vermont," and it may also be the birthplace of baseball fever in Vermont. The sport was so popular in town that by July 1875 the editors of *The Vermont Journal* chided their readership that it may have become too important in the life of the community:

The "national game" of base ball will soon give way to the more useful and practical science of rifle shooting, and the liability to broken bones and blackened eyes is nothing in the latter compared to that of the former. Besides, in case of a public emergency so vital to the country's welfare as the unpleasantness of 1860, the value of an organization of off-hand rifle shooters could scarcely be estimated.

But the readership failed to take heed. In the summer of 1876 *The Journal* reported several matches in Windsor. For example:

The Jones and Lamson mill boys have challenged the town boys to a game of Baseball, to be played on the grounds back of the depot on Saturday, the 22nd at 3:30 o'clock.

The Shoe Shop hands challenged the clerks in the stores in the village to play a game of ball, Wednesday evening which resulted in a victory to the club—after four innings—by a score of 40 to 9. A large crowd collected on the Commons to witness the game. The uniform was unique in the extreme.

A game of baseball was played, on Saturday between the "Livelys," Capt. Wm. Pollard and the "Slowlys," Capt. E. S. Cole—the "Livelys" winning by a score of 14 to 8.

Those games weren't pick-up events, nor part of any organized league, but arranged affairs with captains and commercial or civic sponsors. That was the world of amateur baseball in which Fred Mann learned his trade.

Mann's exact path from Windsor to the major leagues isn't clear, but we know that it was by way of Massachusetts. The *Boston Globe* mentions him playing in 1880 for the Westfield Firemen and the following year for the Hammond "nine" of the Worcester Shop League. Presumably Mann hoped to land a position on a traveling professional club. In those days semipro teams derived much of their revenue from exhibition games with National League teams, and it wasn't unusual for an N.L. team to visit a small city, sign up one or more of the best local players, and take them away.

Mann's first break came on July 28, 1880, when the touring Washington Nationals came to Springfield, Massachusetts. The Nationals had already played exhibitions in Springfield against Cleveland and Chicago earlier that week, and now they were scheduled to play Cincinnati. On the day before the game, however, Washington's right fielder became ill. Because the team toured with only one player per position, a local substitute was needed. In the summer of 1880, the best amateur player in the Springfield area was twenty-two-year-old Fred Mann of

At 5' 10½" and 180 pounds, Fred Mann was more powerfully built than most players of his era. [National Baseball Hall of Fame Library, Cooperstown, New York]

the Westfield Firemen. Batting ninth in the order, Mann failed to hit safely and the *New York Clipper* blamed Washington's one-run loss on the "amateur who played right field." Though the game didn't have a storybook ending, it wouldn't be Mann's last opportunity to break into fast company.

In those days Worcester, the second-largest city in Massachusetts, fielded a National League team called the Ruby Legs. In 1881, while Mann was playing in the Worcester Shop League, the Ruby Legs were finishing last, plagued by dissension, rowdiness, and accusations of game throwing. Vowing to field a team of men with good character in 1882, new manager Freeman Brown purged his roster of all but six of the returning players and recruited Mann as one of the replacements. During Worcester's exhibition season the Vermonter played third base, securing a place on the team by banging out a single, two doubles, and a triple in an 18-12 rout of Harvard College.

Once the National League season began, however, the rookie from the Green Mountain State struggled.

This photo shows that Mann was a lefthanded batter, but it's unknown which arm he used to throw. The catcher shown here, incidentally, is Hall-of-Famer Wilbert Robinson. [Dick Leyden]

In nineteen games, eighteen of them at third base, Mann batted .234 with five doubles. Though he was by no measure the team's worst hitter, his fielding percentage was .703, dismal even for a third baseman in an era when players didn't wear gloves. His teammates fared no better, and after a fourteen-game losing streak and a 9-32 start, Freeman Brown was fired and several of his players released. One of them was Fred Mann.

With the upstart American Association challenging the National League's monopoly, 1882 was a fine time for Mann to be looking for a job as a professional baseball player. Only two weeks passed between his release by Worcester and his first appearance for the A.A.'s Philadelphia Athletics on June 24, 1882. Mann established himself as one of the heaviest hitters in the Philadelphia lineup, batting third in the order and finishing second on the team in slugging average. Fielding remained a problem—game accounts from 1882 are strewn with comments like "Mann muffed an easy one" or "Mann's error contributed to the loss."

To expand to eight teams for 1883, the American Association created new teams in New York City and Co-lumbus, stocking them predominantly with players from existing franchises. The Columbus Buckeyes selected Mann in the expansion draft, and over the next four seasons he became a solid all-around player. After moving from third base to center field, Mann even won accolades for his defense. The *New York Clipper* reported that he was "playing brilliantly in the field," while *The Sporting Life* credited him for "making difficult catches in the outfield."

As for his offense, the *Clipper* called him "one of the hardest hitters in the country." Mann also had a knack for being hit by pitched balls, and by the end of the 1887 season he was the all-time major league leader in that category. Usually batting cleanup, he had his best season in 1884, leading the Buckeyes in slugging average, triples, and home runs. Mann remained one of the club's top hitters in 1885, when Columbus merged with the Pittsburgh Alleghenys to form one of the Association's best teams.

In 1887 Pittsburgh jumped to the National League and became the Pirates, but for some reason Mann was left off the team. Before spring training the Vermonter signed with the Cleveland Blues, a team of castoffs and

Mann's best seasons came with the 1883-84 Columbus Buckeyes. In this team photo he is seated in the front row, far right. [National Baseball Hall of Fame Library, Cooperstown, New York]

untested amateurs hastily thrown together to fill the void in the American Association left by the departing Pittsburgh franchise. Predictably, the Blues quickly dropped to last place. The surprise came on July 22 when Mann, though leading the Blues with a .309 average, was unaccountably released. The release didn't trouble him for long, as he signed the same day for a second tour of duty with the Philadelphia Athletics. Mann did his part to improve the team by batting .275 down the stretch, but Philadelphia failed to catch Charlie Comiskey's St. Louis Browns, who were en route to their third consecutive world championship.

That offseason the Athletics traded Fred Mann and two others to the Browns for shortstop Bill Gleason. On the face of it, the trade must have come as a pleasant surprise for the Vermonter. Everyone expected him to be a starting outfielder on the reigning world's champions, as demonstrated by the inclusion of four different poses of Mann in a Browns uniform in the Old Judge baseball card series. During the preseason he did nothing to disrupt those expectations, playing right field, batting second, and collecting more than his share of hits.

It must have been a huge surprise, then, for Mann to read the following item in the "late news" section of the April 25 edition of *The Sporting Life*:

> Fred Mann, recently signed by President Von der Ahe to cover either right or center field, will be released either today or Monday. Young Lyons is showing up in such good shape fielding, batting and running the bases that he will be kept in right field and

McCarthy will play center. No fault was found with Mann's work, but President Von der Ahe is a convert to young blood.

As it turned out, Mann was indeed released. "Young Lyons" batted a mere .194 in his only full season with St. Louis, but Tommy McCarthy went on to become a Hall of Famer and the Browns won their fourth consecutive American Association pennant in 1888.

After his release by St. Louis, Fred Mann signed a minor league contract with Charleston of the Southern League. When the league folded in late summer, Mann was recruited to become captain of the Tri-State League's Columbus Senators, returning to the city where he'd established himself as a major leaguer five years earlier. In 1889 he signed with Hartford of the newly formed Atlantic Association, but at thirty-one his skills were beginning to fade. Playing first base, Mann batted only .235. The 1890 season, in which he batted a paltry .169 in twenty-two games, was his last.

Settling down at 24 Wilbraham Avenue in Springfield, the city where he'd played his first game against major league competition a decade earlier, Mann spent his last twenty years as a hotel proprietor and bartender. His life was cut short by prostate cancer on April 6, 1916, and he's buried in Springfield's Oak Grove Cemetery. Of the places where Mann worked, both the Feeding Hills House and the Brightside Inn no longer exist. The Gilmore House where Mann once tended bar still stands, along with his indelible record in *Total Baseball* as the first of the Green Mountain Boys of Summer.

DICK LEYDEN

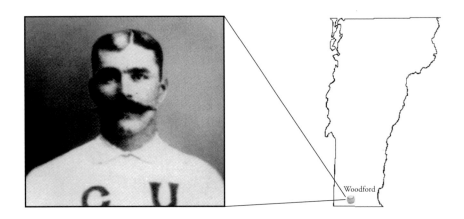

Frank Olin

From Backwoods to Big Business

Franklin Walter Olin was born on January 9, 1860, in a backwoods logging camp in Woodford, near the Vermont-Massachusetts line. From that humble beginning he went on to build a multi-million-dollar business that became the giant Olin Corporation, one of the largest in America's military-industrial complex. On his way to a corporate career of wealth and fame, Olin played one glorious summer in the major leagues, batting over .300 with power.

Frank Olin lived in Vermont for seven formative years before his father, a skilled millwright, found work in a sawmill across the nearby border in New York State. Young Frank went to work at an early age, demonstrating a mastery of tools and an ingenuity that gave promise of his engineering career to come. He scraped together what education he could, partly in public schools, partly on his own at home. It wasn't until after his twenty-first birthday that he gained admittance to Cornell University.

Beginning in the fall of 1881, Olin blossomed at Cornell. He joined no fraternity and shunned most other college diversions, concentrating instead on his studies in civil engineering and taking occasional time off to earn money teaching school or helping his father on mill construction. What time he could spare on campus he devoted to athletics.

In those years college teams received little financial support from the university, instead depending on students to raise and dispense funds. The combined requirements of athletic skill and business acumen per-

fectly suited the talents of young Frank Olin. In his early twenties and having had to work from his earliest years, Olin doubtless was more mature than most of his classmates. He leaped with agile feet into both the sporting events and the business challenges of "running an athletic program on a frayed shoestring," as he later called it.

The strapping freshman won an outfield berth on the varsity nine right away. The next year he shifted to second base, his preferred position. He also took up track, winning the shotput competition at Cornell's field day. He so excelled in marksmanship—a harbinger of his future career in the firearms business—that he was elected captain of the rifle team. In his upperclass years, he rowed with the crew, set school records in putting the shot and slinging the hammer, and emerged as the star of a strong baseball team. Led by "Frankie" Olin, Cornell won the State Intercollegiate League pennant twice and competed against professional clubs. The college newspaper noted with pride: "Olin and the other men are far above college players in general."

Olin hit with authority. In one memorable at-bat on May 1, 1886, against a professional club from Toronto, Frankie tore into a pitch and boomed a shot that would long be celebrated in Cornell legend. More than a half-century later, when the distinguished alumnus returned to inspect an engineering building he'd financed, the batboy of the 1886 team joined his old classmate in pacing off the distance from home plate to the hallowed spot where the ball had landed. It was declared to have traveled 540 feet on the fly.

Besides excelling on the field, Frankie Olin provided leadership in the business management of Cornell athletics. He served as president of the Athletic Association and as a member of the Cornell Athletic Council. His creative engineering genius also came into play on at least a couple occasions. He was instrumental in designing the college's first batting cage, erected within a brick building. He also helped raise funds to pay for both the rent and measures to "protect the windows."

When first confronting curves that dropped, the batsman-engineer conceived and designed a unique response: a curved bat, fashioned from a wagon tongue, which, he reasoned, "allowed him to hit the ball at its exact center." Olin was having difficulty following the ball as it dropped—swinging the bat with the crooked part downward compensated for the extra drop as compared with a straight ball. More than a century later, the Olin-designed bat is regarded as a prized possession in Cornell's athletic office, even though it never caught on with other players.

It was during the summer after his junior year at Cornell that Frank Olin played major league ball. Beginning with the Washington Statesmen of the American Association, one of three major leagues operating in 1884, Olin played twenty-one games and batted .386 for a club that was suffering a disastrous season, dead last in a thirteen-team league. When Washington gave up the ghost in midseason with a 12-51 record, Olin shifted crosstown to the Washington Nationals and was hitless in his only game in the Union Association.

At that point Olin made a move that brought him, for one fleeting moment, in conjunction with a pivotal point in baseball's social history. For the balance of 1884 he returned to the American Association and played for the Toledo Blue Stockings. Also playing for Toledo were the brothers Fleet and Welday Walker, the last two black players allowed on a major league baseball diamond before Jackie Robinson's historic debut in 1947.

The Toledo club fared poorly, slumping to eighth in a twelve-team league with a 46-58 record. Behind their one .300 hitter, rookie second baseman Sam Barkley, Fleet Walker and Frank Olin were the club's second- and third-best hitters. Walker batted .263, while Olin managed .256, playing mostly left field and occasionally relieving Barkley at second. No one else on the team hit better than .240.

Neither Olin nor the Walker brothers intended to terminate their major league careers with their modest 1884 results. The Walkers were, of course, banished by the prevailing racial prejudice of the day. Olin had hoped to play in the National League with the Detroit Wolver-

ines. But for Detroit in 1885 he managed to appear in only one game, going two-for-four and scoring a run, but committing two errors in six chances at third base.

After graduating from Cornell in 1886, Frank Olin launched his career in engineering and business. After one year in a New England patent attorney's office, Olin landed his first engineering job in 1887, assisting the supervising engineer in constructing a powder mill in New Jersey. When the engineer in charge left early, the young Cornell graduate took over and completed the job. That led the following year to an assignment constructing a much bigger mill for the Phoenix Powder Manufacturing Company. The year after that, 1889, Olin set up regular business as the F. W. Olin Company, designing and building powder plants. That same year he married Mary Mott Moulton, who hailed from the Toledo area.

Recognizing the growth potential of America's industrial heartland, Olin moved his business and family to Alton, Illinois, where he lived the rest of his long life. On the Mississippi River twenty-five miles north of St.

More than fifty years after he hit a home run that became a Cornell legend, Frank Olin (right) and the batboy from the 1886 Cornell team step off the distance it traveled. It was determined to have flown 540 feet. [Div. of Rare & Manuscript Collections, Cornell University Library]

Louis, Alton was easily supplied by steamboats, stood close to coal mines, and of course enjoyed unlimited water power. In a succession of business moves, Olin organized companies and created facilities for producing blasting powder for mining operations, ammunition for the newly developed breech-loading shotgun, and a variety of bullets, primers, clay pigeons, and accessories to the firearms and munitions business. Around the turn of the century he fought off a succession of predatory moves by larger companies, including the giant trust, E. I. duPont de Nemours.

As a businessman, Olin was a hard-driving autocrat. A 1953 article in *Fortune* reported that he "ruled with rod of iron," maintaining close personal control of company operations for more than fifty years as chief executive. Olin also had a passion for secrecy. As late as the 1950s, only five of the thirteen directors of the company were allowed to know the breakdown of sales and earnings within the corporation's ten divisions. According to *Fortune*, Olin "never gave a competitor 'good morning' unless the information was already in the public domain."

What transformed Olin's business scope was World War I. Even before American entry, one of his operations landed a fat contract supplying France with ammunition. When the United States finally joined the Allied cause, sales skyrocketed. Wisely avoiding the temptation to overexpand, Olin adjusted to the return of peace and further strengthened his business stability by branching into the growing automotive and appliance markets.

His imaginative but conservative business approach helped him not only to expand during the prosperous 1920s, but also to survive intact the Great Depression of the 1930s. Indeed, in 1931, when one of his chief rivals, Winchester Repeating Arms, collapsed, Olin beat out duPont to take over Winchester's accounts and operations. By 1940 the octogenarian presided over diverse business operations producing annual sales of $45 million.

Just before World War II, Olin stepped down from active management of the business and watched with deep satisfaction as his son John presided over another huge sales bonanza during the war years. Shrewd postwar moves led to the eventual formation of the huge Olin-Mathieson Chemical Corporation in the 1950s. It was the predecessor of today's Olin Corporation, which ranks well up among the "Fortune 500" top corporations of America, with more than $3 billion in annual sales.

Olin Corporation and Olin Hall at Cornell are Frank Olin's visible monuments. But, as one of his classmates reminds us, "buildings are all right in their way but with advancing years it's the memories of home runs and touchdowns that bring comfort." And so it is, in Vermont, that the name of the mighty industrialist is also remembered for his .316 lifetime batting average, his special curved bat for hitting the drop, and that towering home run soaring 540 feet on the fly over the Cornell campus.

GUY WATERMAN

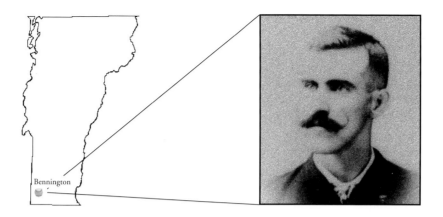

Bennington

Tom Lynch

A Ball Near His Heart

David Nemec's *The Great Encyclopedia of 19th Century Major League Baseball* tells an absorbing story of Thomas J. Lynch.

Nemec's Tom Lynch was a major league ballplayer in the 1880s who went on to umpire in the big time in 1898, 1899, and 1902. He gained brief notoriety in 1890 when he was shot and almost killed in a drunken quarrel in Cohoes, New York. He recovered, however, and assumed prominence in baseball as President of the National League, serving as the N.L.'s chief executive from 1909 to 1913. Nemec then reports that Lynch survived another forty years before succumbing in 1955 at age ninety-four at his home in Cohoes.

The trouble is that Nemec's account combines the lives of two different Thomas J. Lynches. One was an itinerant ballplayer of the 1880s and '90s who enjoyed a brief major league career before returning to his New York home to work for the Cohoes Department of Public Works, dying just a few days short of his ninety-fifth birthday. The other was indeed a well-known umpire who later headed the National League and whose death in New Britain, Connecticut, in 1924 was attended by many of baseball's most significant personages. Nemec's conflation is easy to understand—for years the Hall of Fame's file on League President Thomas J. Lynch mistakenly included *The Sporting Life* item on the other Thomas J. Lynch's ill-fated encounter outside John Donovan's tavern in Cohoes.

Our Tom Lynch is not the dignitary. The Green Mountain Boy is the peripatetic early ballplayer, city la-

borer, and nonagenarian. Even his claim to status as a Vermonter is tenuous. This Thomas James Lynch was born in Bennington, Vermont, on April 3, 1860, the son of Bartholomew and Ann Reilly Lynch, both of County Cavan, Ireland. Shortly after his birth, however, the family moved to Cohoes, and there he grew up, and there he returned when his ballplaying days were over to live out his long life. Vermont, therefore, has only the most literal claim on him (*cf.* Carlton Fisk, among others).

Thomas J. Lynch, the ballplayer, was a rugged and versatile player, well-known for his hitting. *Total Baseball* lists him at 5'10 1/2" and 170 pounds, which was considered large in his time. Lynch played a number of positions on the diamond, including catcher early in his career and later first base and outfield. An item in *The Sporting Life* from 1886 describes him as "a good catcher and a particularly fine hitter." Box scores show him batting in the middle of the order, in the second through fifth spots. While playing for Wilmington in 1884, Lynch was acknowledged in *The Sporting Life* for one game in which he hit three home runs and another when he went five-for-five with two homers. Later in his career, his good batting eye was demonstrated when he reached safely more than ninety times by bases on balls in eighty-one games for Hartford in 1889.

Lynch was a professional ballplayer for at least ten years. On his marriage license in 1884, he listed his occupation as "base ballist." He played in the majors with the 1884 Wilmington [Delaware] Quicksteps of the

10

Union Association and the 1884-85 Philadelphia Quakers of the National League. In his twenty-nine major league games in 1884 (sixteen for Wilmington and thirteen for Philadelphia), Lynch batted a combined .292. When considering Lynch's average, it should be kept in mind that his era was a time of pitching dominance. Pitchers delivered the ball just fifty feet from home plate and generally held the upper hand. The present dimensions of 60' 6" from the pitching box to home plate were not established until 1893, whereupon batting averages skyrocketed.

Lynch's experience in Wilmington in 1884 yielded more than a sterling baseball performance—it also provided him with a wife. In the off-season, on November 3, the twenty-four-year-old Lynch married nineteen-year-old Mary Agnes "Minnie" Batterbury of Wilmington. The *Cohoes Daily Mirror* reported that Lynch and "his fair young bride" were surprised by his schoolmates, "who presented him with an elegant gold-headed cane" and his bride "with a handsome solid silver castor." The next summer, in August 1885, a daughter, Anne Margaret, was born in Wilmington.

In the summer of 1885, Tom Lynch returned to Philadelphia but played in only thirteen games, batting a meager .189. He also spent time later that season with Newark of the Eastern League and Atlanta of the Southern League. In 1886 he went back to Atlanta for the entire season, playing in eighty-six games, coming to the plate 340 times, and batting .279, the tenth-highest average in the league. Then, in 1887, Lynch played the entire season in Syracuse of the International League, a prestigious circuit just a notch below the two major leagues of the time.

Lynch's experience in Syracuse included some trouble that may have foreshadowed his difficulties outside Donovan's Saloon a few years later. Lynch was suspended in September for "drunkenness," a "problem" that had occasioned a fine earlier in the season. *The Sporting Life* acknowledged that Lynch would be "badly missed at this stage of the fight as his hitting qualities are well-known and many games have been pulled out of the fire by Tom's good stick work." Evidently Lynch displayed proper remorse for his indiscretions with alcohol, as *The Sporting Life* reported a few days after the original story that "Tommy Lynch has reestablished himself in the good graces of the Syracuse management."

In the fall of 1887, after Lynch's season in Syracuse and just two years after the birth of his daughter, his marriage ended in tragedy. On November 28, his second child, George, born only six months earlier, died of consumption. On December 8, his wife, Mary Agnes, succumbed at age twenty-two from acute rheumatism.

Lynch had lost a baby and his wife within two weeks of one another. Perhaps deciding that the life of a "base ballist" did not allow for the upbringing of a two-year-old daughter, Lynch left Anne Margaret in the care of his wife's family in Delaware. Though Lynch later remarried and fathered seven more children, he never had a relationship with the daughter of his first marriage. Many years after Lynch's baseball career was over, a meeting was proposed between Lynch and Anne Margaret. Feeling that she'd been abandoned by her father, she chose not to see him, and they lived their whole lives unreconciled.

Lynch continued his baseball career following the deaths of his baby and wife, playing as far south as Birmingham, Alabama, and as far north as Hamilton, Ontario. Then, in the off-season of 1890, Tom was shot and so seriously injured that *The Sporting Life* reported "Ball Player Fatally Wounded in Saloon Row." In Cohoes the incident became known as the "Doyle-Lynch Row" and garnered considerable attention in the *Cohoes Daily News*.

It seems that for some years there had been bad blood between Lynch and Bert Doyle, a local millworker. Doyle

Tom Lynch (far right) stands tall among his teammates on the Atlanta club of the Southern League in 1886. [National Baseball Hall of Fame Library, Cooperstown, New York]

reported that Lynch had "been down on me" since an altercation three years earlier. In the early morning of October 27, 1890, after a night of drinking, Lynch and Doyle revived their quarrel. *The Sporting Life* reported that Lynch was "a muscular fellow and able to hold his own with most anybody" and Doyle was "his inferior in size and strength." After Doyle was struck by Lynch, he left Donovan's Saloon to get a weapon and later returned (to recover his hat, he told police). When Lynch saw him a second time, he said, "You want more, do you?" and knocked him down again. That was when Doyle shot him.

According to the *Cohoes Daily News*, the bullet struck Lynch so perilously close to his heart that the attending physician "dared not to probe for the ball." The coroner was called from Albany and at 9 a.m. the following morning Lynch's "ante-mortem statement" was taken. At the same time *The Sporting Life* was reporting that Lynch was "not expected to live forty-eight hours," the Cohoes newspaper was describing Lynch's "puzzling" condition:

> He apparently suffers no pain or inconvenience from the presence of a thirty-two calibre bullet in his body near the heart. He slept well last night and unless restrained by friends he would be out on the street. . . . No effort has been made to recover the ball. Unless some unforeseen complications arise, he will undoubtedly recover.

It is said that early ballplayers were a tough lot, and Lynch would seem to prove that. Indeed, Lynch did recover. In fact, a "Lynch" played ball for Troy (a neighboring city to Albany, just a few miles from Cohoes) in the Eastern League the following season. This Lynch didn't have much of a year, batting safely only thirty-two times in 157 at bats (.203). Perhaps he was limited by the after-effects of a near fatal shooting some months before.

At that point the trail grows cold. It's fair to surmise that Tom Lynch's injuries effectively ended his baseball career. We know that he lived out his long life in Cohoes, working for twenty-five years as a city laborer (according to his obituary in the *Troy Times-Record*). At some point in the 1890s he re-married and started another family. In the days before his death on March 28, 1955, Lynch was considered to be the oldest surviving major leaguer. His obituary in the *Troy Times-Record* acknowledged his long life and celebrated his baseball career that had him competing with the greatest players of the nineteenth century: "Pop" Anson, Hoss Radbourn, Only Nolan, Bill Purcell, and others.

Thomas James Lynch was not a league president in the majors, but rather a "base ballist" who lived much of his life "with a ball near his heart."

KARL LINDHOLM
RESEARCH ASSISTANCE BY MARGARET CUSICK

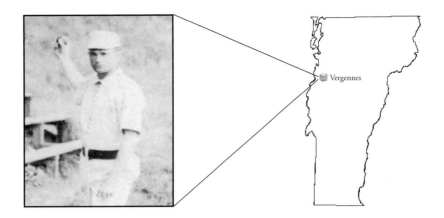

Henry Porter

Big Winner for Losing Teams

Vergennes calls itself "the smallest city in America," and it was in that tiny Addison County city that Henry Porter was born in June 1858. Prior to the War of 1812, Vergennes had been a hotbed of Lake Champlain commerce, but by mid-century its thriving shipping industry had long since faded. The Porters' stay was brief and not noteworthy. City records reveal no evidence of any Porters living in Vergennes in the years just prior to the Civil War, and it's known that Henry's family moved to Brockton, Massachusetts, while he was still quite young.

Henry soon made a name throughout the sandlots and semipro diamonds of eastern Massachusetts. A right-handed pitcher, he teamed with his catcher-brother Albert to form a battery of local notoriety. From 1878 to 1883 Henry pitched for several teams in the Bay State, and his outstanding record for Holyoke earned him a June 1883 tryout with the National League's Cleveland Blues. The Blues gave him his start in organized ball by farming him out to Bay City, Michigan, of the Northwest League.

Porter spent parts of two seasons in Bay City, where he "pitched champion ball, aiding it in securing the pennant." After the 1884 Northwest League season ended, Henry signed on with the Milwaukee Brewers of the short-lived Union Association, making his major league debut with that team on September 27, 1884. Appearing in six games with Milwaukee, Henry achieved an unusual trifecta—three wins, three losses, and a 3.00 ERA. After the Union Association folded

in January, Porter signed on with the Brooklyn Grays of the American Association, also then regarded as a major league.

At Brooklyn's Washington Park on June 4, 1885, a Vermont-born pitcher faced a Vermont-born batter for the first time ever in a major league game. Henry Porter held Fred Mann hitless that day but issued a bases-loaded walk in the eighth inning to force in the winning run in a 5-4 loss to the Pittsburgh Alleghenys. Despite that defeat, Henry enjoyed his best season in the majors in 1885. On a mediocre fifth-place club, Porter was 33-21 with a 2.78 ERA, third in the Association in wins and complete games, fourth in innings pitched, and fifth in strikeouts and winning percentage.

Baseball players tend to be a superstitious lot, and Henry Porter was even more so than most. While pitching for Brooklyn he started wearing a red-trimmed jersey and became convinced that he couldn't win without it. "A story is told of him that one time in St. Louis the jersey was at the laundry and that he cried because he could not get it," *The Sporting News* reported. "One of the directors got it for him before he could pitch."

Porter put together two more solid seasons as the workhorse of the Brooklyn pitching staff, but each year his ERA grew while his wins, innings pitched, and strikeouts shrank. After the 1887 season, St. Louis Browns owner Chris Von Der Ahe dismantled his three-time American Association pennant winner, selling his star pitching tandem of Bob Caruthers and Dave Foutz

Brooklyn vs. Pittsburg.

The fifth game between these clubs was played June 4 in Brooklyn, the Pittsburgs then winning for the fourth time. Morris and Porter pitched with telling effect. Porter gave a base on called balls in the eighth inning, when three of the visitors were on the bases, and this sent in the winning run.

BROOKLYN.	T.	R.	B.	O.	A.	E.	PITTSBURG.	T.	R.	B.	O.	A.	E.
Krieg, 1b	4	2	1	10	1	0	C. Smith, 2b	4	2	1	7	3	1
McClell'n,3b	4	0	0	1	1	0	Whitney, ss	4	0	4	0	2	1
Cassidy, rf	4	0	0	3	0	0	Eden, lf	4	0	0	1	0	0
Pinkney, 2b	4	0	0	4	4	0	Mann, cf	4	1	0	0	0	0
G. Smith, ss	4	1	1	3	2	0	Kuehne, 3b	4	0	1	0	1	1
Hotaling, cf	4	0	0	1	0	0	Brown, rf	4	1	1	3	0	0
Swartw'd, lf	4	1	1	1	0	1	Fields, 1b	4	0	0	11	2	0
Hayes, c	4	0	0	4	0	0	Kemmler, c	3	0	0	4	2	0
Porter, p	3	0	0	1	4	0	Morris, p	3	1	1	1	7	2
Totals	35	4	3	24	12	3	Totals	34	5	5	27	17	5

Brooklyn......1 0 0 0 0 0 0 2 1—4
Pittsburg.....1 0 0 0 0 0 0 2 *—5

Earned runs—Brooklyn, 1; Pittsburg, 1. Base on errors—B., 1; P., 3. On balls—B., 4; P., 2. Struck out—B., 5; P., 4. Umpire, Valentine. Time, 1.45.

Another close contest with the same result marked the meeting between these clubs June 5. Errors by Cassidy and G. Smith and safe hits by Brown, Miller and Eden enabled the visitors to score their three runs. The Brooklyns were helped to two runs on singles by McClellan and Pinkney, a two-bagger by Krieg, and a wild throw by Miller. Smith's second-base play was noteworthy.

BROOKLYN	T.	R.	B.	O.	A.	E.	PITTSBURG	T.	R.	B.	O.	A.	E.
Hotaling, cf	4	0	0	0	0	0	C. Smith, 2b	4	0	0	5	8	1
McClell'n,3b	4	1	1	1	1	1	Whitney, ss	4	0	0	3	2	0
Swartw'd, lf	4	0	0	2	4	0	Eden, lf	4	1	2	1	0	1
Krieg, 1b	4	0	1	6	0	0	Mann, cf	3	0	0	0	1	0
Cassidy, rf	4	0	0	0	0	1	Kuehne, 3b	3	0	0	0	2	0
Pinkney, 2b	4	1	3	4	1	0	Brown, rf	3	1	1	0	0	0
G. Smith, ss	4	0	1	3	4	1	Fields, 1b	3	1	1	14	0	0
Terry, p	4	0	0	0	7	0	Miller, c	3	0	1	4	2	1
Hayes, c	4	0	0	8	4	1	Meegan, p	3	0	1	0	2	0
Totals	36	2	8	24	15	4	Totals	30	3	6	27	16	5

Brooklyn......0 0 0 0 0 1 0 1 0—2
Pittsburg.....0 2 0 0 0 0 0 1 *—3

Base on errors—Brooklyn, 1; Pittsburg, 3. On balls—B., 3; P., 1. Struck out—B., 1; P., 6. Umpire, Valentine. Time, 1.50.

The Brooklyns beat the Pittsburgs for the second time June 6, a result due to timely hitting and almost faultless fielding. Umpire Valentine was hit by a pitched ball in the second inning and gave way to West. Krieg made a home-run, Porter, Hotaling and Kemmler each a three-baser, and Swartwood two double-baggers.

BROOKLYN	T.	R.	B.	O.	A.	E.	PITTSBURG	T.	R.	B.	O.	A.	E.
M'Clellan,3b	5	0	0	1	1	0	Smith, 2b	5	0	0	5	1	1
Pinkney, 2b	5	1	2	6	2	0	Whitney, ss	4	0	1	2	2	0
Cassidy, rf	5	3	1	0	0	0	Eden, lf	4	0	2	0	0	0
Krieg, 1b	5	2	2	6	0	0	Mann, cf	4	0	2	0	0	0
Smith, ss	5	2	1	2	2	0	Kuehne, 3b	4	0	2	1	1	1
Hotaling, cf	5	1	1	4	0	0	Brown, rf	4	0	0	2	0	0
Swartwo'd,lf	5	2	2	0	0	0	Fields, 1b	4	1	0	6	0	2
Hayes, c	5	1	0	8	1	1	Kemmler, c	4	1	1	11	1	1
Porter, p	5	1	1	0	5	0	Morris, p	4	0	2	0	5	1
Totals	45	13	10	27	11	1	Totals	37	2	8	27	10	6

Brooklyn......0 0 0 0 2 6 0 2 0—13
Pittsburg.....0 0 0 0 0 0 1 0 1— 2

Earned runs—Brooklyn, 4; Pittsburg, 1. Base on errors—B., 4. On balls—B., 4; P., 2. Struck out—B., 6; P., 6. Umpire, Valentine. Time, 2.10.

These 1885 box scores show the first games in which two Vermonters faced each other in the major leagues: Henry Porter pitching for Brooklyn and Fred Mann batting for Pittsburgh. [Dick Leyden Collection]

to Brooklyn. With Porter suddenly expendable, the Grays dispatched him to a hastily-assembled new franchise, the Kansas City Cowboys. Predictably, the Cowboys finished dead last in 1888, and Porter led the Association with thirty-seven losses. Still, he won eighteen games for a really terrible team; Kansas City's eight other pitchers combined to win only twenty-one.

At times Porter still sparkled. On June 6, 1888, he tossed a no-hitter against the Baltimore Orioles, the twenty-sixth such accomplishment in the history of the major leagues. At the time, however, the feat went largely unnoticed. A sub-headline in the *Baltimore Sun* mentioned "Porter's Rare Pitching Feat," but the game account focused more on the Orioles' lack of enthusiasm than on Porter's great pitching:

> A game played by eighteen galvanized corpses is a spectacle unexpected in any baseball city, and yet that was the sight to which the spectators of the Baltimore-Kansas City game at the Huntingdon avenue grounds yesterday were treated. Baltimore was defeated, but there was nothing remarkable in that. Baltimore was shut out, but that has happened before. But it never before occurred when every Baltimore player was doing fairly good work that they were shut out without a single hit.

Within a year of the no-hitter, however, the years of overwork took their toll. In 1889 Porter appeared in only four games for Kansas City and lost all three of his decisions, his ERA skyrocketing to 12.52. At the age of thirty-two, his major league career was over.

Henry Porter's career was brief but stunning. Over the course of four seasons, 1885-88, Porter pitched more innings than any other hurler in the American Association. Appearing mainly for second-division teams, he *averaged* twenty-three wins, twenty-five losses, and 430 innings pitched per season, and went the distance in an incredible 98 percent of the games he started. Even by nineteenth-century standards, successive seasons of thirty-three and twenty-seven wins is impressive, especially when his team wasn't exactly a forerunner of Stengel's Yankees. Overlooking Porter's brief but disastrous final season, his career ERA is a solid 3.51. The young man from the shores of Lake Champlain had done the Green Mountain State credit.

With his big league days behind him, Henry returned to his adopted hometown of Brockton and continued pitching, playing with numerous teams throughout southern New England over the next four seasons. In 1893 he finally settled down and went to work in Brockton's famous shoe industry. For more than a decade Henry held a responsible position in one of the Douglas shoe factories.

Henry Porter was only forty-eight when he died on December 30, 1906, at his home on North Montello Street. The *Brockton Enterprise* reported that he died "[a]fter an illness of long duration," and his death certificate lists the cause as complications arising from pneumonia. Thus ended the life of a Green Mountain Boy who, as his obituary reported, "was known throughout the baseball world as one of the cleverest pitchers in his day."

WALT NELSON

Lee Viau

A Short-Lived Blaze of Glory

Corinth, Vermont, is often featured on calendars and postcards portraying idyllic Vermont scenes. It is quiet, rural, and has changed little from when Leon Viau was born there on July 5, 1866. Leon's father, Antoin, was a carpenter. His name invites speculation that he came down from Canada, and, as Corinth town records list no Viaus, it's likely Leon's parents didn't live there long. Then as now, construction projects came and went, and carpenters like Antoin followed the work.

Soon after Leon's birth, the Viaus moved to Hanover, New Hampshire, where Antoin found employment at Dartmouth College. In modern terminology, he was a one-man building-and-grounds crew, not a bad achievement for an itinerant French-Canadian carpenter. At Hanover young Leon, by then nicknamed "Lee," grew up and gained entrance to Dartmouth in the fall of 1884, enrolling in the Chandler Scientific Department.

The young Viau's athletic prowess may have had something to do with his acceptance into the prestigious institution, as this was the era of the rise of intercollegiate athletics. Soon after entering college, Lee played left field and batted lead-off for the freshmen as they won the annual contest held each fall between the four college classes. He batted only .143 in the three intramural games, but his five runs scored led the freshmen in that category. In the spring Lee appeared in two games for the Dartmouth varsity, playing left field and batting seventh in the order. He had three hits (including a double) in nine trips to the plate. *The Dartmouth*, in a rare instance of singling out an individual player, commented, "Viau handled the stick with great effect."

In his sophomore year Viau started the season in left field again, but beginning with the second game he also did some pitching. His mound debut on April 12, 1886, was a disaster. Brown University scored five runs in the first inning on two hits and numerous errors, after which Viau retreated to the relative safety of left field. Brown went on to a 7-4 win, with Viau accounting for four of Dartmouth's miscues. It wasn't a promising beginning for a man destined to pitch in the major leagues, but two days later he started again, this time against MIT. Lee went the distance in a 5-2 win, walking only two and striking out sixteen.

Viau pitched in only two more games for Dartmouth, finishing with a 2-2 record. Though his record provides no basis for professional scouts to take notice, for some reason Lee attracted the attention of Jim Keenan, a catcher for the American Association's Cincinnati Reds. Keenan recommended him to Gus Schmelz, the Reds' newly-appointed manager, and in the fall of 1886 Viau left Dartmouth and signed with a minor league club in St. Paul, Minnesota, for a salary of $275 per month.

After pitching well at St. Paul in 1887 (one newspaper regarded him as the "best pitcher in the league"), Viau signed a $2,500 contract with Cincinnati. The Reds gave him an early chance to prove himself, handing him the ball in their first exhibition game at New Orleans in the spring of 1888. The twenty-one-year-old responded

Viau appears at far left in the front row of this photo of the Dartmouth Class of '88 baseball team. [Dartmouth College Archives]

with a 6-0 shutout. He then opened the regular season with eight straight wins before suffering his first setback on June 1. For the season, Viau went 27-14 (fifth in the Association in wins and fourth in winning percentage), and compiled an ERA of 2.65 (tenth), 387.2 innings pitched (eighth), forty-two complete games (seventh) and 164 strikeouts (tenth). On a pitching staff that included Tony Mullane and Elmer Smith, both thirty-game winners the previous season, Viau emerged as the ace.

Though showing occasional flickers of brilliance, Viau never fulfilled the bright promise of that first season. In 1889 he won twenty-two games but his ERA slipped to 3.79 while his strikeouts declined and his walks increased. He lost twenty games (eighth-most in the Association) and yielded the title of staff ace to rookie Cyclone Jim Duryea, who went 32-19.

The year 1890 was a turbulent one in baseball, with several clubs (including Viau's Reds) deserting the American Association to join the rival National League, and John Montgomery Ward leading an exodus of many of baseball's best players to form the Players League. As recalled in his obituary fifty-seven years later, Viau claimed that "his work suffered because of continuous pressure brought on him by agents of the Players League,

who offered him a big boost in salary if he would jump." He pitched in only thirteen games that season before the Reds traded him to the lackluster Cleveland Spiders.

Viau faired poorly in Cleveland, winning four and losing nine, but his teammates were almost as bad. Cleveland finished 44-88, 43.5 games back of first. His ERA rose to 3.88, and for the first time he walked more batters than he fanned. At that, Viau's four wins ranked third on the Spiders, topped only by Ed Beatin's twenty-two victories and the nine wins of a twenty-three-year-old rookie named Denton True Young. Better known as "Cy," Young won an additional 502 games over the next twenty-one seasons.

Another Brush with a Young Hall of Famer
In a spring training exhibition in Gainesville, Florida, on March 26, 1891, Lee Viau played an unwitting role in launching the career of John McGraw. Charles C. Alexander described the day's events in his biography of the Hall of Famer:

John McGraw, hitherto an obscure minor leaguer, gained a measure of recognition that day. Years later he admitted that Lee Viau, Cleveland's pitcher, was still working his arm into condition and didn't really bear down on the Gainesville batters. Nevertheless, McGraw's performance against the major leaguers—three doubles in five times at bat, three runs (of six Gainesville scored to Cleveland's nine), errorless play at shortstop—made his name widely known when the telegraphed reports of the game appeared in the Cleveland newspapers, were picked up by other dailies, and were also noted in the baseball weeklies *Sporting Life* and *Sporting News*. Within a week or so, McGraw had heard from a score of professional clubs seeking his services for the coming season.

Viau stood only 5' 4", but he had a blazing fastball and ranked among the American Association's strikeout leaders in both 1888 and 1889. Though he started as a left fielder at Dartmouth, Viau batted only .139 in the majors. [Dick Leyden Collection]

Viau nearly revived his career in 1891, improving his ERA to 3.01 and winning eighteen games as Cleveland, with the acquisition of several stars from the now-defunct Players League, climbed to fifth place (65-74). But the 1892 season had scarcely begun when Cleveland dispatched Viau to Louisville, another second-division club. He started sixteen games for the Colonels, posting a dreary 4-11 record before being traded again, this time to Boston. Returning to his native New England, Viau finished his major league career with one

Viau made his pitching debut in this game against Brown on April 14, 1886. [Dartmouth College Archives]

last blaze of glory, giving up no earned runs in a complete-game win in his only appearance for the Beaneaters.

Thereafter, the janitor's son from the quaint Vermont village led an inconspicuous life. Viau drifted to the minors, for a while pitching in the New England League. While records are spotty, he's mentioned as pitching for Fall River and Haverhill in 1894, with a winning percentage of .630 but more wild than ever, issuing 108 walks while racking up only fifty-one strikeouts. Alcohol may have contributed to Viau's decline. In fact, his name appears on a list of notorious drinkers in a book called *Baseball Babylon*.

In 1896 Viau pitched in the Atlantic League for Paterson, where he had a couple more brushes with future Hall of Famers at the start of their careers. His rookie manager was Ed Barrow, the man most responsible for the success of the New York Yankees between 1921 and 1945. One of his teammates was twenty-two-year-old Honus Wagner, the greatest shortstop of all time. In their biography of Wagner, Dennis and Jeanne DeValeria describe an incident that gives a pretty good indication why Viau was no longer in the majors:

> [Barrow] quashed open gambling in the stands, but on two different occasions he had to fine and suspend pitchers for taking the mound while drunk. In another episode, former big league pitcher Lee Viau arrived at the park in an altered state. Several players were upset with him for sampling the spirits when they needed him to pitch, and Wagner expressed their displeasure. Viau, only five feet four inches tall but a stocky power pitcher, grabbed a water bucket and emptied it over Wagner's head. An unamused Wagner wrapped his large hands around the pitcher's throat, lifting him off the floor. After a few seconds, Wagner regained his composure and dropped the shaken man. It was a seldom-seen side of the mild-mannered Wagner.

Despite that altercation, Viau hung on with Paterson a couple more seasons, winding up his career in Organized Baseball there in 1898.

After bouncing around semipro baseball and later umpiring a little, Viau worked as manager of the game room at the Paterson Elks Club. There's no record of his ever marrying. Viau died at age eighty-one in Hopewell, New Jersey, on December 17, 1947.

To have known brief moments in the sun was the lot of many of the Green Mountain Boys of Summer, as it was for Lee Viau. He retired from major league baseball with a winning record (83-77), chiefly as a result of his glorious rookie season with the 1888 Cincinnati Reds.

GUY WATERMAN

Harry Burrell

The Mystery Relative

Sometime after his first major league season of 1977, Pat Putnam, the Texas Rangers' Vermont-born first baseman, filled out a survey sent to him by the National Baseball Library. In response to a question whether any relatives had played professional baseball, Putnam wrote, "Grandfather Burrell may have played (?)." The relative Putnam had in mind was his mother's father, George Burrell, whose career was cut short by a severely broken leg. "Grandfather Burrell" did try out for the Boston Braves back in the 1910s, but he never played organized professional baseball. What Putnam didn't know was that he had another relative who had actually made it to the majors. His name was Harry J. Burrell.

According to *Total Baseball*, Burrell was born in Bethel, Vermont, on May 26, 1869. His death certificate is probably more reliable, however, and it indicates that he was born three years earlier. Harry's father, Peter Burrelle (many family members still retain the French spelling), was a lumberjack from Boucherville, Quebec, ten miles east of Montreal. He had come to Vermont in the fall of 1863 to work a lumber job with his brother Lewis, and the following spring the brothers brought their families to Bethel to settle permanently. "Peter Burrelle was a strong, rugged man and was very skillful in the use of axe and saw," wrote the *Bethel Courier* in 1902. "He had probably worked up more wood than any two men around here."

Like many nineteenth-century athletes, Harry got his start playing for the hometown nine. The above photo-

graph is from the 1886 team picture at the Bethel Historical Society, which bears the caption "Bethel Town Team, Champions in 1886." Burrell must have played well enough to earn a promotion to a larger town, because by 1889 he was playing for Brattleboro. The following year he headed west to play for Dubuque, Iowa, and spent most of the next two seasons playing in western minor leagues.

After a stint in Joliet, Illinois, Harry Burrell won a job in the big time, entering the American Association during its last month of operation as a major league. Joining the roster of the St. Louis Browns, which included Hall-of-Famers Charlie Comiskey, Clark Griffith, and Tommy McCarthy, the right-handed pitcher made his major league debut on September 13, 1891. Over the last month of the season Burrell pitched in seven games, going 4-2 with a 4.81 ERA as the Browns finished second, 8.5 games behind the Boston Reds. The day after Burrell's last appearance, teammate Ted Breitenstein pitched a no-hitter in his first major league start.

Those seven games comprised the entire major league career of Harry Burrell of Bethel, Vermont. In the decade following his month in the majors, Burrell jumped from team to team, his life as an itinerant minor leaguer no doubt simplified by his bachelor status. If he were alive today, he would probably say his greatest thrill in baseball was leading Des Moines to a Western League championship in 1897. Or perhaps he would mention pitching for Taunton, Massachusetts, of the New England League when the great Christy Mathewson made his professional debut with that club in July 1899.

Following his retirement as a player after the 1900 season, Burrell returned to the midwest and kept up his ties with the game. In 1901 a Vermont newspaper, the *White River Herald and News*, reported:

Harry Burrell, the Brattleboro ex-outfielder who afterwards developed into a pitcher, and who has been playing professionally since he left for the West a dozen years ago . . . is now a promoter of the Iowa State League. Burrell, who is a Bethel boy, is teaching penmanship at an Iowa college.

Harry eventually settled in Omaha, where he died of toxemia on December 15, 1914. Sixty-three years later, his descendant Pat Putnam, another confirmed bachelor, carried on the family baseball tradition and became the second Bethel native to reach the majors.

JEFF PURTELL

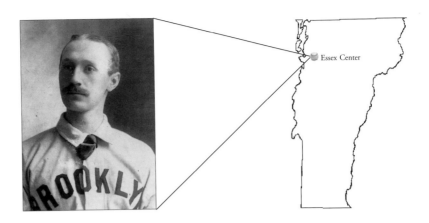

Bert Abbey

The Leader of UVM's "Wonder Team"

Baseball already had a fairly long, though not illustrious, history at the University of Vermont when Bert Abbey arrived on campus in 1887. It had been a club sport as early as 1866, and UVM played its first intercollegiate game, a 44-4 loss to Middlebury, on May 29, 1882. By the time Abbey left to join the Washington Senators in 1892, however, he'd transformed the UVM baseball program into a national powerhouse. In recognition of his efforts, Abbey (along with fellow Green Mountain Boys of Summer Ray Collins, Larry Gardner, and Ralph Lapointe) became one of seven original inductees into UVM's Athletic Hall of Fame in October 1969.

Like so many of the state's early settlers, Abbey's ancestors were farmers who came to Vermont from Connecticut early in the nineteenth century. At their farm on Brown's River Road in Essex Center, the Abbeys raised a variety of crops and livestock. Though he aspired to become a Baptist minister, Bert's father, Pearl Castle Abbey, remained on the farm at Bert's grandfather's insistence. He was still living there on November 29, 1869, when his wife gave birth to a boy with reddish-brown hair, brown eyes, and the distinctive Abbey nose. They named him Bert Wood Abbey after close friend Lambert Wood, shortening the name to Bert because Wood never cared for Lambert.

Like his father, Bert was called by his initials, and the nickname "BW" stuck with him throughout life. Abbey had one sister, Pearl May, who was two years younger. The Abbey children attended the schoolhouse on East Road in Essex and played together since no other children lived near the farm. At the Essex Classical Institute BW's favorite subject was natural history, an interest he carried to college. Initially Abbey studied classical languages at UVM, but, according to family legend, in his sophomore year he stoked the fire with his Greek and Latin texts and enrolled in the natural science course.

BW didn't develop an interest in baseball until the fall of 1886, when he arrived at Vermont Academy in Saxtons River. On September 27, 1886, he played his first organized game against the Putney town team. Though the game's outcome is unknown, Vermont Academy's lineup lists Abbey as starting pitcher, batting clean-up. One day that fall, after returning from a Vermont Academy game, BW experimented with a curveball for the first time. He collected a bunch of baseballs and started snapping off curves at a marked target on a barn. "I finally got so I could curve a ball and still keep it under control," he said. After leaving Vermont Academy in February, BW continued practicing back at the farm, recruiting his sister to serve as catcher.

In the fall of 1887 Abbey entered the University of Vermont and formed the school's first freshman baseball team. "That fall the varsity went to Dartmouth and got trounced," Bert recalled. "When they returned we challenged them to a game. I pitched and struck out sixteen men. (I really struck out eighteen, but in those days they didn't count the first two fouls as strikes.) So we trounced the varsity, too, and they ended up taking five of us onto their team."

Bert Abbey stands at right in this family photo. Bert's father, PC Abbey, served as chaplain of the Vermont legislature, to which he was elected himself in 1902. [Abbey Family Archives]

With Abbey on the mound and a team composed mostly of "medics," UVM dominated the Vermont Intercollegiate Baseball League in 1889, prompting the league's other two members, Middlebury and Norwich, to demand that only "academics" be eligible to play. UVM's refusal caused the V.I.B.L. to disband. "We quit playing St. Joseph's, Middlebury, and Norwich right away, because they offered us no challenge," Bert remembered.

As a junior Abbey was named UVM's coach and captain, and under his direction the team underwent its first "systematic training." Bert required players to exercise at the Burlington YMCA and held winter practices in a room under the university chapel in the basement of the Old Mill. The hard work paid off: "On Decoration Day, 1890, we beat Dartmouth at home for the first time," Abbey remembered. "This called for a night-shirt parade down Pearl and Church streets to celebrate."

That year Bert led a campaign to keep the UVM varsity together as a summer team, convincing Burlington's business leaders to donate more than $500 to cover travel expenses and salaries for the players. Vermont played a heavy schedule against professional teams from all over the East Coast, including the John Morrills (headed by the popular ex-captain of the Boston Red Stockings) and

the Cuban Giants (a well-known Negro barnstorming team), prompting other colleges to complain that UVM's players were no longer true amateurs. Abbey's teammate Lyman Allen hardly denied the charge.

During these years much was said about "professionalism" in this University by representatives of other colleges. While this criticism was to some degree just, still I know positively that other colleges were more blameworthy in the matter than we were, as can be proved by financial offers to many of our players to go to other colleges, which at the same time were pretending to be entirely free from professionalism, and were criticising us.

Putting aside the morality of the issue, summer play vastly improved UVM's baseball fortunes. The 1891 team, with a record of 19-6, was Vermont's best ever. By that time Abbey was joined on the mound by another Green Mountain Boy of Summer, Arlington Pond, and UVM was playing collegiate powers like Harvard and Yale. At that point Abbey received a lesson from one of the most influential men in sports history: "While I was at UVM, Alonzo Stagg, star Yale pitcher of his day and one of the greatest baseball and football coaches of all time, came to Memorial Auditorium. I got him aside in the basement of the auditorium and he showed me how to pitch a curve that wouldn't tip off the batter. That's the only coaching in baseball I ever had."

Because he still hadn't completed all of the courses necessary for graduation, Bert returned to UVM for a fifth year in 1892. That year the UVM players, not lacking in self-confidence, began calling themselves the "wonder team." During Easter recess they took their first-ever southern trip, challenging even major league teams. UVM won all five of its games against collegiate and amateur competition, but its results against the National Leaguers were a different story. The Philadelphia Phillies, with an outfield of Hall-of-Famers Ed Delahanty, Billy Hamilton, and Sam Thompson, gave the precocious

The Abbey farm was a 150-acre parcel two miles north of Essex Center on Brown's River Road. [Abbey Family Archives]

Vermonters a 24-3 drubbing. And on April 5, 1892, the Washington Senators shut out UVM 7-0 in front of a rain-soaked crowd of 550.

Despite the loss, the "wonder team" received high praise from the Senators. Second baseman Tommy Dowd called UVM the "best college team playing baseball." Abbey was particularly impressive, scattering eight hits, striking out seven (the Washington pitcher struck out only five), and not allowing a single earned run. After the game Washington's manager, Billy Barnie, told a reporter that Abbey and his catcher, Larry Kinsella, made up the best amateur battery he'd ever seen.

Abbey remembered the impression he made on the Washington manager: "Somewhere along in the game he called me aside and asked if I had any ideas about professional ball. He said, 'If you ever decide to play, telegraph me!' All the rest of the trip I kept thinking of the offer and the chance to make some money—more than I would make teaching, anyhow. So I telegraphed him and was told to report at once." On June 11, 1892, Bert pitched his last game for UVM, a 6-5 loss to the town team from Northampton, Massachusetts, dropping his record for his college career to 30-12. Three days later he was on the mound for Washington.

Years later Abbey recalled his debut against the St. Louis Browns.

> I was disgusted with my pitching, or the umpiring anyhow! In college I never gave more than one or two bases on balls, but here the umpire called them a lot closer. They had just lengthened the pitching distance by five feet and the catcher stood way back by the grandstand, except for [with two strikes]. When I challenged the umpire on his calls, he replied, "The rules say under both shoulders and over both knees. You're putting the ball over the shoulder [on one pitch] and under the next. You're doing the same with the knees!"

Despite pitching under increased scrutiny, Abbey won the game by a score of 12-7 and went on to compile his best season in the majors. Though his record was 5-18 for the hapless Senators, he compiled a respectable 3.45 ERA.

In the spring of 1893 Washington sold Abbey to the Pittsburgh Pirates, who in turn assigned him to their farm

Bert Abbey, the "pitcher" on the right, poses with the UVM freshman baseball team that defeated the varsity in 1887. [University of Vermont]

UVM's "wonder team" of 1892 challenged even major league competition. In this photo of the team, Bert Abbey is in the middle row, second from right. His Lambda Iota fraternity brother, fellow Green Mountain Boy of Summer Arlie Pond, is seated in the front row, second from left. [University of Vermont]

club in Macon, Georgia. Bert enjoyed his stint in the Southern League immensely. The 5' 11", 175-pound redhead was a favorite of both the southern belles and the team's management, which appreciated his steady, gentlemanly conduct. Unlike many of his teammates, Abbey didn't drink or smoke, and he constantly monitored his weight. He was still having a wonderful time in the south when he received news that Pittsburgh had sold his contract to the Chicago Colts. Though this meant a return to the big time, Abbey was disappointed and threatened not to report.

National League president Nick Young informed him that he'd be suspended if he didn't report immediately, but Abbey stood firm. "I had hoped that I would be allowed to get a full year in the Southern League and then begin a new season with either New York or Boston," Abbey wrote. "I don't want to go to Chicago now. The team is way in the hole and among the tailenders and to go with it this year will injure my chances for next season."

When Abbey returned to the farm in Essex Center, the Colts sent a telegram asking for his demands. "I didn't

want to go to Chicago so I wired a price I thought would scare 'em," he recalled. "I said I'd finish the season for $1,000 and next year will cost $2,400. That was big money in baseball then." Chicago answered almost immediately: "Join the club in Cleveland." Abbey complied.

In hindsight the Colts probably regretted going to so much trouble. Abbey was 2-4 with a 5.46 ERA for the remainder of the 1893 season, then went 2-7 with a 5.18 ERA in 1894. One can only speculate on how he got along with his manager, Hall-of-Famer Cap Anson. An infamous racist, Anson is often cited as a major force in the creation of baseball's color line. Abbey, on the other hand, enjoyed playing in exhibitions against black players. He openly opposed the demeaning but common practice of throwing change on the floor of the hotel as a tip to the Negro bellhops. Instead he handed them the change, even though his teammates knocked him for doing it.

Following the 1894 season, Abbey married Annie Isham on New Year's Eve at her family's home in Burlington. The newlywed Bert pitched in only one game for Chicago in 1895 when the Colts traded him, appropriately

Annie Abbey, a UVM graduate, met her future husband while teaching at the Essex Classical Institute. She kept a diary while traveling with Bert and the Brooklyn team during the 1896 season. [Abbey Family Archives]

enough, to the Brooklyn Bridegrooms. Pitching in eight games for Brooklyn, Bert won five of seven decisions with a 4.35 ERA. One highlight was pitching in a game against the New York Giants at the Polo Grounds before 13,000 fans, at the time one of the largest crowds ever.

Meanwhile, back on the farm in Essex Center, Bert's father was struggling to make ends meet. His heart wasn't in farming—he eventually realized his dream by becoming ordained at age forty—and when he questioned his ability to pay the mortgage, BW lifted his spirits by saying, "If you keep praying and I keep playing ball, we'll make the payments."

But BW's days in baseball were numbered. When he got off to a mediocre start in 1896, Brooklyn farmed him out to Montreal of the Eastern League. In an extra-inning game against Toronto, Abbey uncorked a high fastball and felt something pop in his right arm. At the age of twenty-six, he knew at that moment that his career as a pitcher was over.

Abbey returned to Vermont and founded Central Telephone Company, the state's first independent phone company, installing the telephones, wires, cables, and switchboards himself. In 1909 he sold the business to Northern Telephone Company and returned to farming. Having traveled considerably during his baseball career, Bert took things he'd seen in other parts of the country—from tractors and harvesters to new strains of

Abbey (standing, third from left) reported to the Chicago Colts only after they met his demand for a "big money" contract of $2,400. The Colts may have regretted their investment, given Abbey's mediocre statistics during his time with Chicago. [Abbey Family Archives]

Charles Francis Carter, as he looked during his time in Burlington. [College Street Congregational Church]

Did a Nineteenth-Century Burlington Minister Discover the Curveball?

In a 1962 interview published in the *Burlington Free Press*, Bert Abbey claimed that the curveball was first developed by the Reverend Charles Francis Carter, a former Yale pitcher who served as pastor of the College Street Congregational Church in Burlington from 1886 through 1893. Could Abbey's claim be true?

According to his file in the Yale archives, Carter arrived at Yale in 1874 and played football and baseball. For three years he pitched regularly for the varsity, achieving his greatest fame for "the record game of 5 to 0, against Harvard, when only twenty-seven Harvard men went to the bat, being put out in one-two-three order." In other words, Carter had pitched a perfect game.

Alas, Carter couldn't have invented the curveball. Two years before his arrival at Yale, several pitchers in the professional National Association were already throwing curves: Hall-of-Famer Candy Cummings of the New York Mutuals, generally considered the inventor of the pitch; Phoney Martin of the Troy Haymakers; and Bobby Mathews of the Baltimore Canaries. It's possible, however, that Carter was the first collegiate hurler to master the curveball.

strawberries and blueberries—and introduced them in Vermont. Abbey also obtained an appointment as game warden. "The family felt that BW got himself appointed so he could go hunting whenever he desired," Bert's granddaughter Betty Royce said.

But Annie Abbey, having grown up in the "big city" (at least by Vermont's standards), never enjoyed life on the farm. On a few instances she left spontaneously to spend time with family and friends in Burlington. At Annie's coaxing Bert sold the Abbey Farm in 1921, by which time four generations had tackled its everyday challenges. The Abbeys bought property in Shelburne, and there Bert helped his son Fred operate a nursery and garden center, Gardenside Nurseries, that remains in business to this day. Bert studied ornamental horticulture and grew an incredible vegetable garden, as well as a large collection of grapes.

In his later years BW hunted regularly with his grandson Paul. Walking with a cane and stopping frequently to

In his later years Abbey walked with a cane because he suffered from arthritis, which he attributed to his baseball days. The worst pain was in his left hip, which had endured years of hard sliding. [Abbey Family Archives]

sit, Bert taught Paul to respect nature. He spoke highly of the undeveloped Vermont countryside, pleased that the hunting territory he'd staked out in Chittenden County as a young adult hadn't changed much in a half-century. When interviewed thirty-four years after his grandfather's death, Paul Abbey still had many fond memories.

He was someone you could look up to. It would always be uplifting to see him. I never saw him angry. He always had a good story, a new subject to discuss. BW seemed to enjoy the life of leisure—he didn't want too many projects. Never complained about the cold weather. Always on time and expected others to be prompt. When the family got together, he was always the center of attention. Maybe a little too social conscious by today's standards, but friendly and outgoing and open-minded. As a matter of fact, he was the perfect grandfather.

Bert Abbey was thought to be the oldest living former major league baseball player before his death on June 11, 1962. A few months earlier, the ninety-two-year-old Vermonter told a *Burlington Free Press* reporter: "I have a grandson named for me who wanted to be a better pitcher than I was. I told him I'd shoot him if he played professional ball. Baseball's okay in college, but no place for a man with brains!"

PAT O'CONNOR

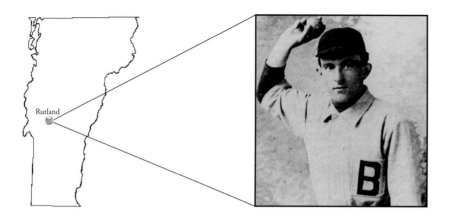

Rutland

Arlington Pond

From Rutland to the Philippines

Though he pitched for the legendary Baltimore Orioles of the mid-1890s, Arlington Pond found more fame on the island of Cebu in the Philippines, some 6,000 miles from his native shores, than he ever gained on the pitching mounds of the National League. His spacious plantation home with thatched roof and woven palm-leaf walls lay at the end of a palm-bordered driveway, a long, long way from Rutland's Merchants Row, where he'd grown up.

According to *Total Baseball*, Erasmus Arlington Pond was born in Rutland on January 19, 1872, but college alumni surveys filled out in Pond's own hand list his birthplace as East Saugus, Massachusetts, and the date as 1873. If the alumni surveys are more accurate, he quickly repaired the damage by becoming a full-fledged Vermont resident by the time he was in grammar school. Arlie's father, Abbott Sequard Pond, worked for his brother Dr. Erasmus Arlington Pond at the Pond Sphygmograph Company, selling surgical instruments out of offices in the Morse Block in downtown Rutland. Young Arlie grew up at the busy corner of Main and Center streets, next door to 114 Main Street, the home of that uncle for whom he was named and in whose career path he followed.

Arlie graduated from Rutland High School in 1888 and spent two years at Norwich University, distinguishing himself as a musician and as pitcher on the baseball team. In 1890 he transferred to the University of Vermont. As an "academic" at UVM Pond was a member of the glee and banjo club, and he also played one season of varsity football, but he earned his greatest fame as a baseball player.

That was the era of Green Mountain Boy of Summer Bert Abbey, Pond's Lambda Iota fraternity brother, and Arlie patrolled center field on the 1891 team, UVM's best ever with a 19-6 record. In 1892 Pond played second base and alternated on the mound with Abbey to give Vermont a devastating pair of hurlers, and UVM's "Wonder Team" finished its season at 21-9. Perhaps the highlight of that season was Arlie Pond's no-hitter against Yale.

Abbey had jumped to the majors by 1893, but enough players returned for UVM to win nine, lose two and tie one against the best teams in the east during a thirteen-day, 2,000-mile southern trip. That record attracted the attention of the University of Chicago's Amos Alonzo Stagg, better known for his contributions to football. Stagg invited UVM to compete against seven of the finest college baseball teams in the country in a double-elimination tournament at the 1893 World's Fair in Chicago. Little Vermont won the hearts of the press and fans at the Columbian Exhibition, finishing second and earning the distinction of being the only team to defeat Stagg's *alma mater*, Yale, the tournament's eventual champion.

Pond graduated from UVM in 1893 but remained in Burlington and enrolled in the Medical School. After receiving his medical degree in 1895, he signed up for a post-graduate surgical course at the College of Physicians and Surgeons in Baltimore. But his reputation as an outstanding collegiate pitcher preceded him to Maryland and became known to Ned Hanlon, manager of the National League's Orioles. Though Pond continued to take advan-

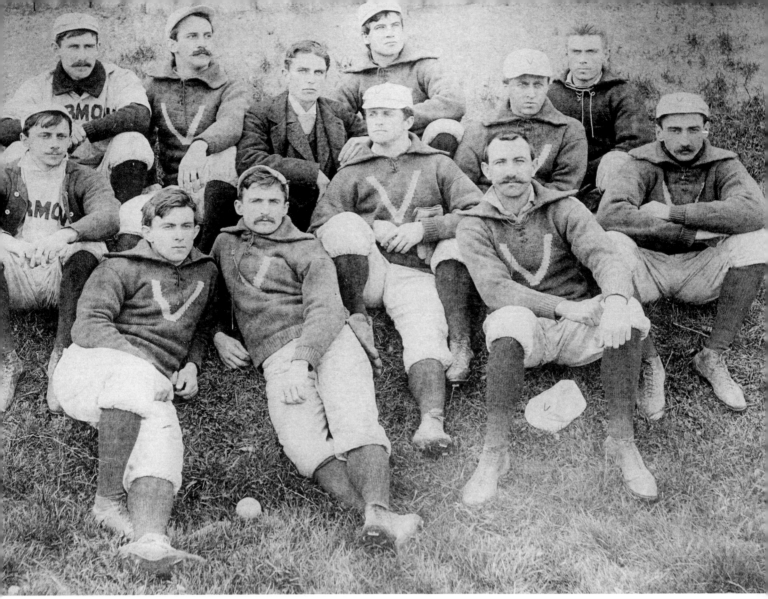

The 1893 University of Vermont baseball team finished second out of eight teams in what may have been the first College World Series ever. In this team photo Pond is reclining at left in the front row. [University of Vermont]

tage of his situation in one of the world's leading medical communities, performing his residency at St. Joseph Hospital and his internship at Baltimore City Hospitals, Hanlon convinced him to spend summers with the Orioles. On June 23, 1895, Pond signed a contract with one of baseball's all-time greatest teams.

His new teammates in orange and black included six future Hall of Famers: manager Hanlon, third baseman John McGraw, shortstop Hughie Jennings, catcher Wilbert Robinson, left fielder Joe Kelley, and right fielder Wee Willie Keeler. If the Orioles had a weakness it was pitching, but Baltimore's staff was hardly pathetic. Rookie Wizard Hoffer was on his way to thirty-one wins, George Hemming was racking up twenty, and Dad Clarkson, Duke Esper, and Sadie McMahon each were en route to double-digit victories. Hanlon hardly needed Pond. Pitching in only six games, the twenty-three-year-old contributed little on the field to Baltimore's second con-

secutive National League pennant. Instead he found other ways of making himself useful, such as serving as team doctor. After one game, the *Baltimore Sun* reported that "Dr. Pond is suffering from a small abscess in his left hand, which he lanced himself."

Baltimore won its third-straight N.L. pennant in 1896, reaching its zenith with an incredible record of 90-39 (.698). Replacing Clarkson in the rotation, Pond contributed heavily to the team's success, starting twenty-six games and compiling a 16-8 record with a 3.49 ERA. At one point he pitched two five-hitters in the same week, and on another occasion he was even better. In a scene at odds with Connie Mack's later reputation as a distinguished gentleman, the thirty-four-year-old player-manager of the Pittsburgh Pirates danced up and down in the third-base coaching box, trying to rattle Pond by yelling, "He can't get 'em over! He can't get 'em over!" Mack's efforts went in vain as Pond pitched a four-hitter.

Pond graced the cover of this scorecard during 1896, another pennant-winning year for the Orioles. [Dick Leyden Collection]

In the 1896 Temple Cup playoffs, a predecessor of the modern World Series pitting the N.L.'s top two teams in a best-of-seven championship, the Orioles faced their hated rivals, the Cleveland Spiders, and their ace pitcher, Cy Young. The Spiders had taken eight of eleven from Baltimore during the regular season, but this time the Orioles swept the series. Though he didn't pitch (Baltimore went with Hoffer and Joe Corbett, a twenty-year-old rookie whose brother "Gentleman Jim" Corbett had been heavyweight champion of the world), Pond was part of the celebration when both teams met in a Cleveland saloon, filled the Temple Cup with seventeen quarts of champagne, and hoisted it around.

In 1897 Hanlon became the first manager ever to employ a four-man pitching rotation with success: Pond, Hoffer, Corbett, and rookie Jerry Nops each won between eighteen and twenty-four games while working between 221 and 313 innings. Though Arlie turned in his best season in the majors, going 18-9 with a 3.52 ERA, the Orioles finished second behind the Boston Beaneaters during the regular season. In what turned out to be the last Temple Cup series ever, Baltimore dropped the opener to the Beaneaters, 13-12, but bounced back to sweep the next four games. Again Pond didn't pitch.

At the start of the 1898 season Hanlon used Pond sparingly. Arlie didn't make his first appearance until May

Pond is seated at far right in the front row of this Baltimore Orioles team photo. The six men to his right in the first and second rows all went on to the Hall of Fame: John McGraw (first row, second from left), Joe Kelley (second row, third from left), Ned Hanlon (in street clothes), Willie Keeler (front row), Wilbert Robinson (to Hanlon's left), and Hughie Jennings. [Babe Ruth Museum, Baltimore]

Although pitching for the Baltimore Orioles was just a sideline to his medical career, Arlie Pond racked up 34 wins during the 1896-97 seasons. [Babe Ruth Museum, Baltimore]

11, when he mopped up in an 8-4 loss to Boston. Nine days later he started and lost a 3-1 decision to Pittsburgh despite giving up no earned runs. On July 6 Pond started the second game of a doubleheader and pitched a five-hit shutout against a Philadelphia lineup that included future Hall-of-Famers Ed Delahanty, Nap Lajoie, and Elmer Flick. That sparkling performance proved to be his last in organized baseball.

As Arlie Pond was whipping his final major league pitches, his country was embarking on its bold adventure in imperialism: the Spanish-American War. On the day before that final shutout, July 5, 1898, the twenty-five-year-old physician-pitcher was appointed acting assistant surgeon of the U.S. Army with orders to report to Fort Myer near Washington, D.C. Though the war was decided sooner than the 1898 pennant race—thanks in large part to a brilliant naval victory by a fellow Vermonter, Commodore George Dewey—the consequences were far-reaching alike for American interests and those of Dr. Erasmus Arlington Pond.

Much of the fighting had taken place in the far-off Philippine Islands. Only 379 Americans died in combat but more than 5,000 eventually succumbed to a variety of tropical diseases, so when the young Dr. Pond ar-

This portrait, taken near the end of World War I, shows Dr. Arlington Pond in the uniform of a lieutenant colonel of the United States Medical Corps. [National Baseball Hall of Fame Library, Cooperstown, New York]

These two photographs of Cebu's Southern Islands Hospital were taken more than two decades apart, one shortly after Pond's arrival in 1906 and the other after his death in 1930. Pond's role in the Philippines can be compared to Albert Schweitzer's later work in central Africa. [Dick Leyden]

rived in the Philippines with the 10th Pennsylvania Regiment, there was plenty to keep him busy. Then the Senate's decision to keep the Philippines as an American colony set off an ugly guerilla war with the islands' nationalists, who hitherto had been fighting the Spaniards.

When the Pennsylvanians returned stateside, Dr. Pond was ordered to remain in the Philippines with a Colorado regiment. The fighting became intense at times. The August 26, 1899, issue of *The Sporting Life* reprinted in full a June 23 letter Pond wrote to his future brother-in-law, C. E. Gambrill of Baltimore (Pond married Elizabeth Gambrill in Rutland on July 2, 1900), that includes a harrowing account of an ambush by the nationalists. The letter effectively documents the horror of the skirmish and the disdain Pond felt for the native islanders. Pond clearly believed in the ideology of imperialism—Anglo-Saxon superiority and the "white man's burden"—and one senses condescension in descriptions of his later work. For instance, his obituary in the *Manila Times* stated, "To the Filipinos he was kindly but firm, and much of his medical life was given gratuitously to these people." Not surprisingly, Pond believed that Filipinos weren't ready for the responsibilities of nationhood, and he didn't live to see President Harry Truman declare Philippine independence in 1946.

Arlie Pond intended to return to major league baseball after his tour of duty. In a letter he wrote while in San Francisco in February 1900, he divulged those intentions to old teammate John McGraw, who had taken over as manager of the Orioles. Even way out in the Pacific, Arlie didn't give up baseball altogether. This excerpt is taken from the history of the baseball team of the all-black 25th Infantry Regiment:

> In the early part of 1902, Major Arlington Pond, Medical Corps, U.S. Volunteers (pitcher for the famous Baltimore National League Team), became manager and coach, and his instructions aided the team greatly, especially the pitchers. The regiment was on the eve of its departure for the United States, being transferred to Malabong, Luzon, P.I., where it was stationed until its departure for the homeland. During its stay at the above station, the team participated in several games in which it was victorious. The main scalp taken was that of the famous Land Transportation Team, the Champions of the Manila League at that time (Major Archie Butt's Quartermaster Team).

By 1902 the United States had suppressed the Philippine Insurrection and had started pouring aid into the archipelago. The new American government knew that a top priority was to stop the spread of plagues like bubonic, cholera, smallpox, and leprosy, which had raged unchecked under the Spanish colonial regime. Dr. Pond set aside his baseball career, and he and his young wife remained in the Philippines as a key part of that humanitarian effort, working under the Islands' first Governor General, future U.S. President William Howard Taft.

On August 11, 1902, Pond was detailed from the Army to the Board of Health of the Philippine Islands for cholera duty. A year later he stepped into a permanent position as medical inspector. With the Rockefeller Foundation's private support, Pond played a lead role in the clean-up of Manila City and the collection and segregation of lepers. Then in 1906 he was appointed first chief of the Southern Islands Hospital, 400 miles south of Manila on the island of Cebu. There Pond founded a hospital for lepers in the historic Spanish capital city and undertook the monumental task of vaccinating the island's entire population.

Aside from his official duties, Pond in 1908 was instrumental in reorganizing and rebuilding the old Army-Navy Club as a social center for the entire American community. He also remained active in athletics, playing cricket, golf, polo, and tennis. In the latter sport Arlie held both the singles and doubles championships of the Philippines for several years. He was also a scratch pool and billiards player. With the help of the Reverend George Dunlap, a former Princeton University catcher, Pond popularized baseball on the island, and the Cebu team won the Interscholastic Championships of 1910, 1912, and 1913.

According to newspaper reports, Dr. Pond more than any other was responsible for the "good feeling" that existed among the various elements in Cebu. The *Manila Times* stated, "Many prominent men in business and public life owe their start to Pond's generosity in providing schooling for them and in caring for their health." Though Cebu was somewhat isolated from Manila, Pond became well known and highly regarded throughout the Philippines.

When World War I broke out, Pond was commissioned a major in the Army Medical Corps and assigned to Medical Officers' Training Camp at Fort Benjamin Harrison, Indiana. He was preparing to go to France when Governor General Harrison of the Philippines asked for his return to the islands. Pond was assigned to Camp Stotsenburg with the 9th U.S. Cavalry and the Philippine Field Artillery, then in August 1918 was named post surgeon of the Cuartel de Espana and placed in charge of the dispensary at Fort Santiago, Manila.

On October 28, 1918, Major Pond reported for duty aboard the transport *U.S.S. Warren* en route to Vladivostok, Siberia. It was one year after the October Revolution, and President Woodrow Wilson had grown wary of the Bolsheviks and their vow to mount an anti-capitalist world revolution. He pursued several policies to topple or at least contain them, finally resorting to military intervention—hence Pond's presence on the *Warren*. The transport arrived in Vladivostok on November 11, the day the Armistice was signed. It was ordered back to its former station, and Pond eventually received his discharge on January 15, 1919.

Still dedicated to the welfare of the Philippines, Dr. Pond returned to civilian life in Cebu. This time he entered private practice, as well as several business ventures, including a coconut plantation, a cattle ranch on the island of Mindanao, and the Pond & Deen Navigation Company. It was commonly known that he was a millionaire. "Our leading citizen," one prominent Filipino financier called him.

On September 10, 1930, while his wife was in Shanghai recovering from a breakdown following the death of her cousin, Arlie underwent surgery for appendicitis at his own hospital in Cebu. At first the operation appeared successful, but then peritonitis set in. A wire requesting an Army surgeon from Manila was sent, but an amphibian plane couldn't be arranged. After showing marked improvement, Dr. Pond suffered a relapse and died at 9:00 a.m. on September 19 in the same hospital where he'd saved so many lives. He was only fifty-eight.

The death of Arlington Pond was mourned as a great loss to the Philippines. Flags flew at half-mast and all business houses and banks were closed on the day his funeral service was held at the Manila Lodge of Elks No. 761. Several prominent people attended the military service, among them Senator Sergio Osmena, a Cebu native and one of the outstanding figures in Filipino politics during the first two decades of American rule. After an honor guard fired three volleys and the bugler played taps, Pond's body was taken to the army morgue where it was cremated. The old baseball player's memory is still revered in Cebu, and Pond Parkway, a downtown thoroughfare in Cebu City, honors his name to this day.

TOM SIMON

Northfield

Ed Doheny

His Mind Was Thought to Be Deranged

Ed Doheny's baseball future looked bright as he entered the 1903 season. He was coming off a sixteen-win season and pitching for the defending National League Champion Pittsburgh Pirates. Unfortunately, while Doheny's body was strong, his mind was on the edge of breaking down—for good.

The son of Irish immigrants, Edward Richard Doheny (pronounced DAH-huh-nee) was born in Northfield, Vermont, on November 24, 1873. The Dohenys' modest cottage still stands on the east side of King Street at the foot of Turkey Hill. A sandlot star in his hometown at age fourteen, Ed soon outgrew the competition he could find in central Vermont, so he crossed the Canadian border and pitched for Farnham, Quebec, in 1894. The next year, when the Northfield native was pitching for St. Albans, a Boston sportswriter earned $100 for putting the National League's New York Giants on to Doheny. Success seemed at hand for the twenty-one-year-old Vermonter.

Doheny started three games for the Giants in September 1895 and lost all three. In his twenty-six innings pitched, he gave up thirty-seven hits, nineteen walks, three hit batsmen and four wild pitches while watching twenty-two runs cross the plate. It was far from an impressive beginning, but still he showed potential. After his second outing, a 13-5 loss, *The New York Times* wrote, "Doheny, though slaughtered, showed the earmarks of a ballplayer."

Ed steadily improved over the next two seasons, whittling his career ERA down to 3.08 despite a lifetime record of 10-14 to that point. Though his innings pitched

were too few to qualify for the league title, Doheny sported an ERA of 2.12 in 1897. Teammate Amos Rusie, who pitched considerably more innings, led the league at 2.54. One reason Doheny pitched so infrequently was that he was frequently suspended from the team for "breaches of discipline."

Whether those suspensions were deserved is difficult to determine this far after the fact. On the one hand, Doheny's behavior could be as wild as his pitching often was. On the other, it was Ed's misfortune to join the Giants in their first year under Andrew Freedman, who has been called "perhaps the most hated team owner in baseball history," quite a statement considering a history that includes Charles Comiskey, Walter O'Malley, George Steinbrenner, and Marge Schott. According to his obituary in *The Sporting News*, Freedman "had an arbitrary disposition, a violent temper, and an ungovernable tongue in anger which was easily provoked, and he was disposed to be arbitrary to the point of tyranny with subordinates." He was hardly an ideal boss for a man as unstable as Doheny.

A Sample of Doheny's Bizarre Behavior

Sometimes Doheny returned to Vermont during his frequent suspensions. On one such occasion he took the mound in a Northern League match-up against Norwood Gibson. A few years later, when Gibson was pitching for the Boston Pilgrims, H. L. Hindley of the *Brattleboro Reformer* recalled the game:

> The good work that young Gibson, pony pitcher, is doing for the Boston Americans reminds me of Gibson's last appearance in a Vermont league. He was pitching for Plattsburg, and Mike Powers, now backstop for the Philadelphia Athletics, was behind the bat. St. Albans had Doheny, the famous Pittsburgh southpaw, who was then on New York's suspended list and playing independent ball. Gibson had held St. Albans level for eight long innings, then Plattsburg got a score in the ninth, St. Albans tying it in her half. It was up to Gibson for the tenth, as Doheny had blanked Plattsburg and St. Albans needed only one to win. Then the little lad from Notre Dame got his.
>
> I said it was a hard game, Gibson pitching against a National Leaguer, and, in that fatal tenth, Doheny went down to the coaching lines and opened up a Dad Clarke repertory of talk. He called attention to Gibson's fatigue, to his lady-like delivery, to various points of interest in his personal appearance, while Mike Powers was too mad to talk. He merely knelt and prayed that the little lad would burn 'em over. Gibson did his best, but the strain was telling and pretty soon a little Texas Leaguer got a St. Albans man to first and Doheny was up to bat!
>
> The big fellow with the larboard wing saw it was up to him to win the game and he grinned on Gibson with a sardonic smirk as he swung the willow experimentally and told the spectators what he would do. The pitcher wasn't worrying much, for Doheny never could hit, but he carelessly sent over a fast, straight one and the man at bat just naturally banged it to deep right field, and, before the ball could be fielded in, darkness and all, the man on first was home and it was all off. And no disgrace to Gibson, either.

By 1898 Doheny seemed to be back in favor with Freedman, and he was even named the Giants' Opening Day pitcher. Finally he appeared to be on the verge of fulfilling the glimpses of talent he'd displayed in his first three seasons. At times Doheny did achieve some extraordinary feats. On August 15, 1899, for example, he made his own distinct mark in the baseball record book by striking out Louisville's Pete Dowling five times in a single nine-inning game. And on May 25, 1899, he pitched a masterful four-hit game only to lose because the opposing pitcher, future teammate Deacon Phillippe, threw a no-hitter. For the most part, though, the 1898-1900 seasons were disastrous for Doheny. He lost fifty games while winning only twenty-one, and each year his ERA increased, as did his wildness. His low point was 1900, when he went 4-14 with a 5.51 ERA, his highest since his rookie season.

In 1901 Doheny's luck seemed to change, as did the results of his labors. He was traded in midseason from the Giants to the Pittsburgh Pirates, then the best team in the National League. For the first half, pitching irregularly, Doheny went 2-5 for the Giants. But with his new team he was 6-2 during the second half of the season. Of course, pitching for a team that was running away with the National League pennant didn't hurt his record. The Giants never finished higher than seventh with Doheny, but the Pirates finished in first place each of his three seasons in the Steel City. Doheny won more games in two and a half years in Pittsburgh than he had in six and a half in New York. He became a mainstay in baseball's best pitching rotation, which also featured Phillippe, Jesse Tannehill, and future Hall-of-Famer Jack Chesbro.

In 1902 Ed Doheny was 16-4 for a winning percentage of .800, second-best in the National League. He racked up another sixteen victories the following year and helped the Pirates pitch an N.L. record six consecutive shutouts. In fact, Doheny set the new record by recording the fourth shutout of the streak, a 9-0 defeat of the Boston Beaneaters.

Still shy of his thirtieth birthday, the Vermonter should have been at the height of his career. His place on an excellent Pirate staff seemed secure for years to come, pitching for an owner, Barney Dreyfuss, considerably different from Andrew Freedman. He should have appeared in the first modern World Series and received a share of the proceeds. But lurking in his psyche was an illness that not only denied him more success but doomed him to disaster.

Off to a 12-6 start in 1903, Doheny began exhibiting strange behavior, exacerbated by his excessive consumption of alcohol. First he had a few unpleasant altercations with teammates. Later he started believing he was being followed by detectives. When he left the team without permission towards the end of July, the *Pittsburgh Post* reported that act with a pitiless but starkly revealing headline: "His Mind Is Thought To Be Deranged."

After a few weeks of rest at his home in Andover, Massachusetts, Doheny returned to the Pirates in Boston during an August road trip. He pitched well, improving his record to 16-8, but another series of behavioral mishaps beset him, finally causing his sanity to be questioned. Granted a leave of absence by the Pirates, he was escorted home to Andover by his clergyman brother on September 22, 1903, and placed under the care of a physician.

Though he received daily medical treatment, Ed's condition didn't improve. Nothing seemed to help, not even a gift of his uniform from the Pirates, which Doheny interpreted as a rejection of his belief that he'd someday return to the team. During the first modern World Series, while the A.L.'s Boston Pilgrims were upsetting his former teammates, Doheny suffered a breakdown that

This modern photo show the Danvers State Asylum, where Ed Doheny was institutionalized following his tragic breakdown in October 1903. [Seamus Kearney]

knocked him out of the game for good. On October 10 he threw his doctor head-first out the door of his home and warned him not to return. Then, in the early morning of October 11, he attacked and felled his male nurse, Oberlin Howarth, with a cast-iron stove leg. Howarth was seriously injured but eventually recovered.

Doheny's wife hurried for assistance, but for more than an hour Ed held a score of neighbors and several policemen at bay, defying them and threatening to kill the first man who attempted to take him. Finally Chief of Police Frye and Officer Mills caught Doheny off his guard and overpowered him, and after an examination by two physicians he was declared insane and committed to an asylum in Danvers, Massachusetts. By 1905 his condition had worsened. A Lowell newspaper reported, "Mrs. Doheny writes that her husband—the

pitcher—shows no sign of improvement at Danvers State Asylum and will never recover his reason. [He's] not able to recognize anybody." Though he lived thirteen more tormented years, Ed Doheny never recuperated from his mental illness, never pitched again, and died in another Massachusetts institution, the Medfield State Asylum, on December 29, 1916.

Thus closed the stormy life of one of the most talented Green Mountain Boys of Summer, tragically struck down just as he was overcoming his early problems and establishing himself as one of baseball's winningest pitchers. Whatever demons controlled his psyche, they turned his life upside down. Instead of realizing his dreams of glory, Ed Doheny plunged into a nightmare from which he never awoke.

SEAMUS KEARNEY AND TOM SIMON

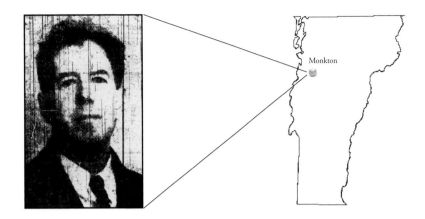

Frank Dupee

From Here to Infinity

Monkton, Vermont, isn't known as a hotbed of athletics, but it was in that tiny Addison County farm community on April 29, 1877, that Frank Oliver Dupee (pronounced "doopy") was born. The second son of immigrant sharecroppers from Quebec, Frank apparently used his extraordinary size—6' 1", 200 pounds, extremely large for his era—and pitching talent to gain an education that should have offered him an escape from a lifetime of poverty.

By the time anything is known of his life, he was enrolled as a student at Maine's Westbrook Seminary. During the summer of 1901, the twenty-four-year-old Dupee—passing himself off as nineteen, a common practice at the time—signed with Augusta, Maine, of the New England League. Joining the team three weeks into the season, Frank was the winning pitcher in his professional debut on June 7, 1901. He went on to win three of his four starts before the franchise moved to Lynn, Massachusetts, during the last week of June. Reluctant to leave Maine, Dupee hooked on with Portland and, according to *The Sporting Life*, "was the star pitcher of the Portland team and the wonder of the New England League." By August 17 Dupee had compiled a record of 10-6 and a 2.47 ERA when Portland sold his contract to the Chicago White Stockings. A bright future seemed assured.

But Dupee's time at the top of his profession turned out to be short-lived, coming one week later on Saturday, August 24, 1901, at Baltimore's Oriole Park. It was the inaugural season of the American League, and the

first-place White Stockings, clinging to a half-game lead over the Boston Americans, were in desperate need of pitching help. Player-manager Clark Griffith, the ace of the staff, had a broken finger, and the usually dependable Nixey Callahan was suffering from stomach trouble. To make matters worse, John Katoll was serving a suspension after throwing a baseball at an umpire three days earlier. That left Griffith with one reliable hurler, rookie Roy Patterson, who'd pitched the day before. Under those circumstances Griff had no choice but to start his new acquisition against John McGraw's feisty Orioles.

Dupee's major league debut started off well enough, his teammates staking him to a 1-0 lead in the top of the first inning on two-out triples by Sandow Mertes and Fred Hartman. Then Dupee took to the mound and, according to the *Chicago Tribune*, "must have had an attack of stage fright or something, for he could not throw the ball anywhere near the plate." The seminarian faced three .300 hitters, left fielder Mike Donlin (.341), right fielder Cy Seymour (.303) and second baseman Jimmy Williams (.317), and walked all three. That was enough for Griffith, who replaced Dupee with Callahan. Steve Brodie hit an infield fly, but Warren Hart and Roger Bresnahan both singled, knocking in all three of the runners Callahan had inherited from Dupee. The Orioles went on to win 10-4, with the loss charged to the rookie from Monkton.

On the train to Philadelphia, where the White Stockings were to open a three-game series against the Athletics on Monday, Dupee explained to reporters that never in his life had he given up so many bases on balls. That wasn't exactly true. In his last start in the New England League he'd walked six, and *The Sporting Life* acknowledged that "his only weakness is occasional lack of control." Despite the fit of wildness, Griffith indicated he'd give the young pitcher another start. Dupee seemed assured of a second chance.

That chance never came. On Sunday, an off-day due to Pennsylvania's blue laws, Griffith signed Wiley Piatt, a veteran lefthander who'd just been released by the A's. Three days later Griff returned Dupee on option to Portland. While the White Sox went on to win the A.L.'s first pennant, Dupee pitched in two more games back in the New England League, winning one and losing one to finish the season at 11-7.

Still another chance seemed to rise the next spring. Before the 1902 season the White Sox sold Dupee to the New York Giants. He went unbeaten in spring exhibition games, and the New York writers described him as the equal of Christy Mathewson, who'd posted a 20-17 record the previous year as a rookie for the seventh-place Giants. Dupee was so impressive, in fact, that "Dirty Jack" Doyle, the Giants' first baseman, dubbed him and Mathewson the "Heavenly Twins" (they were approximately the same height and build). Slated to begin the season as a regular in the New York rotation, Dupee surely was ready to emerge.

Not so. Only days before the season opener, the hard-luck hurler suffered an arm injury that never completely healed. Dupee pitched in the minor leagues another thirteen seasons but never again got a chance to pitch in the majors.

Dupee's frustrations continued after his retirement from baseball. He and his wife, Florence, lived for more than fifty years in West Falmouth, Maine, on a farm they inherited from Florence's parents (currently the site of Falmouth High School). Frank struggled to make a living raising vegetables, supplementing his income by serving occasionally as a hunting and fishing guide and by selling the pelts of muskrats, foxes, skunks, and raccoons he trapped in nearby swamps. It wasn't a happy life. His son Frederick, eighty-eight years old at the time he was interviewed in 1996, didn't recall his father fondly.

Frank Dupee died at the age of seventy-nine on August 14, 1956. His obituary quoted John McGraw as telling sports writers that Dupee was the only pitcher he ever saw who had as much speed as the famed Walter Johnson. But instead of glory, his legacy amounts to this: By yielding three earned runs without recording a single out, Dupee is one of only eighteen pitchers in all major league history with a lifetime ERA of infinity. Of those eighteen, only two gave up more earned runs than Dupee's three. And that makes the once-promising lad from Monkton officially the third-worst pitcher in the history of major league baseball.

Tom Simon

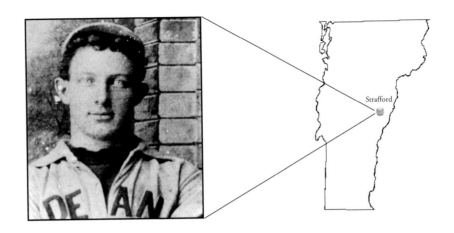

Doc Hazelton

Pride of the First Northern League

There used to be a ballpark on the edge of Burlington's Intervale, near the intersection of North Prospect Street and Riverside Avenue. It was known as Athletic Park, and from 1903 to 1906 it was the home of Burlington's team in the first of Vermont's legendary Northern Leagues. During those years Athletic Park was the site of what may have been the highest caliber of baseball ever played in Vermont. It was where stars like Jack Coombs, Ed Reulbach, Larry Gardner, and Eddie Collins got their start. But none shone brighter in the Northern League than Burlington's captain and two-time batting champion, a former St. Louis Cardinal by the name of Willard "Doc" Hazelton.

Willard Carpenter Hazelton was born in Strafford, Vermont, on August 28, 1876. He was the fourth and youngest son of Henry and Amanda (Carpenter) Hazelton, both of whom were Strafford natives. Henry Hazelton's sister married the brother of Justin Morrill, who served with distinction in the United States Congress as Representative and Senator from Vermont for forty-four years.

The Hazeltons descended from several of Strafford's earliest settlers. One was Willard's great-grandfather, Thomas Hazelton, who fought at Bunker Hill in the initial stages of the American Revolution. The old family homestead was destroyed by fire in 1921, but the hotel operated by Willard's father still stands, though it's now a private residence. It borders the Strafford common where Will played his first ball games. Years later,

when "Doc" signed a major league contract, the *Chelsea Herald* wrote, "His love for baseball dates back to the lad in kilts whose chief fun was in tossing a ball on our little common near his home. One remembers well his laughing, sunshiny face as he caught the ball, beating some other boy not as deft-fingered as he."

Will attended Strafford common schools, the town's public elementary schools, but because Strafford didn't have a high school he was forced to go away to further his education. He spent the 1893-94 school year at Kimball Union Academy in Meriden, New Hampshire, then returned to Strafford in 1894-95 and earned $110 teaching at the common school near Miller's Pond. "The Fall and Winter terms of the Pond school were taught by Mr. Will Hazelton, who spared no pains with the twelve young pupils entrusted to his care," wrote that year's *Strafford Town Report*.

In 1895 Will enrolled at Dean Academy in Franklin, Massachusetts, where his field of study was "Technical Preparation." The school always had a strong baseball program—Hall-of-Famer Gabby Hartnett is an alumnus—and Will pitched for the varsity. He was also elected president of the Class of 1897.

Following a well-developed trend of Dean graduates, Hazelton matriculated at Tufts University in Medford, Massachusetts, where he majored in engineering. "While at Tufts, he endeared himself to his schoolfellows by his quiet, studious and gentlemanly demeanor," wrote the *Chelsea Herald*. As a freshman Will was unanimously

The Hazelton family operated this hotel bordering the Strafford Common, where Will played his first ball. [Strafford Historical Society]

elected captain of the baseball team. In fact, a note in the March 17, 1907, issue of the *Boston Globe* credits him with forming Tufts' first-ever team. He spent summer vacations playing with amateur teams all over New England.

During the summer after Will's sophomore year the sport nearly cost him his life. On August 25, 1899, three days before his twenty-third birthday, he was batting in a game at Fabyan House, a resort on New Hampshire's Mount Washington, when a pitch struck him on the forehead. Will picked himself up and played for three more innings before he fell unconscious. He was rushed to Mary Hitchcock Hospital in Hanover, where he was diagnosed with a skull fracture and a burst artery, which formed a blood clot that was pressing on his brain, causing paralysis on his right side. Within a week of the injury a Dr. Connor of Cincinnati performed surgery to remove the clot and pieces of bone.

"There was little expectation of his recovery," the *Chelsea Herald* reported. "Nearly a week had elapsed before he regained consciousness, but in a month's time he was allowed to come to his home. His physicians told him his perfect physical condition is what saved him." In March the *Herald* reported that Willard had spent two days in Boston recently and expected to return to Tufts to complete his college course. He did in fact return, graduating in June 1901.

The winter following his graduation Will signed a contract with the St. Louis Cardinals, intending to use the money to pay his way through medical school. In February 1902 the *Boston Post* wrote that news of his signing "was read with intense pleasure by that young man's friends, who are legion in Boston and throughout central Massachusetts, where he enjoys a high reputation as a fast and most promising player." Will planned on filling the breach created by the departure of Dan McGann, the Cardinals' regular first baseman in 1901, who had jumped to the rival American League.

In St. Louis on April 17, opening day of the 1902 season, Hazelton made his major league debut against the previous year's National League champions, the Pittsburgh Pirates. The Cardinals were a ragtag assemblage of unknowns, decimated by the American League's raids, and most experts predicted they would finish last. The Pirates, on the other hand, retained their entire lineup from 1901. To make things worse for the Cards, the Pirates were pitching their ace, Deacon Phillippe, one of the N.L.'s best. St. Louis gamblers, perhaps being generous to the home team, made them only 8-to-5 underdogs.

To the surprise and delight of the 11,000 fans who showed up at League Park, the reconstructed Cardinals battled the powerful Pirates nip-and-tuck for nine innings before bowing, 1-0. Despite a badly-skinned knee suffered during the exhibition season, Hazelton, by that time known as "Doc" because of his ambition to study medicine, started at first base and collected his first major league hit, a single off Phillippe. The Cardinals dropped the next contest, 10-4, as Doc picked up his second hit in as many games. He was also the only St.

Louis fielder not to make at least one error. "Medals and other congratulatory testimonials are contemplated," the *St. Louis Post-Dispatch* snickered. In the third Pittsburgh game Hazelton was 0-for-4 and contributed two errors in a 10-2 drubbing.

The Vermonter's slump continued as the Cardinals headed out on the season's first roadtrip. In games at Chicago and Cincinnati, Hazelton was a combined 1-for-15. Before the end of April, with his team off to a dismal 1-6 start, St. Louis manager Patsy Donovan decided he'd seen enough of his big first baseman. Doc was handed his release after starting the first seven games of the season, making contact in each of his twenty-three plate appearances but managing only three singles for a .130 batting average, with no runs scored or batted in. Doc joined Rochester, New York, of the Eastern League, then jumped his contract in June and spent the rest of the season with an independent team in Milford, Massachusetts.

For the next several years Hazelton coached the University of Vermont baseball team in the spring and played for Burlington's Northern League team in the summer. Though it wasn't the majors, it was the apex of his baseball career. In *Disorganized Baseball: Baseball In Vermont (1887-1935)*, baseball historian Merritt Clifton writes:

It is probable that the level of 1901-06 represented the pinnacle of professional baseball in Vermont. An all-star team of Northern League performers could undoubtedly have performed respectably in the major leagues. Many players more than held their own from the first with virtually no other professional experience.

The Burlington team that Hazelton captained in 1903 was a typical Northern League aggregation. In addition to Hazelton, it included four other former or future big leaguers: Bob "Doc" Lawson, who'd pitched in the majors the previous two seasons; Libe Washburn, who'd lost all four of his starts with the Phillies earlier in 1903; Jack Doscher, a pitcher who joined the powerful Chicago Cubs later that season; and Ed McLane, who went on to play one game in the outfield for Brooklyn in 1907.

After starting the 1904 season with Toledo of the American Association, at the highest rung on the minor league ladder, Hazelton jumped his contract and returned to Burlington. He paid a steep price for his contract-jumping when Organized Baseball's ruling body, the National Commission, branded him as a baseball "outlaw," which meant that he couldn't play for any clubs belonging to the National Agreement. But by that time the

Doc Hazelton (wearing a dark cap in this photo of the 1911 team) is the only man in history to serve three separate stints as UVM baseball coach: 1903-05, 1910-11, and 1917. [University of Vermont]

Burlington captain and clean-up hitter had won two consecutive batting titles and established himself as one of the best and most popular players in perhaps the finest outlaw league in the country—right in his native state.

Hazelton Lures Ed Reulbach to UVM

Though forgotten today, Doc Hazelton enjoyed a successful coaching career at UVM. Taking over a program that had fallen on hard times in the years since Bert Abbey and Arlie Pond, Hazelton led the team to an 11-13 record in his first year, then followed up with a 14-5 record in 1904. The 1905 team was undoubtedly his finest, and the man most responsible was a 6' 1", 190-pound, hard-throwing pitcher named Ed Reulbach.

Hazelton had discovered Reulbach in the Northern League the previous summer, when the twenty-two-year-old midwesterner went undefeated for Montpelier-Barre while pitching under the pseudonym of Sheldon to protect his amateur status. "Big Ed" had attended college at Notre Dame the previous three years. He'd come to Vermont intending to stay just for the summer, but he met and married Nellie Whelan of Montpelier, and Hazelton convinced him to forego his senior year at Notre Dame and enroll in medical school at UVM.

After losing to Harvard, Vermont reeled off nine consecutive victories to open the 1905 season. Newspapers called Reulbach the "greatest of all college pitchers." On May 12, following a 1-0 shutout of Syracuse, Big Ed received an offer from Frank Selee, manager of the Chicago Cubs, that "would take the breath away from an average person" (*Burlington Free Press*). The midwesterner couldn't refuse. That night, accompanied by a large group of students and fans, he caught the train to New York. The *Free Press* described the scene as "like a funeral" until the boys gave the departing pitcher the college yell as his train pulled away.

Three days later, Reulbach was on the mound against the world-champion New York Giants, hurling a complete game and yielding only five hits in a 4-0 loss. By the end of the 1905 season, Reulbach's record with the Cubs stood at 18-13 and his ERA at 1.42. In his star pitcher's absence, Hazelton managed the best he could, but losses in five of the last ten games left UVM with a still-impressive 16-6 record.

In 1906 Hazelton turned over the UVM coaching position to Northern League teammate Tom Hays, choosing instead to play during the early part of the season with Johnstown, Pennsylvania, of the Tri-State League, another outlaw circuit. After umpiring several UVM games, Hazelton left Burlington for Johnstown on May 16. To the concern of Burlington baseball fans, the popular first baseman hadn't returned by June 22, the day before the opening of the Northern League sea-

son. Burlington was playing a scrimmage that day against the UVM varsity, featuring Ray Collins on the mound and Larry Gardner at third base. "It was not a happy introduction to Burlington fans that the league team met," the *Free Press* reported, "as the crowd was distinctly pro-Vermont and did not hesitate to jeer the leaguers and roast the umpire at every chance."

At least that was the case until the dramatic arrival of Doc Hazelton, standing out from his teammates by showing up in one of the Burlington team's new gray-and-blue uniforms:

> When the old boy showed up, the only enthusiasm of the afternoon was manifested by the crowd in favor of Burlington. It was very complimentary to Hazelton and he made good by the snap and pepper he put into his play. Bill and his trusty big stick failed to connect for a good biff, but there will be a lot of those coming later.

Hazelton (right) as Dartmouth coach in 1916. An article from Hazelton's playing career mentioned that he "pays strict attention to his diet," but his attention had apparently wandered by the time this photo was taken. [Dartmouth College Archives]

Unfortunately, the optimism of the *Free Press* proved unfounded; Hazelton batted only .258, his lowest average in four Northern League seasons. It was also a disappointing summer for the circuit as a whole, which entered a thirty-year hibernation after 1906.

Though thirty-one, Hazelton still had some baseball left in him. In 1907 he applied to the National Commission for reinstatement but was turned down. A news item from May 1907 states that he was unable to play for Johnstown that season due to a recent baseball injury. No records exist of his whereabouts for the next two years, when he was probably injured or playing in outlaw leagues.

In 1910 Hazelton returned to UVM for a second stint as baseball coach, remaining through 1911. After a brief foray into the automobile business in Burlington, he accepted a coaching position at his *alma mater*, Tufts. Following the 1912 season, Willard returned to Burlington and married Emma Louise Beech. The Hazeltons had one child, a daughter born on May 7, 1913, whom they named Cora Maybelle. In August 1915 Doc was named baseball coach at Dartmouth College. After leading Dartmouth to a 12-9 record in 1916, he signed on for an unprecedented third stint as UVM baseball coach. This time he lasted just one season, and 1917 proved to be the last year of his involvement in baseball.

Moving to New York City, Hazelton worked for a woolen brokerage. The ten-year-old Cora's death on April 20, 1924, according to the Dean alumni magazine, "brought Mr. Hazelton great sorrow from which he never recovered." Following his retirement in 1937, Willard and Emma returned to Burlington, and Willard died of cancer at Mary Fletcher Hospital on March 10, 1941. His obituary in the *Free Press* failed to make any mention whatsoever of his lengthy career in baseball.

Doc Hazelton was laid to rest in beautiful Lakeview Cemetery on Burlington's North Avenue, only a mile or so from the former site of Athletic Park.

FRANCIS JOSEPH O'BOYLE
RESEARCH ASSISTANCE BY GWENDA SMITH

The Gardner Years

(1908-1924)

After four years without a single Vermonter gracing a major league diamond, the 1908 season produced a bumper crop of rookies from the Green Mountains. Though Amby McConnell and Jean Dubuc had more immediate impacts on their clubs' fortunes, it was Larry Gardner of Enosburg Falls who went on to spend seventeen seasons in the major leagues. During the span of his career, 1908 to 1924, Vermont sent thirteen men to the majors, several of them stars, making this the most bountiful era for Green Mountain Boys of Summer.

Gardner replaced McConnell as the regular second baseman of the Boston Red Sox in 1910. Later that fall, Gardner, fellow Vermonter Ray Collins, and the rest of their teammates played an exhibition game at Burlington's Centennial Field. When America entered the Great War seven years later, Vermont provided more than 16,000 servicemen, among them Arlington Pond, Ray Fisher, Heinie Stafford, Dave Keefe, and Bobby Murray. After the armistice, Fisher returned to the majors and pitched in the 1919 World Series.

Two Green Mountain Boys of Summer who played briefly for the Washington Senators during the early 1920s, Elmer Bowman and Bobby Murray, later made modest contributions to another burgeoning entertainment industry—motion pictures. Another Vermonter had a much more imporant impact in Washington. On August 4, 1923, Calvin Coolidge was sworn in as President of the United States at his childhood home in Plymouth, becoming the second native Vermonter to serve in that office.

Ironically, within a year Coolidge found it politically expedient to become a fan of that very team (though it no longer included Bowman or Murray). The Senators were on their way to the World Series in 1924, which also happened to be an election year, and Coolidge's handlers decided they could win votes by making him a baseball fan, even though he really didn't care for the sport. First Lady Grace Coolidge, however, was indeed an avid fan who kept a perfect scorecard, a skill she claimed she developed during her college days at the University of Vermont.

While the Coolidges were attending games in Washington, Larry Gardner was finishing out his stellar career in Cleveland. Following his retirement after the 1924 season, major league baseball endured another brief hiatus without a single Vermonter.

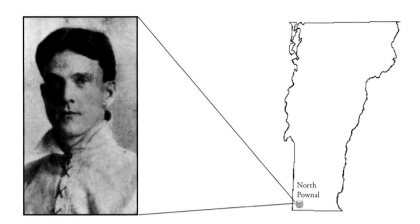

Amby McConnell

Mighty Mite Who Made the Majors

Tucked away in a scenic valley in the southeast corner of Vermont, not far from the Massachusetts and New York borders, North Pownal seems like a town that has been forgotten by time. Jobs are scarce in North Pownal today, and there's little left to remind visitors that the hamlet once produced a major league ballplayer. But less than a mile away from an old tannery, once North Pownal's primary industry, lies a small, grassy diamond, and it was there that an undersized boy began his dreams of big league glory more than a century ago.

Ambrose Moses McConnell was born on April 20, 1883, but exactly where is a matter of debate. Most accounts list his birthplace as North Pownal, but his death certificate lists Cohoes, New York, and still another source places his birth in Williamstown, Massachusetts. From his own personal account we know that as a teenager Amby worked fifty hours per week in the North Pownal tannery, earning the lofty wage of six dollars. He hoped to save money for a trip to Boston to see the champion Beaneaters squad of Hugh Duffy and Kid Nichols, but that opportunity never came.

Amby loved baseball and took advantage of any opportunity to play the game on North Pownal's tiny diamond. Nicknamed "Midget," the speedy 5' 7" infielder became well known in the region for his defensive prowess. Teams in neighboring towns frequently paid his expenses to play on weekends, and on one such occasion McConnell caught the attention of a team from Dalton, Massachusetts. The manager offered him $7.50 a week

to join the squad and Amby jumped at the chance to make a $1.50 raise to play the sport he loved—not knowing that some players on the team were making twice as much. Thus was born a trend of financial misadventure that dogged his professional career.

Leaving Dalton in 1902, McConnell split the 1903 season between Rutland of Vermont's first Northern League and another independent team from Beloit, Wisconsin. A fine showing with the latter squad brought him to Troy in the New York State League in 1904. In 121 games Amby rapped out 150 hits and batted a sterling .318. That earned him a promotion to Rochester in the Eastern League, where he slumped to .254. Returning to the New York State League with Utica in 1906, McConnell stole twenty-two bases and fielded at a .958 clip. He also married a woman from Utica, and in later years he spent his offseasons in upstate New York with his wife and two children.

McConnell returned to the Eastern League with Providence in 1907 and had his best season yet, hitting a robust .320 with fifty stolen bases. At the end of the season the Boston Americans purchased Amby's contract, and on April 17, 1908, two weeks shy of his twenty-fifth birthday, he finally realized his dream of seeing a major league game—and he was playing in it.

The Red Sox, as the team was just starting to be called, were coming off a miserable season, but the nucleus of the championship teams of the next decade was beginning to form. Shortstop Heinie Wagner was already a regular and center fielder Tris Speaker had joined the team at the end of the 1907 season. Aside from McConnell, other rookies in 1908 were pitcher Joe Wood, catcher Bill Carrigan, and infielder Larry Gardner. The Red Sox thought so much of McConnell, however, that they quickly dispatched Gardner to the minors and dealt veteran second baseman Hobe Ferris to make room for him in the lineup.

The Midget didn't disappoint his New England fans during his rookie season. Using a heavier bat than any other Boston player, the left-handed swinger finished second on the team in hits (140) and batting average (.279). Though he struggled a bit defensively in the early going, McConnell was credited with steadying the infield and propelling the team to an improved fifth-place finish. He used his speed to steal a team-leading thirty-one bases, which remains the second-highest total by a rookie in Red Sox history. All in all, it was quite a year.

With Harry Hooper and Ray Collins joining the club in 1909, the surging Red Sox won eighty-eight games on

The 5' 7", 150-pound McConnell was a reliable fielder. Despite leading American League second basemen with a .973 fielding percentage in 1911, he never played another game in the majors. [National Baseball Hall of Fame Library, Cooperstown, New York]

the way to a third-place finish. Though slumping to .238, McConnell played well defensively and stole twenty-six bases as part of the BoSox's heralded "Speed Boys" offense. On July 19 of that season he earned a small place in baseball history. Stepping to the plate with two on against the Cleveland Naps, McConnell hit a liner right at shortstop Neal Ball, who quickly doubled off both baserunners. It was baseball's first unassisted triple play.

The 1910 season proved to be the turning point of Amby McConnell's major league career. After McConnell suffered a serious leg injury, Gardner took over at second base and proved better than his fellow Vermonter. Suddenly expendable, the recovering McConnell was unloaded in what was considered a blockbuster deal: he and third baseman Harry Lord were shipped to the Chicago White Sox for utility infielder Billy Purtell and pitcher Frank "Piano Mover" Smith, who had won twenty-five games the previous year. The change of Sox improved McConnell's fortunes somewhat. After batting .171 for the Red Sox, he hit .275 for the rest of the season.

Amby's new boss in Chicago was the crabby and penurious Charles Comiskey. The Chisox magnate went to great lengths to limit his players' compensation, and the always money-conscious McConnell soon ran afoul of him. In May 1911 Amby suffered a knee injury and was confined to bed for a few days. Unable to go to the local bank to cash his paycheck, he instead mailed it to his wife back in Utica. When she went to the bank, she was told that the check was no good because the account had been closed.

Amby investigated and learned that the Chicago bank from which the check was drawn had closed down. An irate McConnell accused Comiskey of financial misconduct, as the latter refused to settle the debt until the bank's matters were concluded. The issue dragged on throughout the season, with McConnell threatening legal action and Comiskey maintaining that his hands were tied until the courts decided the bank's fate.

Meanwhile Amby played solidly at second base for the White Sox, hitting .280 and leading the league in fielding percentage. At season's end he must have been shocked to learn of his release by Chicago. According to Comiskey, injuries had robbed the second baseman of the speed the White Sox wanted at the position. McConnell had no difficulty locating another baseball job, catching on with Toronto of the International League, where he hit .321 in 1912. He continued his grievance against Comiskey, and the story behind his complaint reveals much about the inner workings of baseball in this period.

The ruling National Commission consisted of an "old boy" network of owners who shared similar interests.

Though he played only four major league seasons, Amby McConnell made his way onto thirteen different baseball cards. This one is from the 1911 gold-border series. [Dick Leyden Collection]

Reading the correspondence between Comiskey and chairman Garry Hermann, it's easy to see that a player like McConnell didn't stand a chance of winning his case. In a condescending tone, the ballplayer was told that he'd receive full payment in due time. Whether he ever did is unknown, but McConnell never returned to the majors, and one is left to wonder if Comiskey made sure of that.

For the next twelve years Ambrose McConnell wandered aimlessly throughout the minor leagues. After playing for Atlanta in the Southern League and returning to the New York State League from 1915 to 1917, McConnell served as player-manager of Richmond in the Virginia League. In 1919 he had his best professional season, winning the batting title with a .338 mark. That success earned him a final trip to the International

League with Syracuse, where he again managed and hit .355 in thirty-two games. But with no big league promotion forthcoming, McConnell resigned and returned to Virginia to manage in Tarboro. Amby was the popular player-manager of the Luddington Mariners of the Central League in 1922, but once again he was struck down by injury. After getting off to a .329 start, he was nailed in the head by a line drive and forced to leave the club. The injury kept him out for the entire 1923 season. Returning home to Utica, McConnell finished his long playing career with a .350 average in 1924.

Baseball remained in Amby's blood. After running a semipro team in Camden, New Jersey, he returned to help rejuvenate baseball in Utica. McConnell purchased the local stadium, Braves Field, and secured a franchise in the Can-Am league. In addition to co-owning the team with Father Martin, a Catholic priest who doubled as president of the league, Amby filled the dual roles of field and general manager. The Utica Braves failed to fulfill McConnell's aspirations. On the field, the team limped to a depressing 45-78 record. Though attendance was excellent, fans complained that ticket prices were too high.

Amby didn't help matters by becoming involved in yet another financial misadventure. He tried to circumvent the Can-Am League's salary cap by signing shortstop Leo Schoppmyer to two different contracts but was busted by his own partner, Father Martin, who disliked Schoppmyer. In his role as league president, Martin fined and suspended McConnell. As he had in the Comiskey affair, Amby brought the case to a higher office. The National Association cut the suspension to two years' probation, but McConnell stepped down as field manager at the end of the season. He continued to serve as Utica's general manager, hiring Schoppmyer as manager in 1939 and then firing him a year later.

On May 20, 1942, Amby McConnell died at age fifty-nine of a massive heart attack. After his death the old ballpark in Utica was re-named McConnell Field, but one year later his widow sold the franchise to the Philadelphia Phillies and it was moved to Williamsport, Pennsylvania. In 1949 engineers ran a New York State Thruway ramp across the infield of McConnell Field, destroying the last earthly vestige of the diminutive infielder from North Pownal.

JOHN BENNETT

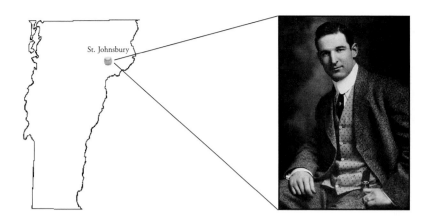

Jean Dubuc

St. Michael's College's Greatest Athlete

For seventy-seven years the 198-foot Gothic spire of Notre Dame des Victoires Church dominated the St. Johnsbury skyline. Standing on Prospect Street, just around the corner from the Fairbanks Museum of Natural History, the church was a familiar landmark to most residents of "St. Jay" until it burned in 1966. But probably no one knew that it was the reason that Jean Dubuc—a pitcher with an 85-76 lifetime record, 3.04 ERA, and surprising .240 batting average in nine major league seasons—was born in the chief city of Vermont's remote Northeast Kingdom.

Before the turn of the century, the Dubuc family owned Granite Construction Company, an itinerant firm that specialized in building churches throughout the northeast. In the spring of 1887 Napoleon Dubuc relocated to Railroad Street in St. Johnsbury to start work on Notre Dame Church. That first summer 150 carloads of Concord granite and thirty carloads of Isle la Motte stone were used to build the church's exterior. In the summer of 1888 the interior was finished in ash, frescoed, and lighted with stained-glass windows—St. Patrick on one side for the Irish parishioners and St. John the Baptist on the other for the French-Canadians.

Later that summer—on September 15, 1888, to be exact—Mathilde Dubuc had a son whose given name at birth is variously reported as Jean Arthur, John Joseph, Jean Baptiste Arthur, and Jean Joseph Octave Arthur. As if those weren't enough, somewhere along the line he picked up the nickname "Chauncey." Despite his French-

Canadian heritage, his first name was pronounced "Gene," at least in American baseball circles, while his last name was pronounced like Dubuque, the city in Iowa.

When Jean was four, the Dubucs moved to Montpelier. The future major leaguer lived in Vermont's capital city for seven years before his parents sent him to the Seminary of St. Theresa in Montreal. There, the *Rutland Herald* reported, Jean "was undefeated in high school games pitched in Canada." As he entered adolescence the family re-located yet again, this time to Fall River, Massachusetts, where Napoleon was the contractor in charge of building St. Ann's Church. In 1904 Jean enrolled in the prep program at the College of the Holy Cross in Worcester, studying electrical engineering. He went out for varsity baseball, but on the second day of practice school authorities informed the fifteen-year-old that he was too young to play.

For the 1905-06 schoolyear, Dubuc attended St. Michael's College in Winooski Park, Vermont. Though he spent only one year at the Edmundite institution, he is generally regarded as its greatest athlete ever. In only its second year of existence, St. Mike's already had a winning baseball team. It was 13-4 the year Dubuc was there, its losses coming to Goddard Seminary, UVM's junior varsity, Plattsburgh High School, and the 23rd Battery team from Fort Ethan Allen. Jean pitched every game, recording double-digit strikeouts routinely, but his exploits at the plate were even more impressive. Batting third in the order, he hit .528 with an .843 slugging average. To put

St. Johnsbury's Notre Dame des Victoires Church was built by Napoleon Dubuc in 1887-88. It was destroyed by fire in 1966. [Scott Cahoon]

that in perspective, subtracting Dubuc's contributions, the team's batting average falls from .300 to .271, and its slugging average plummets from .375 to .316.

The following fall Jean headed west to South Bend, Indiana, and enrolled at the University of Notre Dame. Though his first athletic participation on campus was as

Dubuc (at center, wearing a sweater with a "B" on it) was the star of the 1906 St. Michael's baseball team, batting .528 and compiling a 13-4 mound record. [St. Michael's College Archives]

starting forward on the varsity basketball team, Dubuc showcased his true athletic brilliance on the baseball diamond. In the spring of 1907, the eighteen-year-old Vermonter posted a 5-1 record as the Fighting Irish amassed twenty-one victories against only two losses. The following season Notre Dame was 20-1, with Jean upping his contribution to 9-1. Aside from Dubuc, the 1908 squad featured no less than four future major leaguers: second baseman George Cutshaw, who played regularly for eleven seasons with Brooklyn, Pittsburgh, and Detroit; first baseman Bert Daniels, who patrolled the outfield with the New York Highlanders for four seasons; catcher Ed McDonough, who backstopped for the Phillies for a couple of years; and pitcher Frank Scanlan, who had a cup of coffee with the Phils.

Even in that fast company, Chauncey Dubuc glistened. His nine wins in 1908 stood as a school record until 1989, though later Notre Dame teams played much longer schedules. Of his fourteen wins over two seasons, half were shutouts, and even his two defeats were glorious. In 1907's only loss, Dubuc gave up just one hit and one walk while striking out sixteen—and getting three hits of his own. And his 1908 defeat was one of the most interesting games in the annals of Vermont baseball history.

> **Dubuc's Vermont Homecoming (Part I)**
>
> When Jean Dubuc pitched against UVM at Centennial Field during Notre Dame's 1908 eastern trip, Vermont baseball enjoyed a banner day. The game featured three of history's most distinguished Green Mountain Boys of Summer: Dubuc on the mound for the visitors, Ray Collins for the home nine, and Larry Gardner at shortstop.
>
> In a hard-fought game in which Collins struck out thirteen, UVM handed the Fighting Irish—and Dubuc—their only loss of the season, 6-3. "[Notre Dame], the much heralded champions of the Middle West, came to Burlington with a series of twelve victories," bragged UVM's yearbook, *The Ariel*, "yet even with the far famed Dubuc in the box, they were unable to keep us from scoring six runs."

Jean Dubuc intended to return to Notre Dame in the fall of 1908 but was forced to change plans when a semi-pro game in Chicago cost him his amateur status. Adopting the alias of "Williams," Dubuc pitched a lackluster team called the White Rocks to a 2-1 victory over the powerful Gunthers, but the ruse was detected and reported in the *Chicago Tribune*. Without hesitation, Notre Dame authorities ruled their best pitcher ineligible for further collegiate competition.

Jean barely had time to peel off his White Rocks uniform before receiving offers from seven major league teams.

He signed with the Cincinnati Reds, with whom the nineteen-year-old made his major league debut on June 25, 1908. In his first big league game he was pulled in the fourth inning after severely wrenching his knee, an injury that plagued him for the rest of his career. He pitched only once more until September, when he returned to action as a regular starter. Dubuc ended up 5-6 with a solid 2.74 ERA. One of his victories was a two-hit shutout over the world-champion Chicago Cubs.

That fall Jean won three of his four decisions on Cincinnati's barnstorming tour of Cuba. It looked like 1909 might be a big year for the young Vermonter. But in spring training he contracted malaria, causing him to miss most of the season. In 1910 Reds manager Clark Griffith sent Dubuc to Buffalo of the Eastern League, but when the pitcher continued to struggle, Buffalo released him. Jean went home to Montreal, where his father had moved after Jean's mother's death.

For the French-speaking Vermonter, Montreal was the perfect place to turn around his sagging baseball fortunes. Jean joined the Royals, the local Eastern League

Illness and injury hampered Dubuc during his time with the Cincinnati Reds. This image comes from a T-206 baseball card, circa 1910. [Dick Leyden Collection]

club, and rebounded to 21-11 in 1911, thanks mainly to an effective change-up learned from his catcher, major league veteran Frank Roth. Dubuc also opened a successful business, The Palace Bowling Alley and Pool Room at 282 St. Catherine Street, and bought stock in the Montreal Wanderers, one of two local National Hockey Association franchises. Of course, with twenty-one wins to his credit, Dubuc was eagerly wanted back in the majors—it was said that fifteen big league scouts were in the stands for one of his starts. Montreal's asking price was reportedly $10,000 and a couple of players, but in September the Royals accidentally exposed him to the major league draft. Ten of the sixteen clubs put in claims, with the Detroit Tigers finally obtaining him for the bargain price of $1,500.

Detroit offered Dubuc a salary of $2,250 for 1912. Sitting pretty in Montreal, Jean played coy. In a letter to Tigers owner Frank Navin, he pointed out that $2,250 for seven months' work contrasted poorly with his 1911 salary of $2,196.68 for five months, not to mention the need to hire a manager to run his business if he left Montreal. Dubuc countered with two options: Navin could raise him to $2,800 or allow him to buy out his own contract for $1,500. While that response may seem brazen for an unproven youngster, Dubuc's letter, preserved to this day in his file at the National Baseball Library, is a model of courtesy.

Somehow the differences were resolved, and in 1912 Jean Dubuc began a five-year stint in Detroit with a spectacular first season. Though overshadowed by Walter Johnson's and Smoky Joe Wood's record sixteen-game winning streaks, Dubuc compiled an eleven-game streak of his own en route to a 17-10 record, with two shutouts and an ERA of 2.77. In a feature article in *Baseball Magazine*, F. C. Lane called Dubuc "The Slow Ball Wizard." Another sportswriter dubbed him the "best pitching find of the season." Hall-of-Fame umpire Billy Evans pronounced his change-up the best in the American League.

Over the next four seasons, amid repeated salary wrangles, Dubuc showed flashes of his original glitter but never put together an entire season of distinction. In 1914, for example, he started off in a blaze, winning his first five decisions and bringing forth headlines like "Looks Better Than Ever." According to one newspaper, "Some of the diamond critics believe that he is destined to become the best pitcher in baseball." But for the rest of that year his won-lost record was only 8-14, his ERA for the season escalating to 3.46. He came back in 1915 with a 17-12 record, including a career-high five shutouts (one of them a one-hit, 1-0 triumph over the great Walter Johnson). But when his knee injury resurfaced in 1916, causing him to tail off to 10-10, the Tigers figured he wasn't worth a big salary and sold him to Chattanooga.

After bouncing around the minors for most of 1917-18, the Vermonter's prospects looked brighter when he was acquired by John McGraw's New York Giants before the 1919 season. In an era when relief specialists were unheard of—Firpo Marberry, often credited for launching that role, didn't appear until five seasons later—Dubuc pitched in thirty-six games, only five of them starts, leading the N.L. with thirty-one relief appearances. He won six, lost four, and saved three (tied for second in the league in that category). Dubuc compiled a 2.66 ERA and allowed only 119 hits in 132 innings as the Giants finished in second place. He seemed to have found a niche.

Despite leading the National League in relief appearances with the New York Giants in 1919, Dubuc never again pitched in the majors. [St. Michael's College Archives]

Dubuc's Vermont Homecoming (Part II)

Following the 1919 season, the New York Giants made the only visit a major league team has ever granted to the town of Jean Dubuc's birth. The game occurred on the campus of St. Johnsbury Academy on Friday, October 10, 1919, the Giants taking on a team of St. Johnsbury's local players helped out by pitcher Dana Fillingim of the Boston Braves.

That Dubuc recognized the St. Johnsbury exhibition as a homecoming is evident by the fact that he was New York's starting pitcher, yet the local press made no mention whatsoever of his native status. Weather more typical of mid-July than October helped bring out a huge crowd, which the *Evening Caledonian* described as "cosmopolitan, coming from all parts of northeastern Vermont. Newport, Barton, Island Pond, Wells River, Danville, Hardwick and other places furnished a good sized quota."

The Giants cruised to a 10-4 victory despite five errors. The afternoon's greatest excitement came when Michael Reynolds of Barton was struck by a foul ball. That night rumors of his death spread throughout St. Johnsbury, but the following day's newspaper made clear that he'd suffered only a broken nose. The *Caledonian* quoted Dr. H. H. Miltimore as saying that reports of Reynolds' death "did not take into consideration that he had a good doctor."

The post-game celebration included a dance at the armory, with Sargent's eight-piece orchestra playing all the latest music. "The Giants certainly enjoyed the affair and danced with the pretty local girls to their hearts' content," the *Caledonian* reported. As they boarded a train for Montreal the next morning, the visiting players said that it was "one of the best times they ever had on a baseball trip," and that they'd put St. Johnsbury on their list for future trips. St. Johnsbury is still waiting.

Based on his stellar 1919 performance, Jean Dubuc appeared to have earned another shot at the majors. "He doubtless will festoon the Giant staff for some time to come," was how one writer put it. But after the fall barnstorming tour, McGraw unexpectedly released Dubuc. The thirty-one-year-old veteran hooked on with the Toledo Mud Hens, for whom he played all positions except catcher and middle infield in 1920. In the American Association Dubuc proved his value by winning nine games on the mound with a 2.72 ERA, batting .292, serving as field captain, and even replacing Roger Bresnahan as manager at midseason.

Why did the sage McGraw exile Dubuc to Toledo, and why did the Vermonter never again pitch in the major leagues? The answers to those questions became apparent only as the details of the Black Sox scandal unfolded. On September 24, 1920, pitcher Rube Benton, a former teammate of Dubuc's with the Giants, testified before a grand jury in Chicago that he'd seen a telegram disclosing that the Series was fixed. "I don't know who sent it," Benton said, "but it came to Jean Dubuc, who was barnstorming with us. It simply said: 'Bet on the Cincinnati team today.' I suppose it came from Bill

Burns, who had been close to Dubuc a few weeks before the Series when both were living at the Ansonia Hotel in New York City."

Having his name come up in the baseball bribery investigation wasn't a positive development for Dubuc, to say the least. In the aftermath of Benton's testimony, *The Sporting News* published a piece in its issue of November 11, 1920, entitled "Why Dubuc Was Dropped." The article quoted McGraw as saying that he released Dubuc because he "constantly associated" with Bill Burns, a gambler who'd played with Jean on the 1912 Tigers. According to *The Sporting News*, McGraw suspected that Burns and Hal Chase, who'd also been mentioned in the Chicago hearings, might have caused the Giants to lose out to the Reds in the 1919 pennant race.

While Commissioner Landis was handing out banishments from baseball, Dubuc wisely made himself unobtrusive by leaving the country for the entire 1921 season. Others who were no more implicated in the scandal than Dubuc were banned for life, but Landis failed to notice the newly obscure pitcher in Montreal's Atwater Park Twilight League. By 1922 Jean was back in the United States, pitching in the minors for the Syracuse Stars. *The Sporting News* lifted an offended eyebrow:

> The astounding news comes from Syracuse that President Ernest Landgraf plans to take on Jean Dubuc, former major leaguer and later with Toledo, from which club he

drew his walking papers because he was supposed to know too much about the throwing of the 1919 World's Series.

Still Landis looked the other way, and Dubuc was allowed to carve out a modest living in the minors for the next several years.

In 1927 Jean Dubuc moved to Providence, Rhode Island, where he coached the Brown University baseball and hockey teams and founded the Rhode Island Reds of the American Hockey League. While in Rhode Island he scouted for the Detroit Tigers, signing the great Hank Greenberg among others. New York Yankees scout Paul Krichell recalled spending the better part of a year visiting the Greenberg family and manfully eating Yiddish food, only to watch with dismay as "in stepped Jean Dubuc . . . who called at the Greenberg house, bringing along his own ham sandwich, and signed up Hank right under the very shadow of Yankee Stadium."

In 1936 Dubuc returned to his native state as manager of the Northern League's Burlington Cardinals, but the following year he left sports altogether. For the next two decades he worked as a printer's ink salesman, eventually retiring to Florida. Following a three-year illness, Jean Dubuc passed away in Fort Myers on August 28, 1958. "He was a very dear friend of mine up to the time of his death, was a very fine baseball man, an excellent baseball instructor, and a fine gentleman," said Birdie Tebbetts.

TOM SIMON & GUY WATERMAN
RESEARCH ASSISTANCE BY CAPPY GAGNON

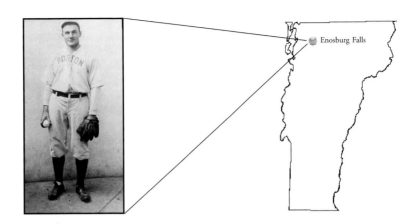

Larry Gardner

A Vermont Baseball Legend

In the foothills of the northernmost Green Mountains, just sixteen miles from the Canadian border, the village of Enosburg Falls, Vermont, proclaims itself "Dairy Center of the World." Like many rural villages, Enosburg Falls is experiencing hard times, but it's fighting to reclaim lost glory. In recent years an energetic village manager and board of aldermen have spruced up Lincoln Park, the quintessential village square with a bandstand and fountain dating from 1897. One recent addition is a Vermont historical site marker commemorating the birthplace of Larry Gardner, long considered the greatest baseball player ever to come out of Vermont.

Back in Gardner's day, Enosburg Falls was one of the most prosperous villages in Vermont. Dairy farming was more lucrative then, but the chief source of the village's prosperity was the world-famous Dr. B. J. Kendall Company, manufacturer of a horse liniment called "Kendall's Spavin Cure." It was in 1872 that Larry's father, Delbert Murancie Gardner, the son of an Episcopal minister, left St. Armand in the Eastern Townships of Quebec. He settled less than twenty miles away, establishing himself in a shop near the Enosburg Falls railroad depot as a "dealer in groceries, provisions, dry goods, Yankee notions, etc."

Five years later, Delbert married a local girl, eighteen-year-old Nettie Lawrence, whose family claimed distant connection to George Washington and a great-grandfather who fought in the Battle of Bunker Hill. Delbert and Nettie had a son, Dwight Murancie, and a daughter, Glenna Maude. Their third and final child, William Lawrence, was born on May 13, 1886.

Larry's childhood days in Enosburg Falls were among his happiest. He enjoyed winter sports and at an early age developed a passion for fishing that lasted his entire life. Larry was also a climber. In an essay entitled "A Daring Adventure" published in a 1904 issue of *The Echo*, a student magazine, he described his dangerous ascent of a 100-foot cliff face at the edge of the Missisquoi River. "I have never attempted to climb the rock since, but I have often stood on its top and wondered how I ever had the nerve to attempt to scale its dark surface," he wrote. In predicting the fates of the next year's editorial staff in that same issue, an astute schoolmate wrote, "This is Mr. Lawrence Gardner, the future athletic editor of *The Echo*. Fame is sure to be his, if he isn't killed first."

But Larry's chief talent lay in team sports, even though the athletic program at tiny Enosburg Falls High School didn't offer a wealth of opportunities. "For lack of an organized leader, not much was done at football, although we had good material," Larry wrote in his column in *The Echo*. "Basketball has created some excitement among the girls, but as yet the boys have not formed a team." Larry was captain of the EFHS hockey club, but "the most popular sport with the townspeople as well as the school," he reported, was baseball.

The first record of Larry Gardner's diamond career dates from 1902, his freshman year. As a junior he pitched every inning of every game and batted an even .400. A

This is the earliest known photograph of Larry Gardner (center). His sister, Glenna, lived her entire life in Enosburg Falls, and his brother, Dwight, settled in Milford Center, Ohio. [Gardner Family Archives]

7-4 record prompted *The Echo* to claim that "we are the champion high school team in Franklin county."

In his senior season of 1905, Gardner rose to what stardom a small village near the Canadian border could offer. The campaign opened with a disappointing 5-3 loss to Brigham Academy, but Larry brought the team back by pitching three consecutive shutouts. On May 20 he was finally scored on but struck out thirteen in a 7-2 win. Two days later Larry pitched against Montpelier Seminary, and in 1943 he told a reporter that "of all the baseball I've ever been connected with, this particular game stands out most vividly in my mind." Thirty-eight years later he recalled the game's details:

Going into the ninth inning we were leading 1-0. "Montpelier Sem" was at bat with bases full and one out. I really was in a tough spot then. The man at bat knocked a hard one that I fielded. I forced the man out at home. The catcher threw to get the man out at first, making a double play and ending the ball game. I can tell you, the men at the corner drug store talked over this game for weeks.

Gardner (front row, left) led Enosburg Falls High School to a 7-1 record and an unofficial state championship during his senior year. [Enosburg Falls Historical Society]

Enosburg Falls celebrated with a band concert, bonfire, and promenade, the Montpelier boys remaining overnight to partake in the festivities.

Larry tossed his fifth shutout in seven games against Newport High School on May 27. More than two weeks later he closed the campaign with a 10-1 win over Newport, which "would have been a shutout, but for a wild throw in the first which let in Newport's only run." The team's 7-1 record, according to the *Enosburg Standard*, clinched the high school championship of Vermont. "The local team has worked hard, has played clean ball, and has made a great 1905 baseball record for Enosburg High School," it proclaimed, "and is entitled to all the honor and credit which the state championship gives them." In eight games on the mound Gardner yielded only eight runs, the majority of which most likely were unearned. He was no weak hitter, either, finishing with a batting average of .432, second-highest on the team.

The summer following Larry's graduation from high school, four of the area's semipro teams banded together to form the Franklin County League. Larry's older teammates appointed him assistant captain of the Enosburg Falls team, called the "Spavin Curers" or "Liniment Makers" by local newspapers. The team from St. Albans was known as the "Railroaders" because the town was the home of the Central Vermont Railway. As the home of a fish hatchery, Swanton was called either the "Fish Hatchers" or the "Bullpout." Newspapermen dubbed the Richford team the "Chinese Spies" because the border town contained a U.S. Customs detention center for illegal immigrants, most of them Chinese.

In a season marred by contract jumping, frequent protests, and a brawl that resulted in criminal charges against participating players, Larry Gardner stood out as the Franklin County League's top all-around talent. He played shortstop and pitched, and after one outing the *St. Albans Messenger* coined him a new nickname: "'Larry' Gardner, the child marvel from Enosburg Falls, pitched rings around the local baseball players yesterday at the local league grounds." From that point on Franklin County newspapers frequently referred to Gardner as the "child marvel." Despite his heroics, the Spavin Curers (12-10) finished in third place, two games behind arch-rival Richford (15-9).

Though the rough-and-tumble circuit lasted only that one season, it had a lasting impact on Larry Gardner's life. Several "ringers" from the University of Vermont baseball team played in the Franklin County League, and they got him interested in attending UVM. In late-September 1905, the nineteen-year-old Gardner became one of eighty-two men and thirty women, only sixteen

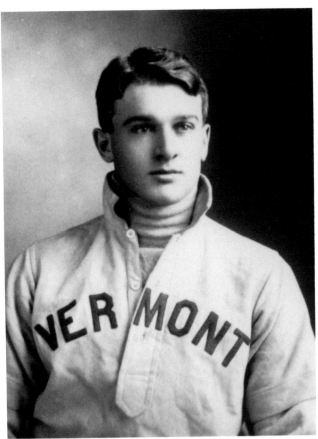

Larry Gardner earned a starting position on the UVM varsity as a freshman and batted safely in each of his first ten games. [Gardner Family Archives]

of whom were from out of state, to make up UVM's Class of 1909. In those days a year's tuition and expenses could run as high as $350, but with a loan from Dwight Gardner, who was working in Ohio as a traveling salesman for the Dr. B. J. Kendall Company, Larry scraped together the money. Even friends helped defray the enormous expense—the Saturday before he left for Burlington, twenty-five of them met at his home and presented him with a five-dollar gold piece as a farewell remembrance.

Larry majored in chemistry at UVM, hoping to go out west to the gold mines and work as an assayer. He was popular among his classmates, and *The Ariel* called him the "'Sunny Jim' of the class," stating that "[his] presence is a sure cure for the 'blues.'"

Though freshmen baseball players typically played for the junior varsity or their class team, Larry was one of two first-year students to make the varsity, the other being fellow Green Mountain Boy of Summer Ray Collins. That season UVM christened a new baseball field, called Centennial Field because the purchase of the land on which it was built was announced on July 6, 1904, at the conclusion of a three-day celebration of the 100th anniversary of UVM's first graduating class. After two years of clearing and grading, Centennial was finally ready for the home opener against Maine on April 17, 1906. Fittingly, Gardner was the first UVM batter in Centennial Field history.

After batting safely in each of his first ten games as a collegian, Larry Gardner led the UVM team with a .350 batting average. The rest of his season was a disaster. In his last seven games, he batted .148 and committed ten of his season's total of fifteen errors. On a team that combined for an .896 fielding percentage, Gardner's .769 was worst among regulars. For the season he batted .269, tied for fourth on the squad. On the positive side, he did steal a team-leading nine bases.

The 1906 Holy Cross Game

The largest crowd of Larry Gardner's freshman season climbed college hill on May 1 to take in the game against Holy Cross, winner of eight in a row before losing at Dartmouth on the way to Burlington. Four players from that Holy Cross team went on to the majors: catcher Bill Carrigan and left fielder Jack Hoey (Boston Red Sox); shortstop Jack Barry (Philadelphia A's); and first baseman John Flynn (Pittsburgh Pirates). With Gardner at third base and Ray Collins in right field for Vermont, the Holy Cross game featured six future major leaguers.

Centennial Field's bleachers were filled to overflowing with students shouting themselves hoarse. Freshmen rules mandated attendance at home athletic contests, though they were hardly necessary, as games were considered major social events. On this day the Holy Cross "Big Four" were held to three hits in fifteen at-bats as UVM won easily, 9-3. Afterwards students thrilled to the traditional tolling of the college bell in the Old Mill belfry.

Then as now, UVM students knew how to celebrate. They marched 300-strong down College Street headed by the college drum corps. When they arrived at the train station, they gave a rousing send-off to Gardner and his teammates, who took the 8:15 train to Rutland, where they spent the night en route to the next day's game against Williams College. On the return march from the station, the students tore down a dilapidated shed and used it to build a bonfire. "The boys gathered around the big fire and spent the remainder of the evening in singing songs, cracking jokes, and telling stories," reported the *Burlington Free Press*, "breaking up about 10:30 well pleased with their celebrations."

In Gardner's era, summer baseball was a legal way for college players to earn money for schoolyear expenses. UVM coach Tom Hays was in charge of stocking Burlington's Northern League team. It was a tradition to announce the players' names at Burlington's "Base Ball Carnival," an annual event to raise money for uniforms and equipment. "[T]he reading of the names at the fair last evening was heartily received," the *Free Press* reported in June 1906, but the last name read, "to be given a trial as utility man," drew a particularly hearty reception. It was Larry Gardner, "whose brilliant plays for Vermont during his first year in college have attracted much attention."

For the summer Larry shared a house with fellow Green Mountain Boy of Summer Doc Hazelton, Burlington's veteran first baseman. Other teammates who went on to the majors included catcher Bob Higgins (Cleveland Naps and Brooklyn Superbas); pitcher Ray Tift (New York Highlanders); and second baseman Harry Pattee (Brooklyn Superbas). In all, no less than twenty-five former or future major leaguers played in the four-team Northern League in 1906, but even in that heady company Gardner held his own. He became Burlington's regular right fielder and batted .296 as the team walked away with the first Northern League's last pennant.

The following spring Larry started receiving attention from major league scouts. George Winter, a pitcher who had twice won sixteen games in a season for the Boston Americans, married a Burlingtonian and lived there during the offseason. To pass the time before spring training, Winter watched UVM work out in the cage and dubbed Gardner a prospect.

Playing shortstop for UVM, Larry was batting .400 after eleven games when, in the words of the *Free Press*, an "inexcusable accident" occurred at Centennial Field in a game against Massachusetts Agricultural College on May 17:

> O'Grady knocked a high fly into short left field and Higgins and Gardner both went after it, no coaching being evident.

Gardner lived in the Delta Sigma fraternity house (currently the Klifa Club) during his junior and senior years at UVM. In this photo, he is seated on the railing on the left side of the front porch. [Gardner Family Archives]

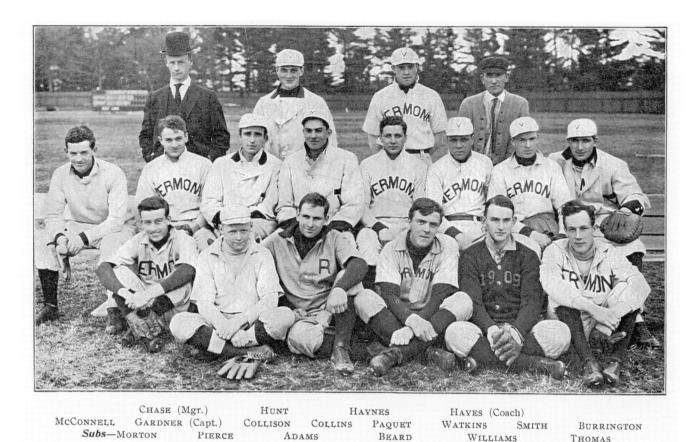

CHASE (Mgr.)   HUNT   HAVNES   HAYES (Coach)
McCONNELL   GARDNER (Capt.) COLLISON COLLINS   PAQUET   WATKINS   SMITH   BURRINGTON
Subs—MORTON   PIERCE   ADAMS   BEARD   WILLIAMS   THOMAS

Univ. of Vt. Baseball Team, Season of 1908.   Champions of the New England States.

This souvenir postcard commemorates UVM's 15-8-2 season, after which both Larry Gardner and Ray Collins were named to the 1908 All-Eastern team. [University of Vermont]

The men came together with terrific force, and both were stretched out almost senseless. Drs. Cloudman and Beecher took the cases in hand and it was discovered that Gardner had sustained a broken collar bone, while Higgins, though not considered dangerously hurt, was reported last night to be delerious and in a more serious condition than Gardner.

When it was announced that Larry would miss the remainder of the season, UVM's student newspaper, *The Cynic*, decried his loss: "Gardner will sorely be missed on the team. He was strong at the bat and wonderful at base running, his fielding was well nigh errorless, while his throwing was swift and sure as fate." Without Larry in the lineup, UVM lost its next three games and finished with a 10-7 record.

By June 30 Gardner had recovered sufficiently to join his UVM teammates, who were playing summer ball in Newport, New Hampshire. As if to answer any question whether his collarbone was fully mended, Larry smashed two home runs to lead Newport to a 5-3 win in its Interstate League opener against Randolph. A couple weeks later he played a brief but full-fledged stint

in organized professional ball. When the Burlington team dropped out of the Class-D Vermont State League, the UVM nine stepped in as replacements. "Many have felt all along that the Vermont team was the one to uphold the Burlington end on any baseball proposition, made up as it is of so many local favorites," the *Free Press* wrote. The collegians fared well, holding the second-best record (4-3) when the league disbanded on July 27.

With still a month to play that summer, both Larry Gardner and Ray Collins joined the Bangor Cubs of the Maine State League. Batting clean-up, Gardner established himself as Bangor's best hitter as the Cubs captured the 1907 pennant. His average of .371 (39 for 105) led the league, and both he and Collins were unanimous selections to the All-Maine team. By that time both players' actions were followed closely by many scouts, especially Fred Lake of the Boston Americans, and newspapers frequently mentioned that they were considered "big league material."

By the spring of 1908 both Gardner and Collins had received offers from major league clubs. In an April 11 letter, which the Gardner family retains to this day, Connie Mack tried to induce Larry to sign a contract immediately for $300 per month, with one month's advance upon signing, and join the Philadelphia Athletics after UVM's season. To allay Gardner's fears that signing a professional contract would make him ineligible for college ball, Mack wrote that "it will not be necessary for anyone but you and I to know that you have signed." During the course of UVM's season Larry also received several offers by telegram from John Taylor, president of the Boston Americans (at that point just starting to be called the "Red Sox").

Gardner rebuffed those offers and remained at UVM. Though he'd missed a good portion of the previous season, his teammates had nonetheless elected him team captain, and he was also elected president of the junior class. Bad weather caused a lack of outdoor practice and a poor 2-4 showing on the southern trip, but the team rebounded to finish 15-8-2 against the toughest schedule UVM had played since the days of Bert Abbey and Arlie Pond. Calling them the "champion baseball team of New England," the *Free Press* wrote, "Capt. Gardner, the hardest hitting man on the team, has been batting at a .300 clip, and it would be hard to find a better shortstop." Nonetheless he was named the third baseman on the *Springfield Republican*'s "All Eastern" Nine, making room for Holy Cross's Jack Barry at shortstop.

When Red Sox utility infielder Frank Laporte went down with an injury in late May, the Red Sox stepped up their efforts to sign Gardner. After UVM's season-ending win over Manhattan College on June 4, Larry's brother, Dwight, and mother, Nettie, came to Burlington to assist Larry with his difficult decision. Signing would mean he could finally re-pay Dwight's loan, but it would also force him to give up his senior season at UVM. Finally Larry succumbed. After final examinations, he reported directly to St. Louis, where the Red Sox were in the midst of a western roadtrip.

Larry remembered feeling "like a lost kid from the green hills" that summer. "Before this time I'd never seen a big league game," he said. "I'd been to the city a few times and while there held on to the hand of an older person for fear of getting lost." If he was nervous, it didn't show in his initial performance. Larry saw his first action on June 22 in an exhibition game in Rochester, New York, as the team made its way back to Boston. He homered in his first at-bat and played shortstop in "whirlwind fashion," handling six chances without error. Three days later, in his first official major league game, Larry replaced an injured Harry Lord in extra innings and ripped a game-winning double to beat the Washington Senators at Boston's Huntington Avenue Grounds.

NEW UTILITY INFIELDER OF THE BOSTON RED SOX

"LARRY" GARDNER,
Hard-Hitting Shortstop Who Played With the University of Vermont Team.

After his junior year, Gardner reported directly from the UVM campus to the Boston Red Sox. [Gardner Family Archives]

On June 27 he appeared in the starting lineup for the first time as the Red Sox took on the New York Highlanders at Hilltop Park in the Bronx. Playing third base and batting fifth, he went 0-for-4 with an error as Boston lost 7-6. To make things worse, Larry was "bunted to death" (his own words) by Wee Willie Keeler, who had two bunt singles among his four hits. That night Cy Young, the legendary pitcher, invited Larry to join him at the hotel bar and consoled the twenty-two-year-old rookie with the help of a bottle of rye whiskey. In his next start, Young, at forty-one the oldest pitcher in the majors, tossed the third no-hitter of his distinguished career.

Gardner had appeared in three official games and was batting an even .300 when "Taylor, the owner of the club, made me a proposition. 'Stay with the Red Sox and gain experience by watching or go to Lynn where there's a place open for a shortstop.'" Larry chose to play regularly, reporting to the New England League's Lynn Shoemakers on July 15. To make room for him, Lynn's regular shortstop moved to second base, and forty-five-year-old Jimmy Connor was forced to the bench. The former regular second baseman of the 1898 Chicago Orphans took no offense, and years later Larry said that Connor "probably helped me as much as anyone to make the big time." In sixty-one games for Lynn, Gardner batted .305 and showed "all the earmarks of another Harry Lord." In September the Red Sox invited him to re-join the team for another western roadtrip, but Larry opted instead to return to UVM for the fall semester.

"With a little extra money in my pocket my senior year I lived the life of Reilly," he remembered. "On occasion I'd even eat at Dorn's Restaurant, a high-class restaurant in town at that time. Heretofore I had eaten at any hash house."

Come spring, Larry watched from the bleachers as Ray Collins led the UVM baseball team to a 13-9 record. Final exams ended in mid-June, but commencement festivities didn't start until June 26, so Larry went down to Boston and actually managed to get into a game. On June 23, 1909, after replacing Harry Lord at third base in a game against the Highlanders, Larry tripled and scored in his only at bat. A couple days later he came back to Burlington for graduation. Only fifty-nine of the 112 students who started at UVM in the fall of 1905 managed to earn diplomas, but Larry was one of six to receive a B.S. in chemistry. Returning to Boston, he appeared in only eighteen more games for the Red Sox in 1909. With Lord a fixture at third and Heinie Wagner at shortstop, Larry spent most of his time on the bench. He performed well when given an opportunity, batting .297 with a .432 slugging percentage.

In 1910 a position opened up in the Boston infield when second baseman Amby McConnell sustained a leg injury only ten games into the season. Larry filled in even though he'd never played second base before. His inexperience showed on one occasion when he took a throw in the baseline with Ty Cobb sliding in. The Georgia Peach could have cut Gardner to shreds, but instead slid around him and was tagged out. Walking off the field, Cobb turned to Wagner and said, "Tell the kid I won't give him a break like that again." But for the most part Larry performed like he belonged, batting .283 in 113 games and winning accolades for his fielding. One sportswriter went so far as to call him "one of the best second basemen in the country." Gardner's development allowed the Red Sox to trade McConnell to the Chicago White Sox.

After spending the offseason in Enosburg Falls ice skating, snowshoeing, and hunting (the current residents of the Gardner house found several of his old Vermont hunt-

ing licenses in the rafters), Larry reported to spring training in Redondo Beach, California, with new confidence. He entertained newspapermen and teammates alike with ventriloquism and sang baritone in the Red Sox barbershop quartet, which included Marty McHale (first tenor), Buck O'Brien (second tenor), and Hugh Bradley (basso).

Despite the speed he'd shown when he first took over at second, Gardner seemed slow and unable to cover territory in 1911. At midseason manager Patsy Donovan, who'd been searching for a third baseman ever since Harry Lord had been sent to Chicago in the McConnell trade, shifted Gardner to the hot corner. "Can it be possible that Larry Gardner has been out of position all this time?" wrote Ring Lardner. "He was certainly a success as a second sacker, but right now it would be hard to convince the uninformed observer that he hadn't been playing third base for years." A Boston scribe wrote, "Third base has not been played so well in Boston since the days when Jimmie Collins was in his prime."

During the 1912 season Gardner and his best friend on the Red Sox, Harry Hooper, lived together in

Gardner excelled both in the field and at the plate after manager Patsy Donovan moved him from second to third base in 1911. [Gardner Family Archives]

Winthrop on Boston's North Shore. After games they cooked shellfish by digging a hole in the sand, throwing in hot rocks and covering the hole with seaweed. Once Larry attempted to duplicate the trick for his family back in Enosburg Falls, using a chicken instead of shellfish and hay instead of seaweed. "It tasted so awful we couldn't eat it," remembered cousin Vadis Rhodes.

That 1912 season was a breakthrough year for both the Red Sox and Larry Gardner. Boston ran away with the American League and Gardner hit .315 with a team-leading eighteen triples. But in a meaningless game in Detroit on September 21, he was injured diving for Donie Bush's grounder down the line. The ball hit the little finger of his bare right hand, snapping it at the first joint and causing the bone to protrude through the flesh. Larry went home to Enosburg Falls to recuperate. Initially it was feared that he'd miss the World Series, but he returned to the lineup on October 6.

Playing with his fingers taped together, Gardner wasn't a factor in the first three games of the World Series against the New York Giants, but in Game Four at the Polo Grounds he blasted a single and a triple and scored two

Larry Gardner's big bat during the regular season and World Series helped the Red Sox win their second world's championship in 1912. [Lou Parelli]

runs in a 3-1 Boston victory. In Game Seven Larry hit Boston's only home run of the Series, but the game for which he'll forever be remembered was the eighth and deciding game at Fenway Park (Game Two had been a tie).

The contest was deadlocked at 1-1 after nine innings, Gardner having driven in Boston's only run on a groundout in the seventh, but in the top half of the tenth the Giants grabbed a 2-1 lead. With Christy Mathewson on the mound for New York, Boston's chances appeared slim. But Fred Snodgrass pulled his infamous muff of Clyde Engle's soft fly, Steve Yerkes walked, and Tris Speaker singled to score Engle with the tying run. With one out and runners on first and third, Mathewson walked Duffy Lewis intentionally to load the bases. Up to the plate stepped Gardner.

Realizing that Mathewson was working him to hit a low ball, Larry allowed two balls to go by before he swung and missed at the third pitch. A walk meant forcing in the winning run, so Matty couldn't afford to be cute. His next pitch was over the inside corner, well above the knee. Larry swung and a shout went up as the ball headed for deep right field. "I was disappointed at first because I thought the ball was going out," Larry remembered, "but when I saw Yerkes tag up, then score to end it, I realized it meant $4,024.68, just about double my earnings for the year."

After a celebration the next day at Boston's Fanueil Hall, Larry returned to a hero's reception in Enosburg Falls. His train arrived bedecked with red lights from engine to rear coach, and explosions of railroad torpedos went off every few rods as it swept into the village. After alighting, Gardner was escorted to the car of honor, beautifully trimmed with American flags, bunting, and "red sox." Seated in the car with Larry were his father, Delbert, and the whole reception committee. Sixteen autos followed in a procession through the village, eventually escorting him to his home.

Gardner's presence was much in demand during the week following the World Series. At a reception in Enosburg Falls sponsored by the Philemon Club, special guest Tim Murnane of the *Boston Globe* talked about how the earnings of baseball players all over the country were a great benefit to rural communities, as players generally hailed from those parts and spent their money there.

The next night Larry, Ray Collins, and 1912 Olympic gold-medal winner Albert Gutterson, all UVM alumni, were feted at Burlington's Hotel Vermont. Among the 450 in attendance were Governor Fletcher, Mayor Burke, and some 300 UVM students. Each of the guests of honor received a silver loving cup presented by UVM President Guy Potter Benton. Gardner's was inscribed as follows:

On a visit to Enosburg Falls, Tim Murnane and Larry Gardner inspect the field where Gardner got his start in baseball. It was laid out in 1904 and is essentially the same field on which the EFHS team plays nearly a century later. [Gardner Family Archives]

From The City of Burlington
and The University of Vermont,
to "Larry" Gardner
in loving appreciation of the deserved
fame he has won for himself, for his
city and his alma mater as third
baseman for the Boston Americans,
world's champions of 1912.

Gardner's 1912 World Series Memorabilia

What became of the ball that Larry Gardner belted to Josh Devore for the sacrifice fly that won the 1912 World Series? The bat's on display in the Hall of Fame Room at UVM's Gutterson Fieldhouse, but the whereabouts of the ball is a mystery.

Initially it was in the possession of Thomas W. Watson, who worked the turnstiles at Fenway Park during the 1912 World Series. After Steve Yerkes crossed the plate with the winning run, Chief Meyers tossed the ball aside and Watson pocketed it. That night he went to the Hotel Putnam and presented it to Gardner. In exchange, Larry gave him a brand new ball autographed by the whole Red Sox team, with the ad-dition of Mayor Fitzgerald's signature. When Larry arrived at Enosburg Falls, both the bat and the ball were displayed at the office of the *Enosburg Standard*. Larry eventually donated the bat to the UVM athletic department, but the Gardner family has no idea what happened to the ball.

Larry Gardner signed a three-year contract with the Red Sox that winter, but still he remained his same humble self. "He has a disposition as sweet as the wild flowers that grow on the mountains of Vermont," wrote Tim Murnane. A few years later, T. C. Cheney wrote that "there is no more modest, unassuming or clean young man in [baseball] than our Green Mountain boy, who is an honor and credit to the game and his state." Larry also carried a reputation as an intellectual: "Off the ball field Gardner prefers to read an essay on Shakespeare's poems than to discuss baseball," wrote one reporter.

Gardner batted a respectable .281 in 1913, but the following two seasons he slumped to .259 and a career-low .258. Then in 1916, despite playing with a dislocated big toe, Larry rebounded to .308, fifth-best in the American League behind only Tris Speaker, Ty Cobb,

Gardner loved his automobiles. Early in his career he shared a Stutz four-cylinder roadster with Harry Hooper, but later he moved up to this fancy six-cylinder convertible. [Gardner Family Archives]

Shoeless Joe Jackson, and Amos Strunk. With Speaker gone to Cleveland, Gardner became the biggest bat in the Boston lineup as the Red Sox won their second consecutive A.L. pennant. Then he enhanced his reputation as a clutch player by smashing two home runs in the 1916 World Series against the Brooklyn Dodgers.

The first one came in Game Three at Ebbets Field. "I hadn't been hitting and I was really mad," Gardner remembered. "Jack Coombs was pitching for the Dodgers and he was a helluva pitcher. He broke off a curve on me, a lefty hitter. I started to swing and tried to stop because I thought it was a bad pitch, but I was committed too far and had to go through with it. I even had my eyes shut. When I opened them, I saw the ball going over the wall. Can you believe that—hitting a home run with your eyes closed?"

In Game Four, with two men on base and Boston down 2-0, Gardner hit a fastball from Rube Marquard for an inside-the-park homer, giving the Red Sox a 3-2 lead they never relinquished. "That one blow, delivered deep into the barren lands of center field, broke Marquard's heart, shattered Brooklyn's wavering defense, and practically closed out the series," wrote Grantland Rice. Boston went on to win in five games, and Larry Gardner was considered the hero. As Tim Murnane put it, he had "a way of rising to the occasion as a trout rises to a fly in one of his favorite Vermont streams."

Despite his heroics, Larry couldn't get a raise. The most Red Sox owner Harry Frazee offered was to pay for Larry's new bride, the former Margaret Fourney of Canton, Ohio, to attend spring training at Hot Springs, Arkansas. "I told my wife to take forty baths a day and ride horses the rest of the time," Larry said. "We really stuck Harry on that one!" In 1917 his batting average

fell from .308 to .265, giving the Red Sox the idea that he was slipping after ten years of service.

On March 1, 1918, Boston traded Gardner, reserve outfielder Tillie Walker, and back-up catcher Hick Cady to the Philadelphia Athletics for first baseman Stuffy McInnis. "While the loss of Walker and Cady might be accepted with cheerful resignation," wrote Paul Shannon in the *Boston Post*, "the going of Gardner, one of the most powerful hitters on the team for years, one of its most dependable members and a model player in every way, will be severely felt." Philadelphia writers, on the other hand, welcomed news of the trade. "The report that Gardner has passed the zenith of his career and is on the decline is all camouflage, probably designed to placate the Boston fans, with whom he was extremely popular," wrote one of them. "His moral and corrective influence upon the younger men of whom the team will mostly consist this year should be invaluable."

Tim Murnane of the Boston Globe *wrote that Larry Gardner "has a disposition as sweet as the wildflowers that grow on the mountains of Vermont." [Gardner Family Archives]*

In his dozen years as a regular third baseman, Gardner was named to Baseball Magazine's *All-America first team four times and to the second team five times. [Gardner Family Archives]*

Though the Red Sox won another World Series in 1918, they sorely missed Larry's presence at third base. "Gardner's absence last year almost cost the Red Sox the world's championship," wrote a Boston reporter. "The Sox tried out more than a dozen third sackers in an attempt to fill his shoes." The thirty-two-year-old Gardner batted a solid .285 for the A's, who finished in the cellar again in the midst of an A.L.-record seven consecutive seasons in last place.

After the season Connie Mack continued his youth movement, trading Gardner, pitcher Elmer Myers, and outfield prospect Charlie Jamieson to the Cleveland Indians for slugging outfielder Braggo Roth. The Indians had finished second in 1918 with a weak platoon of Joe Evans and thirty-seven-year-old Terry Turner at third, so the Cleveland writers thought the deal strengthened the team considerably. In fact, they thought Gardner-for-Roth straight up would have been fair.

Reunited with former Red Sox teammates Tris Speaker and Joe Wood, Larry played every inning of every game in 1919, hitting an even .300 and leading the team with eighty-nine RBIs. Then in 1920 he did even better, batting .310 with a team-leading 118 RBIs to help the Indians finish in first place in the American League. After forty-two years, Cleveland had finally landed on top—of

the eleven cities with major league franchises, Cleveland was the tenth to win a pennant. Larry's leadership was instrumental. When shortstop Ray Chapman was killed by a pitched ball in August, twenty-one-year-old Joe Sewell was called up from the minors in the middle of a tight pennant race. "Larry Gardner helped me a lot," remembered Sewell. "He talked to me all the time when we were in the field, trying to steady me." The rookie batted .329 down the stretch, the beginning of a Hall-of-Fame career.

Cleveland went on to win the 1920 World Series, and on a roadtrip to Washington during the 1921 season the Indians attended a White House reception to receive congratulations from President Warren Harding, who was from Ohio. When it was Gardner's turn to shake hands with the President, Harding said, "I know you are a good player, young man, because way back in the early '80s I knew a player by that name. He was with Cleveland in the old National League and was a mighty good man." Gardner drew a laugh when he said, "That was just about the time I was breaking in." Though thirty-five, Larry had his best season ever in 1921. He established career highs for batting average (.319), runs (101), hits (187), doubles (32), and RBIs (120).

Hampered by nagging injuries, Gardner wasn't quite as good in 1922, though he still played in 137 games and batted .285. He considered retirement when the Indians bought minor league phenom Rube Lutzke, a third baseman, but Speaker convinced him to come back and serve as a coach and occasional pinch hitter. Over the course of his last two seasons, 1923-24, Larry appeared in a combined total of only ninety games, playing the field in only thirty-three.

Larry Gardner had always been concerned about life after baseball. In his early days with the Red Sox he'd

Though in his mid-thirties, Gardner had some of his strongest seasons while in a Cleveland uniform. [Gardner Family Archives]

invested in a Cape Cod cranberry business, but an early frost one year ruined the harvest and destroyed the company. After that Larry went into the automobile business in Enosburg Falls. With his partner, Francis Smith, Larry owned a garage and a Willis-Knight dealership. But when his playing days finally ended, Gardner found he couldn't leave baseball behind. For three years he managed in the minor leagues with Dallas and Asheville. Then, after Cleveland manager Tris Speaker got caught up in a scandal and was fired after the 1926 season, many thought Gardner would step up to the majors. Instead, Cleveland hired Jack McCallister, who had no previous major league playing or managing experience.

Perhaps discouraged by his experience in Cleveland, Larry returned to his garage and automobile business in Enosburg Falls. Margaret hated it there and was relieved when Larry joined the UVM physical education department in 1929. Three years later Larry became head baseball coach at UVM, a position he held until 1952. He always stressed sportsmanship ahead of winning—Gardner's overall record was a lackluster 141-166—and prided himself on developing well-rounded students rather than specialized athletes. "I guess he liked the team to win, but all I remember was how warm and human he was with the players," says Larry Jr., who served as batboy.

Larry Gardner poses with his wife, Margaret, a refined woman who was frequently the butt of Babe Ruth's coarse jokes. [Gardner Family Archives]

Something More Valuable than Winning

Nothing better captures the essence of Larry Gardner's coaching philosophy than a letter he wrote to President Stanley King of Amherst College on May 13, 1938:

I am writing you a somewhat belated letter to express to you the keen pleasure our boys experienced at Amherst on April 21st when we met your Amherst team in a baseball game. While we lost the game, we gained something much more valuable than is expressed by winning or losing.

Coach Gardner hits infield practice at Centennial Field. Former UVM player Tom Clairmont remembers that Gardner was especially adept with a fungo bat. [Gardner Family Archives]

In the ten years I have been connected with baseball at Vermont, I can honestly say that I never saw our boys more impressed by spirit, gentlemanly conduct, and treatment than was given and exemplified by your students.

In the thirty years of my experience in baseball, this was truly the highlight and it pleases me to hand this observation on to you.

Three days later he received this reply from President King:

I would not be honest if I did not say that I am deeply touched by your letter of the 13th. The qualities which you stress in your letter are of course the qualities you and we are trying to develop in our boys in the playing of competitive sports. They are the qualities which seem to me most important in our staff. The teams that you coach at Vermont and which Paul Eckley coaches here may win or lose in individual games but the qualities of sportsmanship which the boys learn from their coaches and their fellows are among the most important by-products of our college education.

I watched the Vermont game from the stands myself and congratulate you on the fine boys on your team. The score of two to one was as close as a score can be. Again my warm appreciation for your letter.

At this baseball banquet Larry Gardner (left) challenged Casey Stengel to remember him when they hadn't seen each other in more than three decades. "I remember you," Stengel said. "You're the feller which made me show the back of my head in the 1916 World Series. You hit one over the wall for a home run." [Gardner Family Archives]

Though the Great Depression took its toll on many retired ballplayers, the Gardners lived a comfortable life in the Queen City. They spent summers at a spectacular camp on Colchester Point, surrounded by cedars and situated on a rocky bluff overlooking Lake Champlain, with stairs leading to a quarter-mile stretch of sandy beach. Larry loved hosting lobster bakes there, and frequent guests included Burlington High School principal Dean Perreault, insurance agent Phillip Bell, and Larry's best friend, UVM track coach Archie Post. The Gardner boys also remember the time Larry's old Red Sox teammate Dick Hoblitzell visited, probably because he was joined by his beautiful daughter. When the south wind came up in early summer, Larry took his rowboat out to catch walleye and pike.

When the kids returned to school in the fall, the Gardners moved back to their comfortable brick cottage at 17 Overlake Park, in one of Burlington's finest neighborhoods. The living room was adorned with no pictures or trophies—they were all upstairs or down in the basement. Larry told visitors he'd left his playing days behind and only took private trips back to the Boston, Philadelphia, and Cleveland of the early part of the century.

In addition to his coaching duties, Gardner was named UVM athletic director in 1942. He also served as commissioner of the second Northern League and as a part-time scout for the Boston Braves. After retiring from the

university in 1952, Larry fished even more frequently and worked a regular schedule at The Camera Shop on Church Street in downtown Burlington. He kept in touch with several old teammates, especially Harry Hooper, and maintained a steady correspondence with Ty Cobb, who at one time owned a fishing camp on Lake Bomoseen.

In their playing days, Gardner and Cobb were intense rivals. "I don't think Ty ever bunted for a hit against me because I found out his secret early," Larry said. "Cobb used to fake a lot of bunts, but I noticed that when he was really going to bunt, he always licked his lips. When I saw that, I'd start in with the pitch. He never realized I'd caught on." In the '50s Cobb wrote long, rambling letters to Gardner, trying to establish a fund for players whose careers had ended before major league baseball's pension system. In a letter dated September 17, 1958, Cobb wrote:

> Nothing would please me more than to have a few days with you and your friends in your home town amongst those <u>real</u> people up there that I know of and their history so well, you being such a true representative. I should tell you now though you must have for years known it so well that I liked you also Ray [editor's note: presumably Ray Collins], also your kind no matter where they lived, we were <u>reared</u> <u>properly</u>.

Larry Gardner received many accolades as the years went on. *Collegiate Baseball* named him the third baseman on its all-time All-America team, and he was an original inductee into the University of Vermont's Hall of Fame in 1969. In 1973, when SABR conducted a survey of its members to determine the greatest baseball player born in each state, Gardner was selected from Vermont. UVM's most valuable player award in baseball was named after him, as was UVM's cage (an honor

Larry Gardner's sons and grandchildren plant a tree in his honor on the University of Vermont green following his death in 1976. [Gardner Family Archives]

Larry Gardner Jr., Tom Simon, and John Gardner pose under the Vermont historical marker that was unveiled in Lincoln Park as part of Enosburg Falls' first annual Larry Gardner Day celebration in August 1996. The house where Larry Gardner was born and raised is in the background. [Carolyn Hanson]

he shared with Ray Collins). He will be inducted into the Boston Red Sox Hall of Fame in the spring of 2000. Still, the ultimate honor—induction into the National Baseball Hall of Fame—has eluded him.

"I remember when Harry Hooper was being considered for the honor and Dad talked with me after I raised the question about *him* being eligible for it," said Larry Jr. "Generally speaking, Dad was very quiet, soft-spoken, reticent about his baseball career when talking with me, but at that one time he got very talkative—very adamant—and told me, 'If you boys *ever* get involved with the campaigning, the politics of getting me into the Hall of Fame, I'll be upset and angry.'"

William Lawrence Gardner died two months short of his ninetieth birthday on March 11, 1976, at Larry Jr.'s home in St. George, Vermont. He left his body to UVM's Department of Anatomy, and his ashes were spread at St. Paul's Cathedral in Burlington. Gardner continued to receive honors even after his death. In 1986 the UVM baseball team wore commemorative patches on their sleeves in honor of his 100th birthday. And when a regional chapter of SABR was founded in the Green Mountains in 1993, its members elected to call it the Larry Gardner Chapter. It was another fitting tribute to a Vermont baseball legend.

TOM SIMON

Interlude

The Day the Red Sox Came to Centennial Field

In the early morning of Monday, October 10, 1910, the Rutland Railway's sleeper train rolled along Burlington Harbor. When it finally inched its way into the smoke-begrimed depot at the foot of College Street, railroad employees gently detached one of the private cars, allowing its occupants a few more hours of sleep.

In that car, Larry Gardner and Ray Collins had just come home. They were joined by some of the best young players in baseball: baby-faced Smoky Joe Wood, one of the fastest pitchers in the league; center fielder Tris Speaker, an established superstar at age twenty-two; right fielder Harry Hooper, also twenty-two, who eventually joined Speaker in the Hall of Fame; and Duffy Lewis, the twenty-one-year-old who rounded out the best outfield in baseball. Though the Red Sox had finished a disappointing

fourth in 1910, the core of the team that would win the World Series two years later was already present.

After checking in at the Van Ness House at the corner of Main and St. Paul streets, the Red Sox had breakfast and went sightseeing in automobiles borrowed from local fans. At 1:30 the players regrouped at the hotel, then paraded up Church Street on their way to Centennial Field. The procession was led by the 10th Cavalry Band from Fort Ethan Allen and included dignitaries like Governor Mead, Senator Powell, Congressman Peck, and horse breeder George Whitney, millionaire heir to inventor Eli Whitney's fortune and former owner of Burlington's team in the first Northern League.

The crowd began assembling at Centennial an hour before gametime in spite of brisk northwest winds that

Larry Gardner receives a loving cup from the citizens of Enosburg Falls. [Gardner Family Archives]

Ray Collins at Centennial Field on October 10, 1910. To that point Collins was undoubtedly the winningest pitcher in Centennial's history, but on that particular day he suffered the loss. [Gardner Family Archives]

The exhibition pitted squads of Red Sox captained by the two local players. Roughly speaking, Collins had the regular outfield and a substitute infield, while Gardner had the regular infield and pitchers for his outfielders. To the delight of the crowd, Gardner led off the game with a clean single to right field off Collins, advanced to second on a bunt by Clyde Engle (who returned to Centennial Field as UVM baseball coach nine years later), and scored on a single by Hugh Bradley. His was the only run until the sixth inning, when Lewis "drove the ball through the ropes in left center, a hit that would have netted him a home run but for the ground rule, which held him at third base." Lewis tied the game for Collins' team moments later on Bill Carrigan's sacrifice fly.

In the seventh Gardner broke the game open with his third hit of the game, a two-out, two-RBI double. Wood pitched three innings of scoreless relief, preserving a 4-1 victory for Gardner's team and prompting the *Burlington Free Press* to comment: "Aside from the interest always taken in Collins' work in the box, the crowd liked to see Wood on the mound. He is a youngster, twenty-one years of age, and certainly has bushels of speed, and all that goes with it."

After the game the Ethan Allen Club entertained Governor Mead and staff, while the Red Sox joined a packed house at the Strong Theatre to take in a Parisian comedy called "The Girl in the Taxi." According to the review in the *Free Press*, the comedy depicted the adventures of three men who "prefer the society of compliant chorus girls and other ladies of the same ilk to that of their wives"—a story line that probably appealed to the ballplayers.

The next day's edition of the *Free Press* shows how little Vermonters have changed over the years, at least when it comes to baseball: "Yesterday's attendance at the base ball exhibition by the Boston Americans shows that Burlington is a base ball city all right, and the same thing can be said of a considerable part of Vermont outside of this city."

TOM SIMON

prevented the temperature from rising much above fifty degrees. The wooden grandstand quickly filled to capacity, so the entire field was roped off and surrounded by spectators and automobiles, making the adoption of ground rules necessary. Even the rooftops of the houses on Colchester Avenue were jammed with viewers. *The Rutland Herald* reported that the attendance of 4,000 "made Centennial Field look like a major league park."

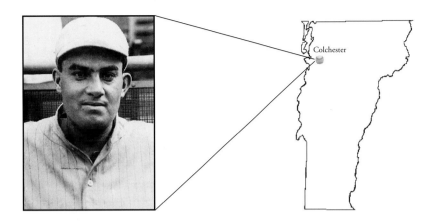

Ray Collins

A Yankee On The Red Sox

Ray Collins' lifetime 2.51 ERA is impressive even for his low-scoring era, and in 1913-14 he won a combined thirty-nine games for the Boston Red Sox. He was a good-hitting pitcher and an outstanding fielder, but the key to his success was his remarkable control. Collins consistently ranked among the league leaders in fewest walks allowed per nine innings, finishing third in the A.L. in 1912 (1.90), second in 1913 (1.35), and fourth in 1914 (1.85).

Though big for his time (6' 1", 185 pounds), the Colchester farmboy didn't throw hard. "Ray Collins hasn't a thing," said Hall-of-Fame manager Clark Griffith at the height of the Vermonter's career, "yet he is one of the best pitchers in the American League—one of the two or three best left-handed pitchers in the business." Hugh Jennings, another Hall-of-Fame manager, concurred: "I class him as the best left hander in the American League, with the possible exception of Eddie Plank."

Ray Collins wasn't kidding when he listed his nationality as "Yankee" on a 1911 *Baseball Magazine* survey. A ninth-generation descendant of William Bradford, second governor of Plymouth Colony, Ray was also the great-great-grandson of Captain John Collins, one of Burlington's original settlers. Captain Collins arrived from Salisbury, Connecticut, on August 19, 1783, and built the first frame house in town near what is now the corner of Battery and King streets. Ethan Allen stayed with the Collins family while building his homestead.

The 375-acre Collins farm on Route 7 in Colchester, originally purchased by Charles Collins in 1835, was where Ray Williston Collins was born on February 11, 1887. Ray's family moved around a lot when he was a kid, renting farms in other parts of the state, but his father, Frank Collins, still owned the Colchester farm. Around 1894 the family returned to the Burlington area and purchased land in the Intervale, an area of rich farmland along the banks of the Winooski River. There, on one of the largest farms in Chittenden County, the Collinses raised a herd of Jersey cows. The brick farmhouse still stands, just down the embankment from the former site of Burlington's Athletic Park.

For a while Ray had an idyllic childhood. "Played ball today" is a common entry in his childhood journal, and he also attended UVM baseball games at Athletic Park. But when Ray was ten his father died of scarlet fever. Ray's mother, Electa, was forced to sell the Intervale property and move to a house in Burlington at 76 Brookes Avenue. She not only survived but prospered, buying and improving lots on Loomis Street and Brookes Avenue and selling them for a profit. Electa rented out the farm in Colchester, where Ray helped with the haying when it didn't interfere with his studies. Later he worked as a conductor on the trolley that ran from Burlington through Winooski and out to Fort Ethan Allen. Ray attended Pomeroy School and later Burlington High School, where he was captain of the tennis, basketball,

This photo of the Collins farm in Colchester dates from 1891. Four-year-old Ray stands to the left of his mother, who is seated on the front porch wearing a white skirt. [Collins Family Archives]

Growing up at 76 Brookes Avenue, Ray attended Pomeroy School and later Burlington High School, which was in the building that is now Edmunds Middle School. [Collins Family Archives]

and baseball teams. He didn't play football in high school because his mother wouldn't let him, even though he was considerably larger than most boys his age.

Ray Collins often recalled his time at the University of Vermont as the four greatest years of his life. Though he lived at home, "Collie" joined the Delta Psi fraternity and got involved in campus social life. Among other activities, he served as committee chairman of the Kake Walk, a mid-winter minstrel show that was banished from campus in the 1960s when it fell out of step with changing racial values. Ray also put his wide-ranging athletic talents to use, playing center on the varsity basketball team as a freshman and varsity tennis as a sophomore.

Ray's greatest accomplishments, of course, came on the baseball diamond. In UVM's home opener on April 17, 1906, the first baseball game ever played at Centennial Field, freshman Collins batted safely twice and pitched a complete game, allowing only one earned run. But the crowning achievement of Ray's freshman year came against Williams at Centennial Field on May 19. The Ephmen entered the game with just one loss, having ruined their undefeated record at Dartmouth the day before. Larry Gardner drew a lead-off walk in the first inning and scored what turned out to be the game's only run. Entering the ninth, Collins was pitching a no-hitter and hadn't walked a single batter. With two outs a Williams batter singled cleanly to right field, but when the runner was thrown

Ray Collins (front row, far left) pitched the 1905 Burlington High School team to an 8-4 record in his senior year. [Tom Simon Collection]

out stealing moments later, Ray was carried off the field on the shoulders of his schoolmates.

Gardner received many accolades for his role on a team that finished 9-8, but the real hero was Ray Collins. Drawing all of the tough pitching assignments, Collie finished with a 4-3 record and a 0.70 ERA, striking out thirty-six and giving up only forty-three hits and ten walks in sixty-four innings. He even gained honorable mention on the *Springfield (Mass.) Republican's* "All Eastern" and "All New England" teams. That notice earned him a summer job in the Adirondack Hotel League for a team sponsored by Paul Smith's Hotel on Lower St. Regis Lake. An old brochure found among his papers boasts that "[t]he Paul Smith's Baseball nine have always been champion of the Adirondacks."

During Ray's sophomore year of 1907, Vermont improved its record to 11-6 and UVM's yearbook, *The Ariel*, praised his performance as "second to that of no college player in the country." By that time Ray had attracted the attention of major league scouts. The Boston Americans followed him throughout the season, and towards the end a New York Highlanders scout offered Ray $3,000 to play from July through October. According to the *Free Press*, "on the advice of older men, Collins has declined the tempting offer, believing that he is yet too young to take up base ball in the fastest league in the world."

That summer Collins pitched for a few semipro teams in Massachusetts, then joined his UVM teammates playing for Newport, New Hampshire, of the Interstate League. In one game Ray struck out twenty-one batters. In July the UVM team played a brief but full-fledged stint in professional baseball in the Vermont State League. In his first minor league start Ray pitched a shutout against first-place Barre-Montpelier, snapping that club's

eight-game winning streak. "Nothing like the pitching of Collins has been seen at Intercity Park since the days of Reulbach," wrote the *Montpelier Argus*.

When the V.S.L. disbanded for good on July 27, Collins joined the Bangor Cubs of the Maine State League. In his first game he shut out a Portland club called "Pine Tree" on four hits. A Portland newspaper stated that Ray's wind-up resembled an "explosion in a leg and arm factory," while a Bangor scribe wrote:

> Collins is a tall, slim young feller from Burlington, Vermont, and is first string man on the University of Vermont team. This university is famous for the ball players it turns out, among whom may be mentioned Reulbach of the Chicago Cubs, and Collins seems to ably sustain the reputation of the university. He has all kinds of speed, curves and shoots, change of pace, good control, and a corkscrew delivery which is enough to scare a batsman away from the plate. Added to these important details, he has all kinds of confidence and a snap that keeps a game a'going.

In 1908, Collins (seated at right) and his catcher, Marcus Burrington, made a formidable battery both at UVM and in Bangor, Maine. [Collins Family Archives]

Ray finished out the season with Bangor and led the Cubs to the 1907 Maine State League pennant. In his last appearance on August 30 at the Eastern Maine State Fair, he pitched both ends of a doubleheader, defeating Portland 11-2 and 5-4 in ten innings.

UVM finished with a 15-8-2 record in 1908, the last year Collins and Gardner played together for the varsity. The highlight of the season for Ray was beating Holy Cross, 1-0, winning his own game by driving in the game's only run with a triple. Students celebrated the victory that evening in traditional UVM fashion, marching to the Collins home on Brookes Avenue, picking Ray up, and carrying him on their shoulders to the foot of Church Street. There they staged a mini-riot:

> The students in their ardor crippled temporarily the trolley service of Pearl Street. The trolley pole on a car was pulled from the wire at the corner of Pearl and Church streets and in front of the Howard Relief hall an attempt was made to block an Essex car; but the motorman applied the juice and the students, deciding that they would be the worse for wear in the encounter with the moving car, cleared the track. The trolley pole on another Pearl Street car coming down the hill from Winooski was pulled from the wire and in the mix-up a window was broken, the splintered glass cutting the conductor, George Rogers, although not seriously injuring him. On the march up Pearl Street, the large bill board at the corner of Prospect Street was taken down and borne in solemn procession by some sixty students to the campus. Here a number of tar barrels were added to the stock of combustibles and an old-fashioned bonfire and war dance took place. After the fire died down the students gradually dispersed.

Following the close of the season, Collins was elected captain for his senior year. Gardner decided to forego his last season of eligibility, signing with the Boston Red Sox, but Ray shunned offers to turn professional. "The president of the Red Sox team of Boston worked hard to land Collins," the *Free Press* reported, "but the college boy, who has one more year at Vermont, decided to pitch college ball for the team of which he was recently elected captain."

Collins received a large increase in pay—reportedly $185 per month—to return to Bangor for a second summer in 1908. He brought with him his college catcher, Marcus Burrington of Pownal, Vermont. Combined with Ralph Good, a Colby College star who later pitched two games in the majors with the Boston Nationals in 1910, Ray led Bangor to its second-straight Maine League pennant. In appointing him to its 1908 All-Maine team, one Maine newspaper called Collins the "premier twirler of the league this season, as he was the last."

Despite returning only five veterans, the 1909 UVM team survived without Larry Gardner, posting a 13-9

During their senior year both Ray Collins (second from left) and Larry Gardner (second from right) were elected to the Boulder Society, UVM's most prestigious honor. [University of Vermont]

record. Captain Collins pitched well throughout the season, but never better than in his last game on June 18. Going out in a "blaze of glory," according to the *Free Press* headline, Ray struck out nineteen and beat a tough Penn State team 4-1. It was a fitting end to an incredible college career in which he won thirty-seven of the fifty games he started, surpassing Bert Abbey, Arlie Pond, and Ed Reulbach as the greatest pitcher in UVM history.

Receiving offers from half of the sixteen major league teams, Collins decided to follow in Gardner's footsteps. Shortly after the Penn State game he went down to Boston and came to terms with Red Sox president John Taylor. "That day I saw my first major league game," he remembered years later. "The Red Sox were playing the Tigers, and Ty Cobb stole second, third, and home." Collins then returned to Burlington for Senior Week. He served as marshal at the baccalaureate sermon and carried the class banner at commencement on June 30, leading a procession of seventy-three undergraduates (including Larry Gardner) down the aisle of Burlington's Strand Theatre. After receiving a B.S. in economics, Ray closed the ceremony with a speech on behalf of the graduating class.

As part of his deal with the Red Sox, Ray received permission to remain in Burlington and pitch an exhibition game commemorating the 300th anniversary of Samuel de Champlain's 1609 discovery of Lake Champlain. The game was part of Tercentenary Week, which included, among other events, Vermont's first-ever marathon (104 times around the oval track surrounding Centennial Field) and a reenactment of the Battle of Champlain on a man-made island in Burlington Harbor, attended by President Taft and the French and English ambassadors to the United States. As 50,000 visitors flooded into the Queen City, Collins held an independent team from Pittsfield, Massachusetts, scoreless for nine innings, then won the game for Burlington with a run-scoring single in the thirteenth.

Ray Collins left Vermont on July 12, 1909. He went first to Boston, then caught up with the Red Sox on a western roadtrip. On July 19, with Boston down 4-0 to Cy Young after three innings at Cleveland, manager Fred Lake figured it was as good a time as any to test his

prized rookie. In five strong innings of relief, Ray yielded two unearned runs and even singled in his first big league at-bat. This game is best-remembered as the one in which Cleveland shortstop Neal Ball made the first unassisted triple play in major league history, but it may also be the only game in which three Green Mountain Boys of Summer saw action for the same team—in addition to Collins, both Amby McConnell and Larry Gardner played for the Red Sox.

Four days later, Ray was the starting pitcher against the hard-hitting Detroit Tigers. Though he lost 4-2, he twice struck out the dangerous Ty Cobb. Collins received a second chance to beat the Tigers on July 25, 1909. Pitching on only one day's rest, Ray tossed the first of his nineteen shutouts in the majors. It was a three-hitter, all three of which were made by Hall-of-Famer Sam Crawford. Collins pitched only sporadically during the rest of the season, going 4-3 with an ERA of 2.81, but he'd proven that he was capable of competing in the majors without any minor league apprenticeship. After

Ray Collins (right) stands with Hap Myers early in the 1910 season. Myers, as Collins noted on the back of this photograph, "did not make good" with the Red Sox, but he became the regular first baseman for the Boston Braves in 1913. [Collins Family Archives]

Collins attributed his success to his unusual sidearm delivery and remarkable control. [Collins Family Archives]

the regular season he matched up against the great Christy Mathewson in an exhibition game on October 13 and defeated him 2-0.

Collins became a regular in the Boston rotation in 1910. In his first full season in the majors, the twenty-three-year-old pitched a one-hitter against the Chicago White Sox and compiled a 13-11 record, making him the second-winningest pitcher on the Red Sox. His ERA of 1.62 was sixth-best in the American League. He also became a fan favorite at the Huntington Avenue Grounds, as demonstrated by the following clipping from the *Boston Evening Record*'s Baseball Chit-Chat column:

> Ray Collins is a star. He is the idol of all the lady fans, those bewitching young women, who coyly gaze from under piles of feathers and ribbons. Is it any wonder that he pitches wonderful ball when those brown and blue and gray and violet orbs are on him? Gee, it's great to be a big, fine pitcher. If I ever have a son that's him, a pitcher and of course he will be a dashing fine chap. Fond expectations.

The Silver King Comes to Vermont

In February 1911 Tim "The Silver King" Murnane, a jovial, white-haired ex-major leaguer of the 1870s who became sports editor of the *Boston Globe*, came to Burlington to visit Ray Collins in his hometown. The following is excerpted from the column Murnane wrote about his visit:

In looking over the list of Boston Red Sox players still in love with their surroundings, living within a day's ride of Boston, I selected Mr. Collins as the player on whom to make a friendly call and wired the young man that I was coming up to see him. I had also intended calling on Larry Gardner, who winters at Enosburgh Falls, about fifty miles farther north, but our signals became crossed and to my surprise Mr. Gardner was on hand to greet me on my arrival at Burlington, where he has many friends as the result of his student days at the University of Vermont, where he, like Collins, was a valuable member of the baseball team.

I was soon tucked away in a roomy sleigh and started for Mr. Collins' home, ten minutes ride from the business section of the city. "I would like to have you see mother" was all the comment that the ball player made as we went slipping over the snow. "This is my home," he remarked as the team drew up in front of a pretty house on a residential street with a grade just right for fine sledding. Before entering the house the camera man snapped a picture of the player and the writer, and Ray pointed to a field close by, saying: "There is where I learned to play ball as a schoolboy. About all that is left to remind me of the old place now is that elm tree."

I was introduced to Mr. Collins' mother as "Mr. Murnane of the Boston Globe" and was informed by the lady that she always has read the Globe baseball news since Ray took up the game as a serious matter. "Ray always loved to play baseball," remarked Mrs. Collins. "When at the primary school he was captain of a team, later at the high school, and finally during his four years at college he kept up his enthusiasm for the game, so I was not surprised to find that he was willing to take a position with the Boston Americans. I never tried to influence my boy to give up the game that he seemed to love so much and his success in which made so many friends for him.

"Ray seldom talks baseball, however, but loves to bring home the pictures of young men he has played with." This was very evident after a glance at his interesting den, where the green and gold colors of his alma mater were the principal decoration, with pictures of baseball parks and Red Sox players strewn around.

We then went for a sleighride around the city, with the ball player handling the ribbons. As we slipped through the main streets it was a continual "Hello, Ray." Everyone in the place seemed to know the player. Collins simply recognized the salute with a "Hello" in each case.

That evening I sat down to supper with the good Mrs. Collins and the pride of her heart. For the first time Ray mentioned baseball. We chatted about the Red Sox players and about the splendid treatment the boys received on their visit to Vermont last fall. Mrs. Collins said she had enjoyed a call from Tris Speaker and other players of whom she had read and had a great desire to see.

The delightful simplicity of the woman, and the good taste displayed in the home, made it quite easy to understand why Ray Collins is modest at all times and deeply considerate of every man's feelings.

In springtime a man's thoughts turn to love and baseball. So it was that during spring training in 1911, while the Red Sox were working out in Redondo Beach, California, Ray Collins became smitten. Her name was Lillian Marie Lovely, and it's said that her surname suited her well. She was the eighteen-year-old sister of Jack Lovely, one of Ray's fraternity brothers who later headed the Jones & Lampson Company, the largest gear factory in Springfield, Vermont. Jack's family had recently moved to Los Angeles from St. Albans, and Jack insisted that Ray look them up while he was there.

Ray apparently left his heart and concentration in California. He was 3-6 at one point in the 1911 season, prompting rumors that he was soon to be released. "Ominous rumblings agitate the atmosphere," wrote one poetic reporter. "The management holds, apparently, that a player who cannot pitch nine games and win, say, 15 or 20, is useless, dangerous and ought to be abolished." But before management did anything rash, Ray turned his season around, finishing at 11-12 with a 2.40 ERA.

During the offseason Ray married Lillian in Los Angeles. In a congratulatory note, Red Sox president James McAleer wrote, "May you live long and prosper and have a million little Collinses. I think you are due for a great year and Mrs. Collins will be proud of her big boy when the season is over." The couple set out like they were taking McAleer's blessing of fertility at face value—their first daughter, Marjorie, was born in December 1912. Four more followed: Ray Jr. in 1914; Janet in 1916; Warren in 1919; and Dorothy in 1923.

During their first winter together Lillian may have made life too comfortable for her new husband. Ray was noticeably overweight when he reported for spring training, and his problems were compounded when a spike wound resulted in an abscess on his knee. Collins missed the first two months of the season, during which time the Red Sox christened their new stadium, Fenway Park. Ray didn't start a game until June 7, nor win one until June 22, but from that point on he was nearly invincible.

A half-century later, Ray's fondest memory of the 1912 season was pitching the first-place Red Sox to two victories in three days over the second-place Athletics at Philadelphia's Shibe Park. When Ray defeated the A's 7-2 on July 3, the headline in the next day's paper, over Ray's photograph, read, "SURPRISED ATHLETICS, RED SOX AND PROBABLY HIMSELF." Then on July 5 he surprised the A's again, 5-3. Collins finished fifth in the American League in shutouts in 1912, but all four of them came in the second half of the season. By October his record stood at 13-8 and his ERA at 2.53, fifth-best in the A.L. The team's only lefthander, Ray was considered the second-best pitcher on the staff behind Smoky Joe Wood (34-5) as the Red Sox walked away with the American League pennant.

Collins started Game Two of the World Series against Christy Mathewson and led 4-2 after seven innings. Then in the eighth he was pulled with only one out after the Giants rallied for three runs. The game was called on account of darkness after eleven innings with the score tied 6-6 (which is why the Series went eight games). The Red Sox led the Series, three games to one, by the time it was Collins' turn to pitch again in Game Six, but player-manager Jake Stahl surprised everyone by starting fireballer Buck O'Brien. O'Brien was no slouch, coming off a 20-13 season, but the Giants shelled him for

Ray and Lillian (Lovely) Collins pose for the camera on their wedding day in Los Angeles. [Collins Family Archives]

Collins (third from right, back row) won a combined thirty-nine games for the Red Sox in 1913-14, but was relegated to the bullpen in 1915. Here he poses with the 1915 team, perhaps the best Red Sox team of all time. The two players to Collins' left (viewer's right) are Tris Speaker and Babe Ruth. Larry Gardner is in the second row, far left. [Bob Wood]

five runs in the first inning. Collins took over and pitched shutout ball for seven innings, but the Red Sox lost 5-2. "Things might have been a little different had Collins been sent in from the first," Stahl admitted.

In 1913 Ray had his best season yet, finishing at 19-8. His .714 winning percentage was second-best in the American League, surpassed only by the great Walter Johnson's .837. On August 29 Collins went head-to-head against Johnson, who entered with a fourteen-game winning streak, and pitched eleven scoreless innings for the victory. Of the three games in which the two pitchers faced each other in 1913, each was decided by a score of 1-0, with the Vermonter winning twice.

That season Collins became involved in the Base Ball Players' Fraternity, an organization founded by Dave Fultz, a lawyer who'd played seven years in the big leagues, 1898-1905, even leading the A.L. in runs scored in 1903. Showing his leadership ability, Collins served as player representative for the Red Sox. Later he was chosen as vice president for the American League and admitted to the BBPF's board of directors and advisory board.

Coming off his best season, Collins expected a substantial increase in his $3,600 salary and was sorely disappointed when the contract he received called for only $4,500. After Ray threatened to jump to the Federal League, the Red Sox met his demands and signed him to a two-year contract at $5,400 per year. With the illness of Smoky Joe Wood, Boston was counting on Collins to become the ace of its pitching staff in 1914, and that's exactly what he did. Ray's six shutouts ranked fourth in the A.L. that season, and he was one of only three A.L. pitchers to reach the twenty-win plateau.

Collins picked up his nineteenth and twentieth victories on September 22, 1914, by pitching complete games in both ends of a doubleheader at Detroit's Navin Field. He won the first game 5-3 and the nightcap 5-0. It's no surprise that the feat came against the Tigers—Ray seemed to own Ty Cobb, Detroit's temperamental superstar. He once walked a batter intentionally to pitch to Cobb, and the tactic worked when Ty grounded weakly back to the mound. The Georgia Peach said that Collins gave him as much trouble as any pitcher he ever faced. Cobb attributed his difficulty to Ray's peculiar wind-up, which caused hitters to "swing at his motion." Nonetheless, Collins and Cobb were friendly, and during one roadtrip to Detroit Ray and Larry Gardner were invited to Cobb's home for dinner. "We went and had a nice time," Ray remembered.

In 1915, because the Boston Red Sox were in the enviable position of having too many good pitchers, Collins was relegated to the bullpen. As early as June newspapers began speculating that he'd soon retire, and one even printed a false rumor that he'd purchased a Rutland hotel. When Collins pitched a two-hitter to beat Cleveland on July 14, the Red Sox reportedly were pleased to see him return to his old form, but the performance turned out to be an aberration. Starting only nine games, the fewest since his rookie year, Ray finished at 4-7 with an abysmal 4.30 ERA.

What caused the sudden downturn in Ray Collins' career? The newspapers made no mention of injury. Perhaps it was just a matter of the Red Sox having better (and younger) pitchers: Rube Foster (20-8), Ernie Shore (19-8), Dutch Leonard (14-7), and a twenty-two-year-old lefty named Babe Ruth (18-6) made up the best rotation in baseball. Incidentally, as an educated man of strong morals, Collins didn't care for Ruth's antics: "Ruth would drink to excess, party all night, get no sleep, and arrive late for games," Ray Jr., now a retired physician living in Middlebury, remembers his father telling him. Still, Ray Sr. was amazed by how well Ruth could play under those circumstances.

Collins didn't pitch a single inning in the 1915 World Series, and after the season the Red Sox expected him to take a cut in pay to $3,500. Rather than suffer that humiliation, Collins announced his retirement from professional baseball on January 3, 1916, stating that he was "discouraged by his failure to show old-time form." He was only twenty-nine years old.

A New York bank offered Ray a job, and with his college and baseball contacts, economics degree, and keen intellect, the position appeared to suit him well. Instead, he chose to return to his family's Colchester farm. It was, according to Ray Jr., "the worst move he ever made." Located just north of Poor Farm Road, the Collins farm was hilly with marshy meadows better suited to growing rush-like swale grass than hay or corn. Because at first he didn't own a tractor, Ray farmed in sweat-intensive, nineteenth-century fashion, walking behind a horse-drawn plow. For a long time the farmhouse lacked indoor plumbing—it had an outhouse, and the family used the Sears catalog as toilet paper. Lillian wasn't used to that sort of lifestyle, but she endured without complaint. Nor did she raise a fuss when Ray's mother moved back to the farm to live with the family for the next twenty-two years.

By the early '20s the knack for pitching that had left Collins in 1915 started to come back. Larry Mayforth, a former catcher then working as UVM graduate manager of athletics, used to come out to the farm a couple nights each week. After supper Ray went out front of the farmhouse and pitched to him until dark. On weekends they drove up to the Montreal suburbs where they received $100 per game to form a battery.

Sometimes the competition was even tougher. On July 4, 1922, thirty-five-year-old Ray Collins took the mound at Centennial Field against the Brooklyn Royal Giants, a black team considered one of the finest of the era. Locked up in a pitchers' duel with Jesse Hubbard, Ray held the Giants scoreless for twelve innings and didn't walk a single batter, but in the thirteenth he finally gave up three runs. "Collins showed the fans that he has not lost the pitching arm, and the head to go with it, which made him at one time one of the most famous twirlers in the major leagues," the

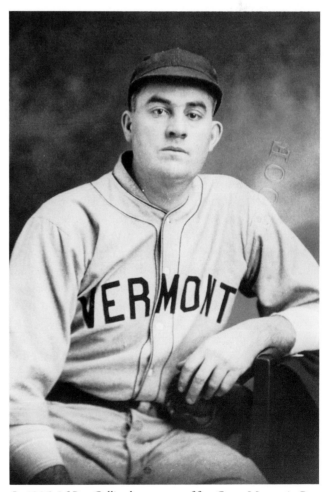

In 1925-26 Ray Collins became one of five Green Mountain Boys of Summer to coach the UVM baseball team. [Collins Family Archives]

In this 1936 photo, Ray boils sap in the Collins sugarhouse. [Collins Family Archives]

Free Press reported. After the game, several of the Royal Giants were boarding their bus when they saw Collins in the Centennial Field parking lot. Unaware that the man who'd just pitched so effectively was a former major leaguer, they approached him and asked, "Man, where did you come from?"

Several local legends developed about the ex-Red Sox star. Colchester resident Harley Monta claimed that Collins would go into his barn on rainy days and pitch baseballs through a small hole in the wall. Eben Wolcott heard that Collins could stand at one end of Sunderland Hollow and throw a baseball to the other. Stories like that are flattering but untrue, says Ray Jr. But he does remember one true incident that occurred at the Champlain Valley Fair in 1924. In a cruel forerunner of the dunking stool, a midway booth advertised "Hit the Nigger, Win a Cigar." An African-American man with his head stuck through a hole waited for someone to throw a medium-soft ball at his head. The crowd urged the former major leaguer with the famous control to take his shot, but Ray refused. Then a man holding real, hard baseballs prepared to throw at the African-American. Collins became enraged. He grabbed the man's shirt with both hands, lifted him off the ground, and said, "You leave him alone!"

After a couple seasons as a part-time assistant, Ray Collins took over as UVM's head baseball coach on January 19, 1925. Following a successful southern trip, highlighted by a meeting with President Coolidge at the White House, the Green and Gold enjoyed a memorable season. After road victories at Syracuse and Colgate, a bonfire celebration was held on campus for the first time in years, and on Decoration Day more than 6,000 people reportedly showed up at Centennial Field for a game against Dartmouth. At the age of thirty-eight, Collins appeared to have finally found a position that suited him. But coaching didn't pay enough to make up

for his time away from the farm, or so he claimed, and after the 1926 season he gave up the job.

It seemed the harder Ray threw himself into farming, the more his luck turned against him. He used some of the money he'd earned in baseball to plant an apple orchard, but the trees failed to take. In 1927 a half-dozen of his cows tested positive for tuberculosis in the state's mandatory testing program; only after Ray took the cows to St. Albans and had them butchered did he learn that the test results were false positives. Then on October 22, 1929, a spark from a blower blade ignited dry grass, and Ray's barn burned to the ground. It had recently been equipped with state-of-the-art milking machines, and its loss was estimated at $15,000. Unfortunately, the fire occurred before Ray had a chance to buy sufficient insurance. He was forced to cash in his life insurance to build its replacement.

The stress and hard work gradually wore down the man who was famous for pitching and winning both ends of a doubleheader. Ray Jr. remembers his father laying down on the couch after dinner. Now, with more than eighty years of living and a career in medicine behind him, he can only guess at the pain his father silently endured. During the winter of 1929-30 Ray came down with a severe strep infection. His physicians identified the germ under their microscopes but couldn't kill it because antibiotics hadn't been invented yet. They told Ray that either his immune system would kill the germ or it would kill him. Months of weakness and delirium later, Ray won.

During World War II Ray chaired the town draft board. Though he probably could have secured an agricultural exemption for one of his sons, both went into harm's way, serving with distinction before returning to successful professional careers. Ray Sr. couldn't carry a

The Collins family gathered together at the farm shortly after the end of World War II. From left to right: Marjorie, Warren, Janet, Lillian, Ray Sr., Dorothy, and Ray Jr. [Collins Family Archives]

Ray Collins (left) and Larry Gardner attend a Burlington Cardinals game at Centennial Field. [Gardner Family Archives]

rifle, but he could drive a tractor—barely, due to severe arthritis in his hip—so he hayed and plowed his neighbors' fields, often until midnight. What drove him to sit his nearly-crippled body onto a tractor night after night, after the sun had set? Money and neighborliness, to some degree, but one can't help but imagine that he felt a sense of obligation to the hundreds of young men his draft board had sent into the armed forces.

For more than three decades the Collins family scraped by. To make ends meet, Ray and Lillian took in travelers in a precursor of today's bed and breakfasts, serving meals and talking baseball with their guests. They also operated a sugarbush, wresting sap from a stand of sugar maples a mile north of the farmhouse. Ray lugged the sap buckets and boiled the sap, and Lillian made and sold a variety of maple products. Eventually Collins won an award from the Vermont Maple Sugar Industry.

His neighbors had no idea that he was struggling financially. To them Ray Collins was a pillar in the community. He was a natural leader—college-educated, well-traveled, well-connected in several levels of society, a star athlete, physically imposing. From 1922, when Winooski split off from Colchester, until the 1960s, when the IBM influx

occurred, an oligarchy of civic-minded, Republican farmers represented Colchester in the Vermont legislature, and Ray took his turn from 1943 to 1946. In 1953 Ray was named Colchester's first zoning administrator. For many years he was moderator of town meetings, and he was always the foreman during his frequent jury duty.

The Relationship Between Ray Collins and Larry Gardner

They were teammates at UVM and on the Boston Red Sox. For nearly a half-century they lived within ten miles of each other. Their names are linked in history, as they are in the name of UVM's cage at Gutterson Fieldhouse. One might expect, then, that Ray Collins and Larry Gardner were close friends.

They weren't.

It wasn't that there was any animosity between them—they just chose to spend their free time in the company of others. At UVM Gardner hung out with an Enosburg crowd, which centered around the Delta Sigma fraternity house. Collins was a Delta Psi. On the Red Sox Gardner and outfielder Harry Hooper were inseparable, while Collins' best friend was fellow pitcher

Every year during UVM reunions Ray Collins hosted a Sunday brunch for the Class of '09. Gardner and Collins are second and third from left, respectively, in this photograph from the late 1960s. [University of Vermont]

Hugh Bedient. In later years Collins visited regularly with Bert Abbey, from whom he obtained tomato plants. He and Gardner socialized only at organized UVM or baseball functions, like the time Ray threw and Larry caught the honorary first pitch of the 1947 Northern League season.

Family members confirm the distant relationship but are at a loss for an explanation. Perhaps it was simply a matter of differing personalities. Collins was reserved and serious, while Gardner was fun-loving and outgoing. It shows in photographs—Collins often wears a somber expression, whereas Gardner usually appears happy-go-lucky.

Gardner and Collins weren't close, but at the Collins farmhouse, which remained practically unchanged until the Collins family sold it in 1999, Larry Gardner's phone number could still be found under the Gs in the old rolodex that sat on the desk.

Finally Ray's arthritis got so bad that he couldn't operate the family farm, so around 1960 he sold it to Ray Jr. By the time of Fenway Park's fiftieth anniversary in 1962, Ray needed two canes just to walk. But he'd missed Fenway's 1912 opening due to a knee injury, and this time he was determined to be there. "My legs aren't what they used to be," he told the *Boston Globe* weeks before the big day, "so I've been out to the airport finding out how I can climb the staircase to get into the plane." On Saturday, April 21, 1962, Collins was one of nine members of the 1912 team to make it back for the celebration (others were Larry Gardner, Bill Carrigan, Joe Wood, Harry Hooper, Duffy Lewis, Hugh Bedient, Steve Yerkes, and Olaf Henricksen). They saw Boston's Don Schwall defeat the Detroit Tigers 4-3 despite home runs by Norm Cash and Al Kaline.

Collins was an active alumnus of the University of Vermont. During the 1950s he served on UVM's board of trustees, presiding over the school's transition from private to public university. Every year during reunions Ray hosted a Sunday brunch for the Class of '09, and ten or so classmates would make their way out to the farm to feast on fried eggs, ham, pancakes, and Ray's famous maple syrup. It was during one of those breakfasts in 1969 that he suffered a minor stroke. His condition gradually worsened until he died at Fanny Allen Hospital on January 9, 1970. He was buried in the Village Cemetery in Colchester.

Respect for athletic success goes only so far, and many stars squander it. Ray Collins used it as capital to serve his town, county, and *alma mater*. Maybe returning to Colchester and taking over the family farm wasn't such a bad move after all.

TOM SIMON
RESEARCH ASSISTANCE BY GUY PAGE

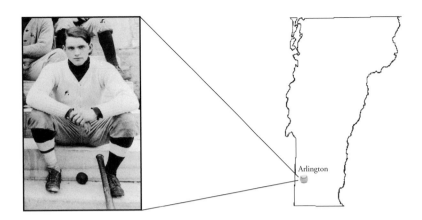

Chick Evans

Boy Wonder from Burr & Burton

In the decade after the turn of the last century, the Knights of Columbus of the towns of Bennington, Vermont, and Hoosick Falls, New York, staged an annual Columbus Day baseball contest. With a $100 wager at stake, the rival towns went to great lengths to stock their teams. In 1910, for instance, Hoosick Falls engaged a Bennington-area major league pitcher, Chick Evans of the Boston Doves, and backed him up with an all-star ensemble of minor leaguers. The New Yorkers must have felt confident of victory.

Little did they know that the Bennington council had hired the Boston Red Sox, who'd played an exhibition game in Burlington just two days earlier. With Smoky Joe Wood and Ray Collins sharing mound duties, the "Bensox" ran away with an 11-1 win. Chick Evans was the losing pitcher in his homecoming, giving up nine runs in just four innings. It proved to be his last game against major league competition.

Charles Franklin Evans was born in Arlington, Vermont, on October 15, 1889. His nickname may have been short for "Chickory," as he was called by at least one sportswriter, but more likely it was just a common sobriquet for baseball players named Charles. Evans grew up in North Bennington and attended Burr & Burton Seminary in Manchester, where he was captain and star pitcher of the baseball team. The 1906 edition of the school's yearbook, *The Burtonian*, gives an indication of his ability: "The battery work this year is such as has never before been exhibited on these grounds. Captain

Evans has been a power in the box that all opposing teams found was not to be trifled with."

Evans' high school career included at least two match-ups against a pitcher named "Fisher" from Middlebury High School. Later a teammate of Chick's at Hartford in 1908, "Fisher" of course was the great Ray Fisher, who won 100 big league games and outlived Evans by sixty-six years. In their first duel, at the fairgrounds in Manchester Center on May 6, 1905, Evans pitched a three-hitter and struck out fourteen en route to a 7-1 victory. One month later, Fisher was the winner in a ten-inning, 4-3 contest at Middlebury College that the *Rutland Herald* described as "one of the fastest played on the college diamond for a long time."

After graduating from Burr & Burton in 1907, Evans joined a semipro team in Hoosick Falls (hence his appearance in the 1910 Columbus Day grudge match), where he was spotted by Tommy Dowd, a ten-year big league veteran who was managing Hartford of the Connecticut State League at the time. Dowd signed Evans to a contract for the 1908 season, and the eighteen-year-old rookie won thirteen games. But what really made major league teams take notice was his outing against Bridgeport on July 21, 1908. The following account is from the *Hartford Times*:

> There was not a fly or a ground ball handled by the Hartford outfielders during the entire game. Only twenty-seven men faced Evans in the nine innings. Ten of these struck out. He fanned at least one man in eight of the nine

Evans is seated in the front row, second from right, in this photo of the 1905 Burr & Burton team. That season he matched up twice against Middlebury High School's Ray Fisher, winning once and losing once. [Burr & Burton Archives]

innings, and in the sixth and ninth had two in each to his credit. Nearly all of the crowd of 1,500 stayed until the end, hoping that Chick would turn the trick. He fanned the last two in the ninth inning. After the game the crowd gathered around Evans and congratulated him on his great pitching feat.

After Chick won ten games by the midpoint of the 1909 season, Hartford sold him to the Boston Nationals on July 21. The Doves, as they were then known, stood at the bottom of the National League standings, but manager Harry Smith nonetheless kept Evans on the bench until September 19. He pitched in a total of only four games for Boston, finishing with a record of 0-3.

The 1910 season started on a much better note for Chick Evans. On opening day, April 14, the Doves beat the New York Giants 3-2 in eleven innings, and Evans pitched one-hit ball over the last three innings to pick up the win. It was his only major league victory, though *The Sporting Life* credited him with additional wins on July 7 and July 20. For a while, in fact, Evans, with a record of 3-0, appeared in some newspapers at the top of the list of the leading pitchers in the National League (at the time it was customary to rank pitchers in order of winning percentage). *Total Baseball*, however, lists his 1910 record as 1-1 (he lost his only start on August 27). What happened to Chick Evans' two additional wins?

For the answer we turn to SABR-member Frank Williams, an expert on won-lost decisions prior to 1920. Williams writes:

> Evans' official record in 1910 is 1-1. The listing in *Sporting Life*, the *New York Times*, etc., for the most part gave the win to the pitcher who was pitching when his team took the lead in the game. The official scorers in the A.L. and the N.L. followed the practices set forth by Ban Johnson and Irwin M. Howe in the A.L., and John Heydler in the N.L. These practices were basically the same for both leagues and were different than the ones used by *Sporting Life*, the *New York Times*, etc. They were official, however, and that is why all the record books show Evans at 1-1 in 1910.

After just seventeen games and 52.2 innings pitched, Chick Evans' time in the major leagues was over. His baseball career and life went downhill after 1910. He pitched briefly with Montreal of the Eastern League in 1911 (teaming with fellow Vermonters Jean Dubuc and George Leclair), then with Syracuse of the New York State League in 1912. Newspaper reports indicate that he developed arm trouble. By 1916 he was living in Schenectady, New York, where he worked in the munitions department of the General Electric Company. He also played the outfield for the company baseball team.

Evans became ill later that year. He was hospitalized in Schenectady's Ellis Hospital from the end of July until his death on September 2, 1916, a few weeks short of his twenty-seventh birthday. Evans' death certificate lists the cause of death as complications arising from gonorrhea. His funeral was held at his brother's home in North Bennington. There the Green Mountain Boy of Summer with the shortest life span was laid to rest on September 4, 1916, less than six years after pitching against Ray Collins and the rest of the Bennington Red Sox.

DICK THOMPSON

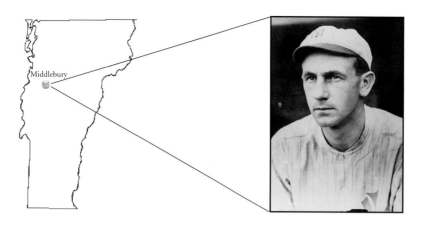

Ray Fisher

Hail To A Victor

Ray Fisher has been justly honored for his thirty-eight years as head baseball coach at the University of Michigan. He was inducted into Michigan's Sports Hall of Fame in 1959, the American Association of College Baseball Coaches Hall of Fame in 1966, and the University of Michigan Hall of Honor in 1979. And on May 23, 1970, he received his greatest honor when the ballpark at the University of Michigan was renamed Ray Fisher Stadium. "In Ann Arbor his name is almost as revered as 'The Victors,' Michigan's famous fight song," said Eric Johnson, president of the University of Michigan Alumni Club of Vermont.

Fisher's legacy in Michigan only began when he was in his mid-thirties, however, and his ties to Vermont run deep. He attended high school and college in his hometown of Middlebury, coached in Vermont summer leagues for years, and in later life spent summers at a camp on Lake Champlain. Nevertheless, few Vermonters today have even heard of him. The pitcher who won 100 games over ten seasons (1910-17, 1919-20), compiled a lifetime 2.82 ERA, and was considered one of the dozen best pitchers of his era by both Ty Cobb and Napoleon Lajoie has no monuments to his achievements in his home state. Oddly, the only recognition he's received in Vermont was induction into the Middlebury High School Hall of Fame in 1986.

Ray Lyle Fisher was born on October 4, 1887, on a farm just south of Middlebury. The Fishers were poor—their first farmhouse had no glass windows, only oil pa-

per—and Ray remembered his mother leaving the farm only twice, once to go to Poultney and another time to Ripton. The youngest of four sons, Ray honed his pitching arm by firing rocks at chickens in the barnyard and at rats inside the grain silo.

Ray's two oldest brothers, Bert and Llewellyn, never made it past elementary school, working their entire lives as farmers. Early on Ray appeared destined for a similar future. But through hard work the Fishers prospered, and Ray and his older brother Harry attended Middlebury High School, walking the four miles to and from school.

The youngest Fisher excelled in athletics at MHS. "My parents only let me play sports if I kept up my share of the farm work," he recalled. Ray played halfback on a football team that won the state championship. In baseball he mainly played catcher, and during a practice game against Middlebury College he attracted the attention of Cy Stackpole, an old minor leaguer who coached the college varsity. Graduating in 1906 after only three years of high school, Ray turned down football scholarships from the University of Vermont and Wesleyan University in Connecticut to join his brother Harry at Middlebury.

"Pick" (short for "Pickerel"), as he was called by schoolmates, set the Middlebury College shot-put record and played varsity football, basketball, and baseball. During his freshman year he started the season at catcher, but before long Stackpole converted him into a pitcher.

Ray (top center) was the youngest of four sons. [Fisher Family Archives]

Ray remembered the day:

"Go out on the mound and throw me a few," Cy said one day in practice. So I went out, tried a curve or two when Stackpole, standing in the box with a bat, told me to. Then I up and threw a fastball. It zipped pretty good. Stackpole just stood there looking at me for a long time with a half-smile on his lips. Finally he said, "How'd you like to pitch against Colgate tomorrow?" I said fine. Colgate

was a major baseball power and was expecting to mop us up. But I had quite a day, fanned eighteen, and shut them out.

That summer Ray received an offer to play semipro baseball in Valleyfield, Quebec. But his father, expecting Ray to work on the family farm, allowed him to go to Canada only on the condition that he send home a dollar per day to hire a farmhand. He did so and had plenty to spare, earning room, board, and ten dollars per week for pitching, and an additional $1.35 per day as a machinist's assistant at the Montreal Cottons factory. The 5' 11", 195-pound righthander did well, receiving offers to play in Cuba and to try out for the Montreal Royals. His father no longer criticized baseball when Ray came home from Valleyfield with savings of $100.

While Fisher was pitching in Quebec that summer, Cy Stackpole recommended him to former major leaguer Tommy Dowd, then managing at Holyoke, Massachusetts. The following year Dowd became manager of Hartford in the Connecticut State League, and he signed Ray after Middlebury's season ended. During the summer of 1908, his first partial season as a professional, Fisher went 12-1, his .923 winning percentage standing as a minor league record for over a half-century. He didn't pitch for Middlebury in his junior year of 1909—as a

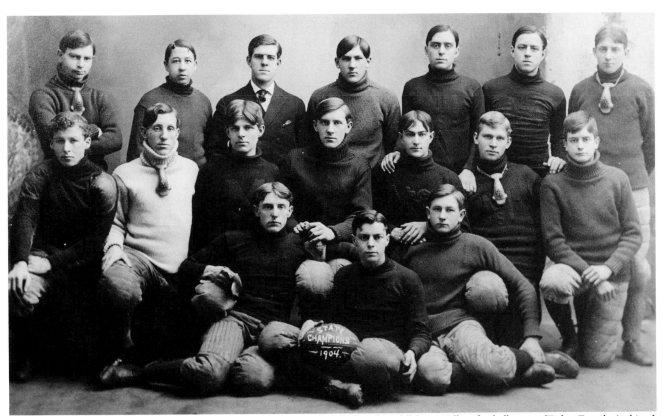

Fisher (front row, right) starred at halfback for the Middlebury High School and Middlebury College football teams. [Fisher Family Archives]

Ray started as a catcher at Middlebury College. [Middlebury College Archives]

homemade bat, to the amusement of his new teammates. Despite his apparent naivete, and perhaps a bit spoiled by Middlebury College's fine facilities, Ray was unimpressed by his new surroundings. "They called it Hilltop Park," he said, "and it wasn't even a good college field. The foul lines were cockeyed and the outfield sloped downhill, so when the batter hit one out there it actually rolled toward the fences."

One of Fisher's first starts came against future Hall-of-Famer Ed Walsh of the Chicago White Sox. "[Manager George] Stallings figured he was going to lose the game and didn't want to waste one of his regular pitchers, so he put me in," Ray remembered. "To be sure I wouldn't hurt any of his regular catchers—I was a bit wild, no doubt—he brought out Lou Criger, who was the famous batterymate of Cy Young. I think my first game in the majors was his last." Fisher surprised everyone by earning a 5-1 victory.

Early in Ray's career, sportswriters often compared him to Hall-of-Famer Jack Chesbro, another New England-born pitcher who'd pitched for the New York Americans

professional he was no longer eligible for collegiate competition—but he returned to Hartford in the summer and led the team to its first-ever pennant, registering one of the greatest minor league seasons ever—a 24-5 record with 243 strikeouts.

It's hard to believe considering his remarkable success, but Fisher claimed that to that point he'd never considered baseball as a post-college profession. But back on the Middlebury campus that fall, one of Ray's classmates received a major league contract. "When I saw that contract," Ray said, "I never envied anybody more. But I never thought anyone was after me. Two days later Arthur Irwin came up for the Yankees, offered me a contract, and I signed. The day after Billy Lush came up for the Giants, so I just missed being a Giant by one day." Ray Collins later told Fisher that the Boston Red Sox also were interested in signing him, on Collins' recommendation.

Fisher's contract with the Yankees allowed him to return to college for his senior year, and he graduated with Middlebury's Class of 1910. After graduation, the twenty-one-year-old Vermonter reported to New York carrying a

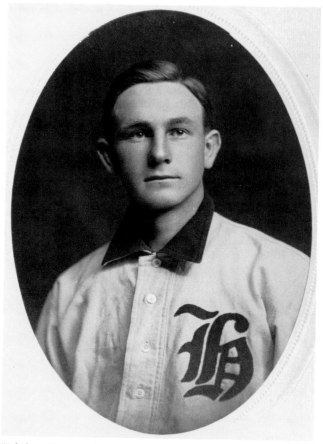

While still a student at Middlebury, "Kid" Fisher pitched professionally for Hartford during the summers of 1908-09. [Fisher Family Archives]

Because Fisher taught Latin at a private school in New Jersey in the offseason, New York sportswriters dubbed him "The Vermont Schoolmaster." [Fisher Family Archives]

the Yankees in 1913-14. "He didn't know any of us," Ray said, "but he had that book [containing statistics from previous seasons]. When you were working, he sized you up and then he would look in the book and see what you did and then he would decide the reason."

Relations between Fisher and Chance were strained until an incident during the 1913 season:

One day I was pitching and they hit a ball back to me with a man on first and I hesitated on my play. I wasn't sure if Peck [Roger Peckinpaugh] or [Roy] Hartzel was covering so I only got one man. They would have gotten me out of the inning.

[Chance] hollered something at me and I hollered something back. Then I saw him making room for me on the bench. And I'm telling you we had it out. People in the boxes were all leaning over and listening. In the meantime, the inning was going. He was so intent on me he forgot to have any pitcher warmed up to take my place.

When the inning was over he didn't have any pitcher warmed up. He said, "Do you want to pitch?" And I said, "I don't give a damn if I ever pitch another game." He said, "Go out there and pitch."

The argument actually improved Ray's standing with his fiery manager.

[Chance's] second year I reported [for spring training] in Houston and there was a boy who went to school with me in Middlebury who lived outside of Houston. They in-

when they were best known as the Highlanders. "Ray Fisher, kid Yankee pitcher, looks like Jack Chesbro, moves like old 'Happy Jack,' and his teammates say he is sure to be the reincarnation of the king of the spit ballers," wrote one New York scribe. "He has plenty of speed and a spit ball just like Chesbro's, but he hasn't learned the control that made the old Yankee star a winner." Another writer made the same comparison: "[Fisher] laughs, talks, acts, and pitches with the same motion as the North Adams farmer. He has a spit ball which, according to [catcher] Ed Sweeney, is just as dangerous as the one Chesbro exhibited."

After posting a 5-3 record as a rookie, Fisher ended up with losing records in each of the next four seasons with the Yankees, at the time a perennial second-division club. His biggest problem was lack of support—in 1913, for example, he lost five games in a row, and the scores were 6-5, 5-4, 3-2, 2-1, and 1-0. "This little example," wrote one reporter, "shows that pitching records have to be studied very carefully in order to get a real line on the actual work of the pitcher, irrespective of whether he wins or loses." But Fisher's record made a negative impression on Frank Chance, who managed

Alice Seeley and Ray Fisher at Lake Dunmore, prior to their 1912 marriage. The two Middlebury natives remained happily married until Alice passed away in 1976. [Fisher Family Archives]

"The Three Rays" of the 1912-16 New York Yankees pitching staff: Ray Keating (left), Ray Fisher (middle), and Ray Caldwell (right). [Fisher Family Archives]

vited me out and I didn't know whether I would be home in time [for curfew]. I said to him, "I'm going to so-and-so's and I expect to be back in time, but I want you to know where I'll be."

And he said, "No rules for you this year," and that was it. He decided I was an alright guy. Never said boo to me. If I didn't come to the ballpark the day after I pitched, no questions asked. Never a better manager than Frank Chance, once we got to know each other.

In 1914 Ray had his best season to that point—10-12 and a 2.28 ERA in 209 innings for the sixth-place Yankees. The next year he pitched even better, going 18-11 with a 2.11 ERA, fifth-best in the A.L. With competition from the Federal League driving up salaries, the Yankees rewarded Ray with a three-year, $19,500 contract.

Close Encounters With A Ferocious Tiger

Ty Cobb is known for the violence with which he played baseball, but Ray Fisher saw a sweeter side of Cobb.

Although they say a lot of things about him, I remember distinctly in Detroit that he hit a ball towards first base

---

and I had to go cover. The ball was real slow along the foul line and I was trying to get the bag and catch the ball at the same time. I ended up with my leg across the bag. He could have stepped on it, and had the perfect right to, but he jumped the bag! If his reputation were true, he would have stepped on it and cut my leg.

Ray also remembered one particular relief appearance in New York when he tamed the Tigers.

It was the eighth inning and [Ray] Caldwell got hit with a liner and split his hand. They put me in there and [Detroit] had the top of the order up. I fooled around and gave a base on balls to Donie Bush, and then Vitt pushed him over. I had Cobb and Crawford coming up.

I could pitch [to Cobb] if I had my stuff, 'cause he stood right on the plate. I got two strikes on him—you couldn't have shot them in any better. I had slippery elm in my mouth and when I saw that second one go by, I put that spit on there and he never knew it. No one ever told him. He swung for a fast one and missed. I could have lost the game then and people still would have been for me! I will always remember that as a highlight because they had the tying run on second base and I got [Cobb] with three pitches.

> [Then] Crawford grounded out to short. I remember I
> came up to bat—the umpires in those days were really good
> fellas. I remember as I came to bat—you wouldn't hear it
> now—that ump said to me, "Ray, you've got pretty good
> stuff out there today." They wouldn't say that now, or even
> think of it.

Until then Ray had spent offseasons in Middlebury. He'd married his high school sweetheart, Alice Seeley—a direct descendant of one of Ethan Allen's Green Mountain Boys—and each winter he'd lived with his wife and in-laws at 8 High Street, serving as physical director at Middlebury College and studying law with a local judge. But by 1915 Ray was so popular in New York City that Middlebury's president thought Ray could do more for the college by wintering in the Gotham area. One might speculate that but for the president's "wisdom," Ray might have spent the next half-century at Middlebury rather than Michigan.

Fisher pitched for the Yankees until 1917, when he came down with pleurisy, a disease related to tuberculosis. Shortness of breath and overall weakness caused him to miss a substantial part of the season. On the day Ray returned to the mound following his bout with illness, his opponent was none other than the great Walter Johnson. "He threw a fastball by me and, I'll tell ya, it looked to me like he just opened his hand and it went by me," Ray remembered. "Then he threw me a curveball and that was just right for me. And I got to second and the second baseman said, 'What did he do, throw you a curveball?'" What Fisher characteristically omitted is that he threw a shutout that day to beat Johnson, 2–0.

Fisher finished the 1917 season, which turned out to be his last with the Yankees, with an 8–9 record despite a 2.19 ERA. "His seven years with the New York Yankees

Ray Fisher was one of the few bright spots for the the New York Yankees during the seven years he pitched for them. His fortunes—and his won-loss record—immediately improved when he joined the Cincinnati Reds in 1919. [Fisher Family Archives]

had been heartbreakers," wrote a Middlebury classmate. "Day after day I saw him at the Polo Grounds pitch games that should have been his with a real team behind him. But he seemed destined to retire from the pastime with nothing but a record as an average pitcher."

Fisher missed the entire 1918 season when he was drafted into the military. Though frustrated at the time, he later believed that his induction may have saved his baseball career. Rather than spending April through October traveling the country in smoke-filled trains, eating poorly, and getting little rest, Fisher regained his health under the watchful eye of army physicians at Fort Slocum outside New Rochelle, New York. He used his managerial skills to run the camp's athletics program.

While Fisher was in the service, the Yankees obtained waivers on him and traded him to the National League's Cincinnati Reds for Pete Schneider, a twenty-game winner as recently as 1917 whose career had also taken a sudden downturn. The Reds lowered Ray's salary from $6,500 to $3,500, and the thirty-one-year-old feared that his playing days were nearly over. But in 1919 Ray bounced back

During his early years with the Yankees, Ray returned to Middlebury during the offseason and served as the college's physical director. [Middlebury College Archives]

by winning his first five starts for his new team. "I have made a long study of pitchers in my career as manager," said Cincinnati's Pat Moran, "and I do not hesitate to say that rarely have I seen a twirler show any better form than Ray Fisher has produced to date for the Reds."

Then Ray dropped five of his next six decisions and lost his place in the rotation. But when the Reds played three consecutive doubleheaders against the New York Giants, Moran was forced to start Fisher, and the Vermonter pitched a shutout. Fisher won eight consecutive games to finish out the season, ending up with a 14-5 record and a 2.17 ERA as the Reds won their first-ever N.L. pennant. Cincinnati had a good team built around Heinie Groh, Edd Roush, and a strong pitching staff, but their World Series victory over the Chicago White Sox will be forever tainted by the Black Sox scandal. Fisher was the losing pitcher in the famous Game Three when honest Dickie Kerr shut out the Reds on three hits, one of them Ray's.

Prior to the 1920 season the National Commission decided to ban Fisher's bread-and-butter pitch, the spitball. Fortunately for Ray, the leagues allowed those who already used it to continue for the rest of their careers, and he was one of seventeen pitchers exempted from the new rule. Like in his Yankee years, Fisher pitched well, posting a 2.73 ERA, but the Reds faltered and his won-lost record sank to 10-11.

By the spring of 1921 Ray's daughter, Janet, was nearing two years old, and Ray was beginning to grow tired of the nomadic life of a baseball player. Deciding it was time to settle into a "real" job, he applied for a coaching position at Cornell University but was turned down. He reported to training camp with the Reds but was on the lookout for other opportunities.

While returning from spring training Fisher learned that Del Pratt, formerly of the Browns and Yankees, had resigned as baseball coach at the University of Michigan to return to the majors. Unhappy with Cincinnati's salary offer of $4,500, a $1,000 cut from the $5,500 he'd earned in 1920, Ray spoke to Pat Moran about interviewing for the Michigan job. Aware that the Vermonter was unhappy with his salary, Cincinnati management did nothing to prevent him from leaving the club. After pitching the last five innings of the Reds' final exhibition game in Indianapolis, Ray drove to Ann Arbor to interview. The press reported that he'd been given his release.

Michigan in fact offered the job to Ray, but around the same time one of Cincinnati's better pitchers came down with a sore arm, while another was suffering from a venereal disease. Suddenly Fisher's services were needed. But Reds owner Garry Herrmann refused Ray's request for a three-year contract, and Ray turned down a one-year contract for the same salary he'd earned the previous season. With the parties at impasse, Ray picked up the telephone on Herrmann's desk, called Ann Arbor, and accepted the coaching job at Michigan. He thought the Reds would place him on the voluntarily retired list.

But that isn't what happened. In late-April 1921 Herrmann wrote N.L. President John Heydler expressing his dismay that Fisher had quit the Reds after giving only seven days' notice—not the proper ten days required by his contract. Heydler declared that Fisher was thus ineligible to play Organized Baseball. Ray was shocked when he heard the news. When his Michigan team was in Chicago, he sought out Commissioner Landis for a face-to-face meeting. Landis contacted Pat Moran and asked him if he'd permitted Fisher to interview for the Michigan position. "I positively refused to grant [such permission] and told him to take up the matter over long-distance telephone with President Herrmann, which I understand he did not do, but took it upon himself to leave the next day," Moran responded.

Ray Fisher poses with his wife, Alice, and daughter, Janet, in this passport photo taken shortly before the Michigan baseball team's 1929 tour of Japan. [Fisher Family Archives]

Like the majors, college baseball returned to segregation around the turn of the century, but Ray Fisher integrated his Michigan team long before it became normal practice at other colleges and universities. This photo dates from the 1950s, some three decades after Fisher re-integrated the Wolverines. [Fisher Family Archives]

For three decades Fisher remained ignorant of Moran's response, which he vehemently contested. But in June 1921, Commissioner Landis sent Fisher a telegram informing him that he was ineligible to participate in organized baseball, and so he remained for sixty years.

At Michigan Ray became the dean of college baseball coaches. In nearly 1,000 regular season games, 1921 to 1958, Fisher's teams went 661-292 (.694) and won fifteen Big Ten titles and an NCAA championship in 1953, the year he was voted NCAA Coach of the Year. Ray's policy was that anyone could play on his team regardless of race, creed, or color, and in 1923 he re-integrated the Michigan varsity, which had not included an African-American player since the 1880s. He was also among the first Americans to take a team to Japan, leading the Wolverines on summer tours in 1929 and 1932. Fisher also coached freshman football and served as an assistant basketball coach at Michigan.

Returning during summers to his wife's family's camp overlooking Lake Champlain on Long Point in North Ferrisburgh, Ray became one of the driving forces be-

hind semipro baseball in Vermont. Occasionally he pitched for the team from Long Point or Vergennes, as on this occasion described in the September 10, 1934, edition of the *Burlington Free Press*:

Fisher spent many summers at this camp on Long Point overlooking Lake Champlain. [Fisher Family Archives]

In the years after World War II, Ray Fisher's Montpelier-based Twin City Trojans were always considered the team to beat in Vermont's Northern League. [Fisher Family Archives]

Ray Fisher, a forty-seven-year-old veteran of the majors, pitched himself into the local baseball hall of fame here this afternoon with a no-hit, no-run victory over the Queen City Blues team of Burlington. He leaves tonight to resume his coaching duties at the University of Michigan. Today's game was played in the remarkably short time of fifty-five minutes, so easily did Fisher dispose of the opposing batsmen.

But to the extent he's remembered in in his native state, it's mostly as the fiery manager of the Burlington Cardinals and the Montpelier-based Twin City Trojans of Vermont's famous Northern League.

With his national reputation, Fisher had little difficulty attracting top-notch talent to Vermont, but the best player undoubtedly was Robin Roberts. Though the future Hall of Famer pitched for rival Michigan State, Ray signed him to play for the Trojans in 1946 and 1947. Roberts has fond memories of his time in the Green Mountains, particularly the second season: "[W]e were really good then. I won seventeen straight starts that year

in Vermont, and that was the year the scouts became interested. I signed with the Phillies in September of that year and was in the big leagues the next June." To the chagrin of his coaches at Michigan State and Philadelphia, Roberts consistently credited his success to Fisher: "Ray taught me everything," he said.

Fisher's rambunctious coaching style brought out the fans. Ray's school-year persona paled in comparison to the summer character known as "Angry Ray"—or "Rowdy Ray," "Violent Fisher," or "Cry Baby Ray," to mention just a few of the nicknames he received from the Vermont press. He was constantly tossed out of games, frequently requiring assistance from police officers—not only to get him to leave the ballpark, but to protect him from rowdy fans once he got outside. Though sometimes accompanied by equipment-tossing, Ray's tirades generally were limited to pointed verbal abuse, but never any expletives.

One story is recounted by R.W. Manville, a former Northern League player, in a letter written in May 1970:

One night, after a particularly harrowing series of umpires' bad decisions, Ray managed (with a few "Lord-a-mighties!" thrown in) to get himself excused from the game in the fifth or sixth inning. In his easily recognizable yankee-spiced voice, he soon had everyone in the stands in arms over his comments wafting gently from somewhere behind the clubhouse. This ultimately led to disaster, and my final remembrance of that evening is Mother Fisher standing by her car, all four tires having been deflated by the crowd, asking the team to go rescue Ray from the clubhouse. As we surrounded him, bats in hand, on leaving the park, Ray couldn't resist one more fling at the hostile crowd: "This is a five-cent town, three-cent team, and a penny's worth of umpire!"

Branch Rickey (right) returned to his alma mater for Ray Fisher Day in 1955. In the early 1920s Rickey was interested in signing the young Michigan coach for the St. Louis Cardinals, but was prevented from doing so by Fisher's blacklisting. [Fisher Family Archives]

Much of that behavior was an act, as demonstrated in this excerpt from the *Burlington Free Press*:

[Ray] went striding out to the plate umpire at Centennial Field one day after a close play, his hands shoved into his pockets like Casey Stengel. He waved his arguing player into the dugout.

Then, with out-thrust jaw, he harangued the umpire. Once in a while he waved an arm while the crowd hooted and yelled. He whirled and went back to the dugout, the umpire glaring at him. After the game, we asked the umpire what Ray had said and got this answer:

"In a quiet voice, despite his arm swinging, Ray said, 'I want you fellows to come down to my camp and we'll have a cookout. We can get some fishing in there.' Then he turned and walked away."

A huge uproar followed Fisher's resignation as coach of the Twin City Trojans in 1949. At the time he was feeling the pressure of coaching year-round, and at age sixty-two he wanted to spend more time on Lake Champlain. The local media, however, focused on an ongoing problem Ray was having with a particular umpire who'd ejected him from three contests. "In my dealings with him, I've learned that he is competent at one thing—and that's his consistency in being usually wrong," Fisher said of the umpire. After his appeal to the league commissioner failed, Ray quit in midseason, citing a conspiracy against him. A month after his resignation he received a testimonial of several-hundred signatures expressing appreciation for his work at Twin City.

Fisher (right) with Charlie Ross after a good day of fishing off Long Point. [Ross Family Archives]

Ray Fisher and Charlie Ross

During the 1930s Ray Fisher befriended a Middlebury boy named Charlie Ross, whose father had died when he was only nine. Charlie spent summers at his family's camp on Long Point, near Ray's camp. He and Ray fished together each morning, and during afternoons they pitched to each other in the pasture next to Ray's camp. "Ray Fisher was like a father to me," says Charlie, now age seventy-nine.

When Charlie graduated from Middlebury High School in 1937, Ray convinced him to turn down a scholarship offer from the University of Vermont to attend the University of Michigan—and lined up several part-time jobs to cover his expenses. Ray also introduced Charlie to his future wife, Charlotte, who was the daughter of Michigan's track coach. Charlie played halfback on the freshman football team—in the same backfield with Tom Harmon, who went on to win the Heisman Trophy in 1940—and pitched for the varsity baseball team. A badly broken arm forced him to give up baseball, but he turned to ice hockey and became Michigan's captain and top goal scorer, earning a tryout with the Boston Olympics, a feeder team for the Boston Bruins.

On the day of his tryout, Charlie learned that the Japanese had attacked Pearl Harbor. He enlisted in the air force and spent nearly three years in England, then returned to Michigan for his law and business degrees. After practicing law in Burlington and serving on the Vermont Public Service Board, Charlie was appointed to the Federal Power Commission by President Kennedy. He later served nineteen years on the International Joint Commission between the United States and Canada before returning to Vermont and operating the Taproot Morgan Horse Farm in Hinesburg.

During Charlie's rise to prominence in government, he still kept in close contact with Ray Fisher. Charlie, in fact, was the last person to take Ray fishing. It was on Lake Champlain in 1982, the last year of Ray's life, by which time Ray had to crawl on the dock to be able to reach the boat.

Ray Fisher coached at Michigan until 1958, when age forced him into mandatory retirement. Though "The Old Fox," as he had come to be known, continued to provide guidance in an unofficial manner, that year marked the beginning of his slow departure from the sport he loved. Ray spent much of his retirement fishing and relaxing at his Vermont camp. There were still plenty of chores, and a Saturday morning was as likely to find Ray on his roof repairing shingles as baiting another hook. Then, in Fisher's later years, two events transpired to bring closure to his life in baseball.

The major leagues had presented him in 1935 with a silver lifetime pass inscribed "To Ray Fisher for Long and Meritorious Service to Baseball," which he'd interpreted to mean that his banishment from organized baseball had been lifted. As a result, he never thought twice when he worked as a spring training instructor for the Detroit Tigers and Milwaukee Braves during the early 1960s. In truth, however, silver passes had been sent to all ten-year major league veterans. Fisher remained on baseball's blacklist, a fact that became apparent when Michigan history professor Don Proctor wrote an analysis of his banishment in 1980. But a couple months after Proctor's article appeared in a magazine called *Ann Arbor Scene*, Commissioner Bowie Kuhn announced that he considered Ray Fisher a retired player in good standing, responding to letters from Henry Caswell of Burlington, a friend of Ray's who'd read the Proctor article, and also from President Gerald

Ford, whom Ray had coached in freshman football at Michigan.

Then in the summer of 1982, just short of his ninety-fifth birthday, Ray attended an Old-Timers' Game at Yankee Stadium. By that point Legionnaires' Disease and hip arthritis had weakened him so much that he had to use a wheelchair for the occasion. Ray's grandson, John Leidy, remembered the events of that weekend:

> When we got there the first evening, there was a reception and I was taken aback by the sheer number of the old-time players who were there. Many Hall of Famers: Mickey Mantle, Joe DiMaggio, Whitey Ford, Lefty Gomez. As a bystander, I was a little disappointed that almost none of the others went out of their way to speak to my grandfather.
>
> Of course, to be fair, almost none of them knew him. None of them had played with him. Next to my grandfather, the oldest player there was Joe Sewell and I believe he went back to the '20s. Grandpa was the only person there who had played in the teens.
>
> I may be reading into this, but I also felt that those guys had a hard time relating to someone who was as old and as weakened as he was. I felt that these athletes were proud of

The ballpark at the University of Michigan was renamed Ray L. Fisher Stadium on May 23, 1970. [Fisher Family Archives]

The oldest living Yankee, 94-year-old Ray Fisher shakes hands with Rick Cerone after throwing out the first ball at Yankee Stadium during the summer of 1982. [Fisher Family Archives]

their physical condition and maybe it was difficult to accept the fact that they would age themselves.

Lefty Gomez came across the room right away and Joe Sewell spoke to him, too. But I will be forever in debt to, and appreciative of, Joe DiMaggio. He was the only person who had not previously known my grandfather who came over and paid his respects.

When we first arrived at Yankee Stadium and stepped out of the limousine, all these youngsters came up wanting autographs. We were in the dugout and they introduced the players one at a time, out on the line, all suited up. Of course my grandfather couldn't play, but they introduced him as the oldest living Yankee, and they wheeled him out onto the field. He waved to the crowd and they had a long, loud standing ovation, second only to DiMaggio. Grandpa began to break

down as the crowd was cheering. I saw the look on his face as he began to get teary as the cheering increased.

We had a dinner Saturday after the game and my grandfather was seated at the head of our table. When the dinner was over, Joe DiMaggio got up to leave a bit ahead of everyone else. He walked to the head of our table and paid his respects to my grandfather before leaving.

A couple months later, when Grandpa was ill, he said to me, "At least we made it to Yankee Stadium."

Three months after his trip to New York, Ray Fisher died in Ann Arbor on November 3, 1982. A few days earlier, he told his nurse, "Well, I guess I'm going up to make my last pitch."

CHIP HART
RESEARCH ASSISTANCE BY JOHN LEIDY

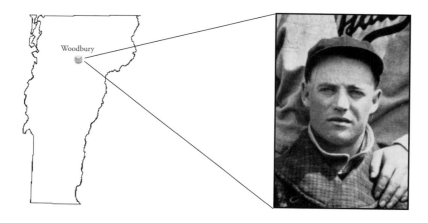

Woodbury

Bob Smith

From Vermont to Vermont Avenue

All four of the Bob Smiths who have played in the major leagues were pitchers, but only one was born in Vermont. A 5' 11", 160-pound righthander, that Bob Smith pitched in seventeen games over three seasons, two of them in the Federal League. He finished his major league career without a single win or loss.

The son of a Canadian-born lumberman, Robert Ashley Smith was born in the central Vermont village of Woodbury on July 20, 1890. He went to high school at Barre's Goddard Seminary, which also produced Green Mountain Boys of Summer Dave Keefe and Crip Polli. Bob's family had moved to Hardwick by the time he entered Tufts University in September 1910. He attended Tufts for only one year, leaving his mark in the school's record books by striking out fourteen batters in a May 1911 game against Bowdoin.

Smith went professional later that summer, signing with Vancouver of the Class-B Northwestern League. He pitched sparingly and was winless in four decisions. Unimpressed by his performance, Vancouver assigned his contract to Boise of the Class-D Western Tri-State League. Smith had his winningest professional season for Boise in 1912, though his eleven wins paled in comparison to the twenty-two of teammate Carl Mays. Best remembered for throwing the pitch that killed Ray Chapman, Mays went on to win 208 games in the majors.

After spending the winter in Riverside, California, Smith tuned up for the 1913 season by pitching for a local team. In a spring training exhibition against the Chicago White Sox "seconds," he caught the attention of Kid Gleason, then a White Sox coach but later the team's manager. In the words of the March 25, 1913, issue of the *Boston Globe,*

Here is what happened to Bob. Up in Redlands, California, the other day, Kid Gleason was managing the White Sox Colts and he couldn't keep his eyes off the opposing pitcher. The White Sox won the game, 3-1, through no fault of the boy on the mound. The game over, Kid "kidnapped" the lad and took him back to Los Angeles for Jimmy Callahan's approval. It was found that Bob belonged to the Boise, Idaho, club so Callahan bought and signed him on Gleason's approval.

Smith started the 1913 season with the White Sox, making his major league debut on April 19. In relief of Frank Lange, he gave up three runs on three hits and three walks in a 9-2 loss to the Cleveland Naps. Chicago then sent him to Minneapolis of the American Association where he went 0-3 in nine games, last appearing on June 26. Whether he was hurt at that point or sent to a team in a lower-classified league is unknown.

In 1914 Smith returned to the majors with Buffalo of the Federal League, a short-lived third major league that competed for players with teams in Organized Baseball. He compiled a respectable 3.44 ERA in fifteen games, good enough to secure a place on the team for the following season. But on April 19, 1915, the second anniversary of his lone outing with the White Sox, Smith made what turned out to be his last major league appearance. He pitched one inning and gave up two earned runs on one hit and two walks, after which Buffalo optioned him to Springfield of the Colonial League, a Federal-affiliated minor league. Smith lost all four of the games he appeared in for Springfield.

The Mystery of Robert M. Brown

Early editions of *The Baseball Encyclopedia* listed a player named Robert M. Brown who pitched for Buffalo of the Federal League in 1914. For years baseball historians tried in vain to find biographical information on Brown, but in 1991 Bill Haber, a member of SABR's biographical committee, realized that Brown was actually Robert Ashley Smith playing under an assumed name.

The key to Haber's solving the mystery was an article entitled "Unholy Compact and Well Broken" in the March 18, 1915, issue of *The Sporting News*. "Robert A. Smith, pitcher, will perform with the Buffalo Federal League team this year under his right name," the article stated. "Last year he pitched for Larry Schlafly's outlaws under the name Brown and therein lies a story from which Mike and Joe Cantillon of the Minneapolis American Association Club can draw the moral that Federal promises and pledges are made only to be broken."

In the spring of 1914 the Cantillons had struck a deal with the Federal League under which the Feds had agreed not to steal any players from the Minneapolis team. But over the winter the Buffalo Federals had signed Bob Smith to a two-year contract and didn't discover that he was already Minneapolis property until he reported for spring training. Wanting to hold onto Smith, Buffalo manager Schlafly convinced the Vermonter to play the entire 1914 season under the alias of "Brown." "Frank Delahanty and Nick Allen, who had played on the Minneapolis club but were free agents when they went to the Buffalo Federals, were the only players who knew the true identity of Brown," *The Sporting News* reported.

Before the 1915 season Schlafly decided that the agreement with the Cantillons was no longer in effect. "Just before the Buffeds left for the training camp at Athens, Georgia, this spring," reported *The Sporting News*, "Manager Schlafly announced that Pitcher Brown would be Pitcher Smith on the score cards this summer."

Little is known of Bob Smith's life after 1915. He may have continued to play baseball in the minors, but his name is too common to trace effectively. On June 5, 1917, he filled out a World War I registration card in Detroit, but it's not known what he was doing there.

Smith died of heart disease in a Veterans Administration hospital in West Los Angeles on December 27, 1965. His death certificate indicates that he and his wife, Millie, had lived in the Westlake section of Los Angeles, where he'd worked as a self-employed real estate broker. Though there's no indication that Smith ever returned to his native state after his baseball career ended, the funeral home that handled his cremation was located on Vermont Avenue.

Dick Thompson

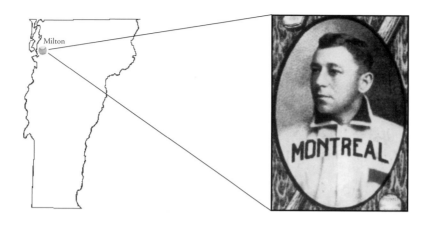

George Leclair

The French-Canadian Federal Leaguer

Tens of thousands of French-Canadians emigrated to the United States during the nineteenth century. In Vermont alone there were 55,000 Franco-Americans by 1900, meaning one-sixth of all Vermonters could trace their lineage to Quebec. One was George "Frenchy" Leclair, a right-handed pitcher who compiled a 7-12 record and 3.36 ERA in the Federal League during its only two years of existence.

According to *Total Baseball*, George Lewis LaClaire was born in Milton, Vermont, on October 18, 1886. The spelling of his last name appears to be an anglicization of the common French name Leclair. George himself preferred the French spelling, which is what appears on his tombstone at the St. Romuald Roman Catholic Cemetery in Farnham, Quebec. There's also some question whether he actually was born in Milton. No birth certificate exists, and there's no record of his baptism at the Catholic church in Milton or any neighboring parish. The only evidence is a form filled out around 1914 and contained in the "LaClaire" file at the National Baseball Library. In his own hand, apparently, he listed his date of birth and Milton as his birthplace.

The only thing known of George's childhood is that his family returned to Quebec, operating a shoestore in Farnham, not far from the Vermont border. The first direct news we have of the boy is when he attracted notice as a nineteen-year-old pitching star for the Farnham team in the Eastern Canada League. In the 1906 season opener, George pitched Farnham to a 9-2 victory. Two

weeks later he notched sixteen strikeouts in a 5-4 win over St. Jean. Leclair stayed with Farnham for five seasons, pitching well enough to earn a shot at Organized Baseball in the fall of 1910.

After the Boston Red Sox played an exhibition game in Burlington, manager Patsy Donovan announced the signing of a local player on Larry Gardner's recommendation. "The new man is George L. LeClair," the *Burlington Free Press* reported, "a native of Farnham, P.Q., who did the twirling at some hard games for Montreal during the past season." Actually Leclair had pitched in only a single game for Montreal. On the last weekend of the 1910 season, he'd started the second game of a doubleheader against Rochester, champions of the Eastern League. After striking out the leadoff man, a nervous Leclair was hit hard by four consecutive batters, resulting in two runs. He regained his composure, however, and allowed only two hits over the next four innings. The Royals scored once in the bottom of the first and four times in the fourth to give Leclair a rain-shortened 5-2 victory in his professional debut.

Whatever happened to Leclair's contract with the Red Sox remains a mystery. He showed up with the Montreal Royals again at spring training in Newport News, Virginia, on March 27, 1911. Accompanying Leclair was Jean Dubuc, who'd been retained as special correspondent by *La Presse*, one of Montreal's French-language daily newspapers. On April 1 Leclair pitched six strong innings for the regulars in a 9-1 victory over the rookies.

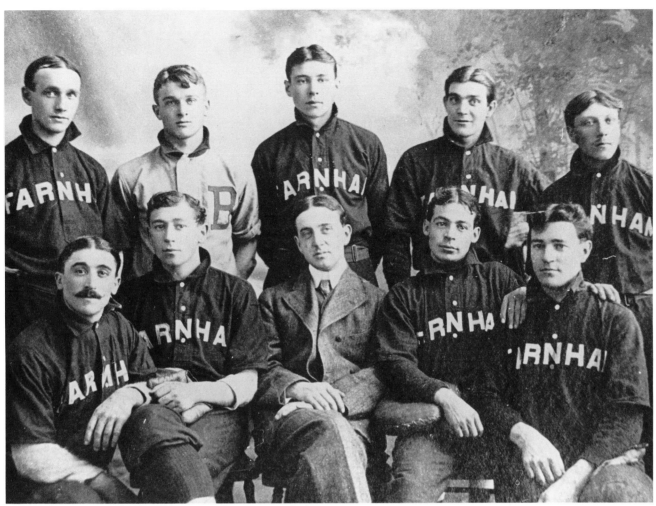

Leclair is seated in the front row, second from left, in this photograph of the 1907 Farnham team. The "ringer" standing directly behind Leclair, wearing his Bangor, Maine, uniform, is Larry Gardner. [Farnham Historical Society]

"Leclair is making a very good impression," Dubuc wrote in *La Presse*. "He just has to keep going to secure a place on the team."

Apparently Leclair kept going because he was one of Montreal's six pitchers when the regular season opened on April 21. Over the course of the 1911 season, however, Leclair appeared in only ten games for the Royals, pitching just 29.1 innings. Montreal invited him to spring training again in 1912, and again he made the team. But before the season was a month old the Royals shipped Leclair to Bridgeport of the Class-B Connecticut League. The following year Montreal released him after only one spring training appearance.

Leclair spent the 1913 season with LaCrosse, Wisconsin, of the Class-C Northern League (not to be confused with the Vermont outlaw league of the same name). He finished with the league's worst winning percentage, prevailing in just two of his sixteen decisions and yielding 161 hits in 133 innings. Although his career in base-

ball appeared to be headed downward, his days in the big leagues were just around the corner.

This telegram, sent by A. J. Choquette, explains Larry Gardner's presence in the above photograph. Three years later Gardner reco- mmended Leclair to the Boston Red Sox. [Gardner Family Archives]

After operating as a minor league the previous season, Federal League owners decided to compete with the two existing major leagues in 1914. To bolster their credibility they signed a number of established major leaguers. George Leclair's teammates on the 1914 Pittsburgh Stogies, for example, included Rebel Oakes, formerly of the Cardinals; ex-Tiger Davy Jones; and Howie Camnitz, a former Pirate. Still, that Leclair could make a Federal League roster may say more about the negative quality of that league's play than the positive quality of his pitching.

The Milton native signed with Pittsburgh in April but didn't make his major league debut until June 5, 1914. The Stogies were already down 6-0 to the Baltimore Terrapins that day when he entered in the fifth inning. The game ended as a 14-3 Baltimore rout, with George finishing out the massacre. It was a typical game for the Stogies, who finished seventh in an eight-team race. Leclair fared better than his teammates, compiling a 5-2 record in twenty-two games, mostly in relief.

George saw several new faces when he returned to Pittsburgh in 1915. Over the winter the Stogies had stolen the crosstown Pirates' corner infielders, slugging first baseman Ed Konetchy and slick-fielding third baseman Mike Mowrey. Even though Pittsburgh improved to second place in the Federal League, Leclair's record actually suffered, and he was only 1-2 when the Buffeds acquired him in late June. Joining Bob Smith, the only other Green Mountain Boy to throw in with the Feds, Leclair stayed in Buffalo less than a month before he was dispatched to the last-place Baltimore Terrapins.

Wearing the uniform of his third Federal League team of the season, he pitched much better than his dismal 1-8 record reflects. For the entire 1915 season, he pitched in thirty-three games, gave up 123 hits in 132.2 innings, and finished with a 2.85 ERA. The demise of the Federal League after the 1915 season meant the end of George Leclair's career as a major leaguer. In the Feds' peace settlement with the traditional circuits, the rights to Leclair went to the American League's St. Louis Browns. Before the 1916 season the Browns assigned him to Little Rock of the Southern Association, where he pitched poorly and infrequently. In September Leclair was demoted to Peoria of the Class-B Three-I League.

In 1917 George was pitching well as a regular starter for Peoria when World War I caused the Three-I League to disband on July 8. His performance slipped somewhat after Peoria transferred to the Central League. Still, when Leclair returned to Farnham to pitch in a postseason exhibition, *La Presse* reported that he'd won both ends of three doubleheaders that summer and was sought after by several International League teams.

After pitching for Elmira of the New York State League in 1918, Leclair returned to Farnham in the offseason and found work with the Canadian Pacific Railway. He died suddenly on October 14, four days short of his thirty-second birthday, a victim of the Spanish Flu. Contrary to reports, the flu epidemic did not wipe out his entire family. In fact, George's wife gave birth to a daughter seven months after his death, and his namesake grandson, Georges Leclair III, currently lives in Iberville, Quebec.

YVES CHARTRAND

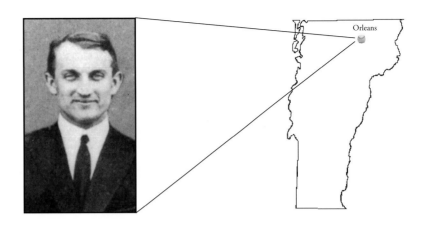

Heinie Stafford

Giant For A Day

"I kept telling myself, this is it. You've hit the top. The major leagues. You can say for the rest of your life, 'I played for the New York Giants.'"

Those are the words of Moonlight Graham in W. P. Kinsella's novel *Shoeless Joe*, the basis for the well-known movie "Field of Dreams," but they could have been spoken by Vermont's Heinie Stafford. Like Graham, Stafford played but one game for the New York Giants, then went on to live a full and productive life. Unlike Graham, however, Stafford doesn't need Kevin Costner to grant his ultimate wish. Heinie Stafford can rest in peace—he got to bat in the majors, albeit only once.

Henry Alexander Stafford was born on November 1, 1891, in the remote Northeast Kingdom village of Barton Landing. The Staffords didn't have much money, so when Henry was in high school he worked as a horse-and-buggy driver for the local physician, sometimes going out in the middle of night for baby deliveries or other emergencies. His father, a painter by trade, was said to have been the quintessential taciturn Vermonter, with the gift for understated quips. Henry acquired his father's sense of humor and thick Vermont accent. To those he added superlative athletic prowess and a life-long touch for getting along with people.

In 1910, when Henry was a senior in high school, Barton Landing changed its name to Orleans, though for years he still referred to it by its former name. At Orleans High School Heinie emerged as an excellent student and star of both high school and town baseball

teams. He received a scholarship for one year of post-high school study at Dean Academy in Franklin, Massachusetts. Baseball was serious business at Dean—its 1911 team played games as far south as Maryland and Virginia. Stafford started at second base and was elected captain, the first of many honors that flowed his way throughout life. During summers he played in the flourishing hotel leagues of the Adirondacks, starring for Oneonta in 1911 and Saranac Lake in 1912.

While at Dean, Henry met and fell in love with Leila Cushing, also from Vermont and also a grand free spirit who loved tobogganing, camping—and baseball. After his first year Henry still hadn't saved enough money to pay for college, and Leila still had another year to go at Dean, so he found a way to spend a second year there. After that Leila was off to Vassar College and Henry won a scholarship to Tufts University. As Stafford arrived on the Tufts campus that fall, his fellow Vermonters Larry Gardner and Ray Collins were playing just a few miles away at Fenway Park against his future team, the New York Giants, in the epic 1912 World Series.

At Tufts Stafford excelled in all facets of campus life. He was elected class president his sophomore, junior, and senior years, also serving as president of the Theta Delta Chi fraternity, inter-fraternity council, the junior and senior honor societies, and the athletic association. One of the fastest collegiate sprinters of his time, Heinie earned two varsity letters in track and was anchorman on the relay team. During his senior year he received a

Stafford is seated in the second row at far right in this photo of the 1910 Orleans High School baseball team. [Stafford Family Archives]

mer. Besides Stafford, catcher Red Carroll made his debut with the Philadelphia Athletics against the pitching of Boston's Babe Ruth only three days after Tufts' final game, and pitcher Walter Whittaker joined the A's in July. The team was not only talented, it was deep. Stafford's backup at second, Horace Ford, made it to the majors in 1919 and ended up eclipsing his college teammates by spending fifteen solid seasons in the big leagues. It was that kind of year at Tufts in 1916.

Heinie Stafford graduated from Tufts with a degree in chemistry on June 21, 1916. That same day he signed to play for John McGraw's New York Giants at the rate of $1,750 for the season. The Giants assigned Stafford under option to their top farm club, the International League's Newark Indians. Splitting time between shortstop and left field, Stafford played in forty-one games for Newark and batted just .230, though he used his speed to steal eight bases. At the end of Newark's season

$100 prize as the "member of the College who best exemplified the combination of ability in athletics and excellence in scholarship."

Heinie also found great success in his four years of varsity baseball. A 1971 article in the *Tufts Criterion* called him "probably the finest second baseman ever to play at Tufts." In his senior year he batted .404, scored thirty runs and stole twenty-four bases, leading the nation in the latter two categories. With Heinie as captain and lead-off hitter, the 1916 Tufts team amassed a glittering 20-2 record and may have been one of the greatest college squads ever.

Including Stafford, six Tufts players were selected first-team All-Eastern in 1916 by *Spalding's Official Base Ball Record*, and three appeared in the majors that very sum-

Heinie Stafford was "probably the finest second baseman ever to play at Tufts." [Stafford Family Archives]

Wearing his Dean Academy uniform, Heinie is seated in the front row at far left of this photo of the 1912 Saranac Lake team. [Stafford Family Archives]

The 1916 Tufts team was 20-2 and produced six All-Eastern selections. Stafford is seated fourth from the right, next to the team's coach, ex-major leaguer Jack Slattery. [Stafford Family Archives]

on September 17, the Giants exercised their option and called him up to the majors.

So excited to be in the big leagues that he had his new teammates autograph a baseball (which he donated to the Hall of Fame in 1959), Stafford joined New York in the midst of the longest winning streak in major league history. Though it was a great time to be young and a Giant, it was a bad time to be a rookie trying to crack the lineup.

Only when a team of Giants played an exhibition game in New Haven, Connecticut, on September 24 was Heinie given an opportunity. Many New York regulars received the day off, but the lineup still included Hans Lobert, Benny Kauff, Heinie Zimmerman, and an unknown rookie named George Kelly, who was bound for Cooperstown even though he didn't become a regular for another three seasons. Playing left field and batting leadoff, Stafford went 1-for-5 and contributed a run to the Giants' 8-5 win over a semipro team.

Despite the remarkable win streak, which, according to the *New York Times*, "has gained more reknown for the local team than would be achieved by the winning of a brace of pennants," the Giants rose no higher than fourth in the National League standings. And even when the streak was over, ending at twenty-six on September 30, Stafford remained on the bench. By October 5, the last day of the season, the talented youngster still hadn't broken into an official game.

The only known photograph depicting Stafford as a professional shows him as a member of the 1916 Newark Indians. [Stafford Family Archives]

Two days earlier, McGraw had become so disgusted by the Giants' play that he'd deserted the team in the middle of the fifth inning. "The Dodgers beat us to clinch the pennant," Stafford told Harold Kaese of the *Boston Globe* in 1966, "and I was sitting beside John McGraw when he exploded, said his team wasn't bearing down, and walked out of the dugout." Reportedly McGraw was in Laurel, Maryland, engaging in his favorite pastime, gambling on horse races. In his absence, the team was managed by second baseman Buck Herzog, the Giants' field captain.

The final game of the 1916 season pitted the Giants against the Brooklyn Dodgers, on their way to their first-ever World Series appearance just two days later against the Boston Red Sox. Only 2,000 fans showed up at Ebbets Field for the meaningless contest. Both Herzog and Brooklyn's manager, Wilbert Robinson, gave several regulars the afternoon off, but even then Stafford didn't crack the starting lineup. On the mound for the Dodgers was Ed Appleton, winless to that point in 1916. Pitching in what proved to be his last game ever in the majors, Appleton clung to a 7-5 lead after eight innings, and still Stafford hadn't played. But with two outs in the top of the ninth and nobody on base, Herzog called on the rookie from Vermont to pinch hit for the Giants' pitcher, George Smith. Here came his big moment at last!

It would be nice to report that Heinie Stafford batted safely at Ebbets Field that afternoon to ignite a game-winning rally for the Giants. It would be nicer still to record that this performance touched off a long, glorious career in the majors. Heinie Stafford—young, fast, bright, a natural leader—stepped up to destiny's challenge. But that's the stuff of Hollywood, not Brooklyn. What actually happened is that Stafford made an out to end the game and the 1916 season. Although the exact type of out he made isn't apparent from newspaper accounts, family members recall him mentioning that he hit an infield grounder.

After tasting the big time, Heinie Stafford never played another game in Organized Baseball. In those days a college-educated man could earn more money in business than in baseball, so Heinie left the game despite his obvious potential. In the fall of 1916 he accepted a position as a research chemist with a textile company in Chester, Pennsylvania. But McGraw wasn't willing to let Stafford go so easily, as demonstrated by the following letter, written just before the next year's spring training:

> When you were procured by the New York Base Ball Club I felt quite confident that you had a future for yourself. One of the reasons why I engaged you and why I practically re-engaged you was that I would have you where I

could be sure to take you south with me and give you a thorough spring schooling in base ball at Marlin.

> If you take advantage of this I believe that I can help you far more than you anticipate in becoming a skillful base ball player. If you do not take advantage of it I am just as confident that you are wasting a first class opportunity. There is enough promise to you to make me positive that it is worth your while to go from Chester with our first squad and train.

> I wish you would write me at once and tell me that you have decided upon this course. I should not advise it to you if I did not believe it the proper thing for you to do.
> Sincerely yours,
> /s/ John J. McGraw

Ignoring McGraw's advice, Heinie remained a research chemist, and on June 15, 1917, he married Leila in the Brick Church in her hometown of Bethel. A clipping from a local newspaper indicates that the couple "went to Burlington, planning a trip, mostly by water, to New York City, after which they will live at Upland, Pa., a suburb of Chester, Pa., where Mr. Stafford is employed as a chemist in an industrial plant."

Heinie and Leila Stafford had two daughters over the next five years. With his background in chemistry, Heinie spent a brief stateside tour of duty with the chemical warfare service during World War I. He didn't give up baseball entirely during this period—during the war he managed and played for his company's strong industrial league team, when many professionals were playing in such leagues to avoid being drafted. Later he joined Upland of the so-called "Millionaires' League," where teammates included future Hall-of-Famers Chief Bender and Frank "Home Run" Baker.

While living near Philadelphia, Heinie loved taking the entire family to Phillies and Athletics games at Shibe Park. "It wasn't uncommon for my mother to wake up

Stafford is seated in the second row, second from left, in this World War I-era photograph of the Upland team of the Millionaires' League. Seated in the same row, wearing a Philadelphia Phillies uniform, is Hall-of-Famer Chief Bender. [Stafford Family Archives]

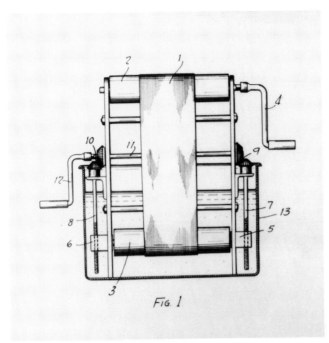

While working for Ewing-Thomas, Stafford patented a chemical process for "mercerizing" silk that revolutionized the industry for women's hose. [Stafford Family Archives]

on Mother's Day and say, 'Let's go to a ballgame,'" daughter Harriet recalls. Stafford always got good seats for his family and sometimes took them to the dugout to meet Connie Mack, Lefty Grove, Jimmie Foxx, and the rest of the great A's of 1929-31. The Stafford girls spent those summers at their grandfather's lakeside farm in Barnard, Vermont, but their father never joined them. Spurning vacations, Heinie only drove to Vermont each Labor Day to bring them back to Pennsylvania for the school year.

Meanwhile Stafford's career thrived at Ewing-Thomas Corporation, a subsidiary of North Carolina's giant Cannon Mills, at the time the largest textile manufacturer in the country. As late as the 1920s, women's stockings had been made of cotton. Stafford developed and patented a chemical process for "mercerizing" silk, making it shiny and strong enough to be worked by machines without breaking. "That patent was a big deal for the company," recalls Harriet.

Stafford worked his way up to vice president and general manager of Ewing-Thomas, but he paid a high price for business success. The DuPont Company was on the verge of developing nylon, which Heinie knew would revolutionize the industry, making silk stockings obsolete. The Great Depression, unionization of the workforce, and ever more aggressive competition from DuPont all took their toll. When Stafford developed a heart murmur, his physician advised him to get out of competitive business. But the event that tipped the scales was the death of his middle

daughter, Jane, a 1936 victim of leukemia. "I think that was when he finally decided to cut back on work and enjoy his life," says daughter Harriet.

So, in that same year, Heinie began laying the groundwork for retiring before his fiftieth birthday. First he bought a 340-acre hill farm a mile north of Bethel village. Then on April 4, 1941, with his youngest daughter off to college, Stafford shocked co-workers by announcing his retirement. "Mr. Stafford has been our friend as well as our employer," reads a testimonial signed by 312 Ewing-Thomas employees. "He has always been fair and considerate. We will miss him in many ways."

Back in Vermont, Heinie Stafford's new home was a run-down, brick cape farmhouse built in 1832. Gradually he fixed it up, calling it Tamarack Farm after the tamarack trees he planted in the front yard. The farm became a large dairy operation, producing 225,000 gallons of milk a year. Heinie's herd eventually grew to include sixty Jerseys, which, he once told a reporter, he "wouldn't swap for twice as many of any other brand you could name."

At Tamarack Stafford turned his analytical talents to the breeding of purebred Jersey cattle. Will Harvey, his roommate at Tufts, was the Universalist minister in Bethel, and he introduced Heinie to Harold "Boss" Turner, Harvey's partner in running the local Boy Scout troop. Together Stafford and Turner spent hours at the kitchen table making huge genetic charts, and their meticulous records are now prized possessions of the breeding programs at UVM and Vermont Technical College. At its height in the early '50s, the Stafford-Turner breeding partnership attracted national attention for the high prices it received for cattle. They once sold a bull called Advancer Regal for $7,000, at the time the highest price ever paid for a Vermont-bred Jersey bull.

Tamarack Farm is located in Bethel at a fork between Route 12 and Camp Brook Road near the Randolph border. Today a sign for Stafford Meadows Road on the opposite side of Route 12 is a reminder of the farm's former owner. [Stafford Family Archives]

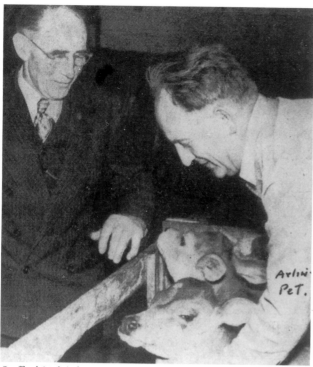

Stafford (right) shows a pair of his prized Jersey calves. He printed the calves' names on this newspaper clipping. [Stafford Family Archives]

Many of Stafford's Jersey strains are still prominent in the UVM and Vermont Tech breeding programs.

In the spring of 1956 Heinie suffered a heart attack, and during his hospitalization he determined to auction off his herd. The catalog for the auction is yet another testimonial to Stafford's remarkable qualities:

> Herd averages, Superior Sires, Tested Dams, Gold Medals—all these are part of a Jersey herd. The other part is the man, and Heinie Stafford is the other part of the Tamarack Farm herd. In this catalogue are the official figures; those who knew him (and they are legion) know what Heinie has been to the Jersey fraternity. Always a loyal worker for any Jersey promotion, always in the forefront of any Jersey gathering, Heinie has been good for us all.

Heinie was still in the hospital at the time of the auction, which his daughter Harriet believes was just as well since it would have broken his already fragile heart to attend. "Prices obtained for some of the herd's top animals were perhaps the highest ever received at a local auction," wrote the *White River Valley Herald*.

Forced to give up dairy farming, Heinie Stafford tinkered in real estate and eventually became active in Republican politics, serving first as a town selectman and later representing Bethel in the Vermont General Assembly. He served four terms in the house, running for his first term the same year that Robert Stafford (no relation) was elected governor of Vermont. In the legislature Heinie served on the agriculture, fish and game, and institutional committees, and was one of the sponsors of the Simpson Bill on Education, an early attempt at property-tax reform. Along with education financing, helping family farms was Stafford's pet issue. "The small dairy farmer will just be eased out," he once told a *Rutland Herald* reporter. "Take a look at the disparity. We buy grain at 90% and our milk is supported at 75%—you figure it out! The farmer is in a tough spot today."

Leila Stafford died of cancer in 1959 during Heinie's first term in the legislature. After her death, Heinie took up furniture refinishing and got a cocker spaniel named Shadow to keep him company. He re-married in 1965 to Gladys Durkee, a widow whose former husband, Robert, had died the same year as Leila. For years the Durkees had been close friends of the Staffords, and Robert was the son of Heinie's favorite professor at Tufts. Later in 1965 Stafford sold Tamarack Farm and moved into the Durkee Homestead, one of the oldest houses in Tunbridge.

Gladys's daughter Nancy lived in Lake Worth, Florida, and she turned her garage into an apartment for her mother and Heinie. There they spent each winter, traveling all over Florida to exhibition baseball games once spring arrived. It was an ideal existence for Stafford, who could name every player on every team. Unlike many Green Mountain Boys of Summer, Heinie didn't go in for hunting or fishing—his hobby was baseball, and he followed the sport throughout his life.

Stafford died on January 29, 1972, while wintering in Lake Worth. It had been a rich, varied, and on the whole happy and successful life. But a part of Heinie Stafford— the inner man for whom baseball was prime—never forgot the glory of his one appearance in the majors. In the last years of his life, more than a half-century after that memorable walk to the plate at Ebbets Field, Stafford still received autograph requests in the mail. He invariably signed "'Heinie' Stafford, N.Y. Giants 1916."

TOM SIMON

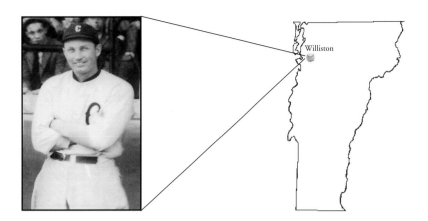

Dave Keefe

Father of the Forkball

Williston, Vermont, today is a Burlington suburb with big stores, housing developments, and plenty of supervised activities for children. A century ago, when Dave Keefe was growing up there, however, Williston was a farm village offering few entertainment options for youngsters. One day Dave and his older brother and sisters were playing out back of their farmhouse, daring each other to place a hand as close as possible to the blades of a corn-cutting machine. Dave won the dare but lost most of the middle finger of his right hand in the process. Eventually his ring finger grew to be larger than normal, and when he was old enough to play baseball he discovered that by placing the ball between his first and ring fingers he could impart an unusual spin. That might have been the origin of the forkball—some credit "Three-Fingered" Keefe as its inventor.

David Edwin Keefe was born in Williston on January 9, 1897. Sixty years earlier, his grandparents Charles and Mary Keefe came from County Fermanagh, Northern Ireland, settling in a red clapboard house near the Old Round Church in Richmond, Vermont. Tragedy struck the young couple when three of their four children died of scarlet fever on the same day. Undaunted, they had nine more. One of them—Charles Jr., Dave's father—grew up, bought a farm a few miles west in Williston, and started a family. He moved the family to a larger farm in East Montpelier, but when he died in 1911 the family moved back to Richmond to be closer to relatives. Dave was sent to boarding school at Goddard

Seminary, where he discovered baseball, eventually attracting the attention of Whitey Witt, a young shortstop with the Philadelphia Athletics.

The A's signed Keefe, and on April 21, 1917, he made his major league debut. He appeared in three games, picking up his first big league win and compiling a 1.80 ERA before Philadelphia farmed him out to Harrisburg. There he compiled a record of 2-13 for a team that withdrew from the league on July 10 with an 11-41 record. Going from one last-place team to another, Dave finished the season with Hartford and was 4-9 despite a 1.43 ERA. He missed the entire 1918 season after enlisting in the navy but returned to baseball in 1919 and once again started the season with Philadelphia. In his only appearance Keefe pitched a complete game, but again the A's sent him to the minors. This time he was 10-17 with a 3.71 ERA for Reading, yet another last-place club.

In 1920 Keefe finally spent an entire season in the majors, putting up decent numbers: 6-7 with a 2.97 ERA in thirty-one games. Predictably, the A's finished last. That year Dave had some memorable encounters with Babe Ruth. On September 6 he struck out the Bambino three times. Three weeks later, however, he had the dubious honor of serving up Ruth's fifty-fourth and last home run of the season, setting a new major league record. In keeping with the pattern, Philadelphia finished last again in 1921 and Dave went 2-9 with a 4.68 ERA, with career highs in appearances (forty-four) and innings pitched (173).

Visible from Interstate 89, Keefe's birthplace on Route 2 in Williston is just down the road from the cemetery where Thomas Chittenden, Vermont's first governor, is buried. [Tom Simon]

After the season the A's released Keefe and he was claimed on waivers by the Cleveland Indians. Teaming with fellow Vermonter Larry Gardner, who became a life-long friend, Dave pitched in eighteen games in 1922, but his ERA shot up to 6.25. At least the Tribe finished out of the basement, but at the age of twenty-five, Keefe's career as a major league pitcher was over. He spent the next ten seasons in the minors, playing with Milwaukee, Portland (Oregon), Waterbury, Buffalo, Sacramento, Memphis, Knoxville, Providence, Norfolk, and Wilkes-Barre.

While playing with Wilkes-Barre in 1932, Keefe went to Philadelphia on an off-day to take in a game at Shibe Park. Needing some work, he asked his old manager Connie Mack if he could pitch batting practice. Mack thought it was a good idea, as it would save wear and tear on his regular pitchers. Keefe took the mound and was a huge success, serving up soft ones to the likes of Al Simmons, Jimmie Foxx, and Mickey Cochrane. After the game Mack asked him to stay on as full-time batting practice pitcher. Realizing he was going nowhere as a player, Dave decided to accept the offer, thus becoming the first man ever hired by a major league team for the exclusive purpose of pitching batting practice. He remained in that capacity for nineteen years.

"The thing I remember most about pitching batting practice," Keefe said, "was the number of times I was hit by a ball. They didn't have screens in front of us in those days and I was struck everywhere except on the bottom of my feet." Vermont relatives remember that Dave was often limping because of the hits he'd taken. He also had the distinction of pitching batting practice for the American League before nine All-Star Games. "That's not a bad record," he cracked, "when you consider I never even had a winning season in the majors."

One All-Star Game Keefe missed was in 1938 when the Athletics came to Centennial Field during the break to play an exhibition game against the Northern League's Burlington Cardinals. Before a crowd of 4,500, including many of Keefe's relatives, Bud Kimball and future major leaguer Lennie Merullo homered to give Burlington a 5-2 lead entering the ninth inning. With two outs, up came Philadelphia center fielder Ace Parker, a two-sport star whose gridiron exploits later earned him a place in the Pro Football Hall of Fame. Parker dribbled a slow roller to the left side of the infield that should have ended the game, but the Burlington third baseman fumbled it to load the bases. The next batter, Billy Werber, doubled to clear the bases. The A's held on for a 6-5 win.

Dave Keefe stayed in close contact with his siblings, and his nieces and nephews looked forward to his occasional trips to Vermont when the A's were in Boston. They remember him as a quiet, ruddy-complexioned man who looked younger than his age. Uncle Dave took particular pride in his posture, standing with his back to a wall fifteen minutes each day to make sure he stood up straight. He brought them bats, balls, and gloves, including a game-used catcher's mitt formerly belonging

This photo was taken not long after Keefe became the first full-time batting practice pitcher in the history of the major leagues. [National Baseball Hall of Fame Library, Cooperstown, New York]

to Buddy Rosar. A sharp dresser who wore expensive suits and silk stockings, Keefe also sent dozens of ties to his nephews, some of which still hang in their closets.

In 1950 Keefe became traveling secretary, staying on when the Athletics moved to Kansas City in 1955. The job involved arranging tickets, rooms, and details for every member of the team's road party. Because of Keefe's meticulous attention to detail, traveling with the A's was usually trouble-free, but even Dave had his awkward moments. Once some of the players became confused and boarded the wrong train. As it pulled out, the players on the correct train laughingly waved goodbye to their teammates. The sight wasn't amusing to Keefe, who had the train stopped so he could retrieve his players.

Dave Keefe was a lifelong bachelor. "I'm not sure why he didn't marry and I never asked because he was a man who didn't like to talk about himself," wrote Joe McGuff, sports editor of the *Kansas City Star*, "but I suspect he'd concluded that a wife might object to the amount of time he spent at the ball park or traveling with the team, and he wasn't the sort of man who liked to make changes in his lifestyle." Keefe's only major concession to change was in regard to the automobile. He got along without learning to drive for a long time, but at age sixty-five he purchased an expensive car, taught himself to drive in the parking lot behind the left-field fence at Kansas City's Municipal Stadium, and drove to Florida for spring training.

Keefe loved his job as traveling secretary. "I've always considered it, and still do, the best and only position in baseball for me," he told an interviewer in 1967. Later that year, however, the A's announced that the franchise was re-locating to Oakland. Rather than move to California, Keefe retired. Though his fifty-year career in professional baseball had come to an end, he still spent much of his time around baseball diamonds. During the Kansas City Royals' inaugural season of 1969 Dave accompanied the team on a roadtrip at the invitation of owner Ewing Kaufmann. Every year he went to the Royals' spring training camp in Fort Myers, Florida.

Keefe took a room at Kansas City's Berkshire Towers Hotel in 1955 and remained in that same room for twenty-three years, even after the hotel was sold and renamed the Baptist Retirement Towers (and in spite of the fact that he was a devout Catholic). In February 1978, Dave was preparing to attend spring training when the Towers went up in flames. The eighty-one-year-old es-

As a batting practice pitcher, Keefe claimed that he was struck by the ball everywhere except on the bottom of his feet. [Keefe Family Archives]

caped unharmed but re-entered the building when he realized a friend was trapped on the top floor. Dave inhaled too much smoke on his way out and died at St. Mary's Hospital in Kansas City on February 4, 1978. His body was transported to Richmond, Vermont, where he was buried in the Our Lady of the Holy Rosary Cemetery, just down the street from an old ballfield where he probably played as a youth.

Two days after Keefe's death, Joe McGuff wrote the following tribute in the *Kansas City Star*:

> The awards that are presented on baseball's winter dinner circuit usually go to someone who has led his league in home runs, saved a franchise or developed a pennant winner. Dave Keefe didn't qualify in any of these categories and as a result was never called on to step before a microphone and receive a standing ovation. It is a shame because Dave did something much more important: He devoted his lifetime to baseball.

TOM SIMON

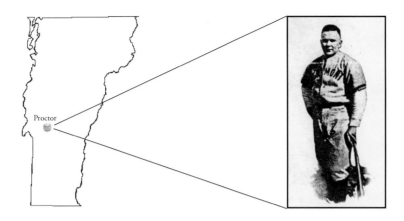

Elmer Bowman

From Marble Mines to the Silver Screen

Tourists under the thrall of the Jefferson Memorial or the United States Supreme Court building in Washington, D.C., little reflect on the source of the elegant marble used to construct them. It came from the hard marble quarries of the Vermont Marble Company in Proctor, Vermont, five miles northwest of Rutland. There, around the turn of the century, the difficult and dangerous work of extracting and processing the stone was mastered by European immigrants.

Elmari Wilhelm Bowman was born in Proctor on March 19, 1897. His parents, Oscar and Rose Bowman, came to Proctor from Finland in the 1890s. Foreign-born and first-generation arrivals—Swedes mostly, but also Finns, Hungarians, Italians, and Poles—made up 2,146 of the town's total 1910 population of 2,756. To this day the Proctor Free Library houses an unusual collection of turn-of-the-century children's books in a variety of languages. Oscar worked long hours at hard and dangerous labor. A 1921 survey by Vermont Marble Company foremen rated the elder Bowman "BX"—"B" indicating "less efficient than 'A,'" and "X" denoting "physical hardship due to illness or accident."

The Bowmans and their four children lived in a modest house at 18 North Street. As everywhere in the American melting pot, the children of immigrants gained opportunities for a better life. Elmer was one of a dozen students who graduated in 1916 from Proctor High School, where he excelled in football and baseball and won a scholarship to attend the University of Vermont.

During summers he returned to Proctor and played baseball locally. "I used to play semipro ball in Rutland with Harry Shedd, who used to manage the Rutland team," Bowman said. "They called them town teams in those days, and we played teams from Barre, Burlington, and other places."

During his four years at UVM, Elmer played first base under the tutelage of two former big league first basemen, Doc Hazelton and Clyde Engle. The Bowman era was the most successful for UVM baseball since the days of Collins and Gardner—during his junior and senior years the team compiled a two-year record of 26-10. A right-handed hitter and thrower, Elmer typically batted clean-up, and he served as captain during his senior year.

Those were the days when UVM had a football team, and Bowman's exploits on the gridiron rivaled his baseball accomplishments. Nicknamed "Big Bow" because of his size (6' 1", 196 pounds), Elmer started at fullback as a freshman and earned a reputation as one of the toughest runners in UVM history. But professional football was in its infancy, so the twenty-three-year-old Bowman chose baseball as his career. He signed with Clark Griffith's Washington Senators in the spring of 1920, just a few weeks short of graduation. "I didn't get anything from them," Elmer recalled. "In those days they didn't do much of that. If you wanted to play ball, they gave you a contract, but there wasn't any of that big money that there is nowadays."

Washington sent Bowman to the Minneapolis Millers of the American Association. Even though he batted a meager .186 in thirty-eight games, Griffith called him up to the majors on July 26, 1920, just as the Senators were setting out on a western roadtrip. With Joe Judge a fixture at first base, Bowman had no chance of cracking Washington's starting lineup. He sat on the bench and observed a cavalcade of great stars of that era—Tris Speaker and fellow UVM alumnus Larry Gardner at Cleveland, Ty Cobb at Detroit, the infamous Black Sox in Chicago. "When the Senators went to Chicago, I remember looking at all the players curiously, trying to figure out which ones did what," Bowman later recalled.

It was in Cleveland a week after his call-up that Elmer Bowman finally made his major league debut. On August 3, 1920, with the Senators trailing 10-5 in the top of the ninth, Griffith called on Big Bow to pinch hit for pitcher Jose Acosta. Facing Cleveland ace Jim Bagby, in relief of starter Ray Caldwell, Bowman lofted a fly ball to center

fielder Tris Speaker. Bagby retired the Senators in order to record one of the thirty-one wins he notched that season.

At Comiskey Park on August 9, 1920, Bowman got a second look at one of the Black Sox culprits—this time from a distance of sixty feet, six inches. Lefty Williams, one of the "eight men out" destined for banishment after the 1920 season, was on the mound when Elmer made his second and last appearance in the majors, pinch hitting for pitcher Harry Courtney. This time he drew a walk but was replaced by a pinch runner.

That was it. Before the Senators returned to Washington on August 14, Griffith sent Bowman and a large sum of cash to Reading in exchange for the International League's leading hitter, Frank "Turkeyfoot" Brower. Known as "The Babe Ruth of the Bushes," Brower batted .311 in thirty-six games for Washington but never produced Ruthian statistics in the majors (in 1923, his best year, he hit sixteen homers for Cleveland). For his part, Bowman batted .296 in thirty-five games with Reading over the remainder of the season.

Elmer Bowman (standing, second from left) is pictured as a senior at Proctor High School in 1916. Four years later he joined the Washington Senators, making two appearances as a pinch hitter. [Proctor Historical Society]

That Elmer Bowman never received a second chance in the majors is surprising in light of his subsequent minor league accomplishments. With Norfolk in 1921, Bowman batted .356 and led the Virginia League in extra-base hits, slashing forty-two doubles, eighteen triples, and nine homers. The following year, playing for New Haven, Elmer beat out the great Native American athlete Jim Thorpe for the batting title, setting an all-time Eastern League record with a .365 average. For that accomplishment, the Winchester Arms Company (coincidentally owned by Frank Olin, another Green Mountain Boy of Summer) presented Bowman with a three-foot-high silver trophy, which he proudly displayed for the rest of his life.

Bowman's Eastern League batting record stood for only one year. In 1923 he topped his previous mark by hitting .366, only to finish second to Worcester's Wade Lefler, who batted .369. Though primarily a line-drive hitter, Bowman socked nineteen home runs during his second year in New Haven. Moving up to the Pacific Coast League in 1924, he hit a solid .301 for Seattle using a bat he jokingly claimed was made of "iron." It was given to him by the P.C.L.'s leading hitter that year, Salt Lake City manager and former Boston Red Sox outfielder Duffy Lewis.

In 1925 Elmer was sent to Birmingham of the Southern League where his average slipped to .290. It was reported that the "tropical heat did not agree with him," and that offseason he obtained his release from the Barons and re-joined New Haven. Bowman had his best season in 1926, smacking fifteen homers and hitting .377 for the Profs to lead the Eastern League for a second time, again setting a new all-time league record (this time the record lasted for two seasons before it was broken). But his average for New Haven slipped to .282 in 1927, and by 1929 Bowman had retired from professional baseball.

In the mid-1920s Elmer Bowman spent offseasons with his wife's family in Los Angeles. A friend from New Haven helped him obtain work as an electrician on the movie lots—his major had been electrical engineering at UVM—where he tended to the lighting of sets used by famous silent-screen stars like Bebe Daniels and Pola Negri. On Sundays he played winter baseball with the Pasadena team, which included Dick Cox, Fred Haney, and other major leaguers.

During the winter of 1926-27 a New Haven newspaper reported that Elmer had arranged a leave of absence from his electrical work to play a "prominent role" in the silent-screen version of "Casey at the Bat." Advertising a rare screening of the film seventy years after its 1927 release, a Southern California silent film society summarized its plot as follows:

Casey, the oversized junk dealer (Wallace Beery), and Putnam, the undersized barber (Sterling Holloway), compete for the charming hand of Camille (ZaSu Pitts). Shady baseball scout O'Dowd (Ford Sterling) turns romantic competition into a baseball free-for-all in this grand farce. Throw in Coney Island, the New York Giants, and the Florodora Sextette and you have nine full innings of entertainment!

Apparently Bowman showed little acting ability—he failed to make the final cut of "Casey at the Bat."

"I did get into some movies as an extra," Elmer said. "In one movie MGM did, they needed over 1,000 extras for a prison yard scene. The union couldn't get them, so some of us electricians had to serve as set extras. We just hung around. I'd get in a few mob scenes every now and then, but they didn't amount to anything."

Bowman worked for Warner Brothers Studios for thirty-six years before retiring in 1960. Over the years he returned to Vermont on many occasions to visit a brother who operated Pullman's Garage in Proctor. Elmer lived twenty-five years in retirement, and he always retained his interest in baseball. "I read the sports page first—I have glaucoma, which makes it hard for me to read, I have to use a magnifying glass—and if I still feel good, I read the main section," he told a telephone interviewer when he was eighty-four years old.

By the 1970s, more than a half-century had passed since Elmer Bowman had played baseball at the University of Vermont, but Burlington banker David Webster still remembered him.

When I was a kid, oh, ten or twelve years old, we used to live on Fletcher Place, which was near Centennial Field, and we used to hang around the ballpark. And of course the UVM players were our heroes. The field was much different then. It had a big wooden fence around it and a poke to center field was a home run in any league. Elmer Bowman was the only one who could ever hit the ball over the center-field fence. I never forgot about him.

Webster was a member of the UVM Hall-of-Fame Committee. With help from former UVM baseball player Ed Donnelly, he successfully pushed for Bowman's induction. "I was really glad to get him in when he was still alive and could appreciate it," Webster said. Bowman was inducted on October 20, 1978.

That was the culmination of an interesting and varied eighty-eight-year life for the son of a Finnish marble worker. Seven years after his induction he died in Los Angeles on December 17, 1985.

BOB BENNETT

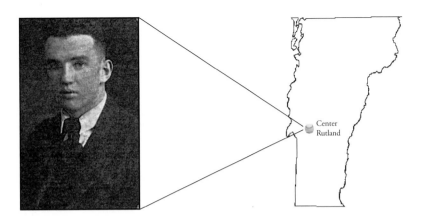

Harry Hulihan

You Can Come Home Again

The village of Center Rutland, Vermont, lies several miles from the real center of Rutland. At the time Harry Joseph Hulihan was born there on April 18, 1899, Center Rutland was populated largely by immigrant families, clustered in valleys amidst large marble quarries. Harry grew up at 375 West Street, just down the street from Hulihan Bros., wholesale and retail dealers in granite and marble. Strangely, both Hulihan brothers were named Patrick, and whether Harry's father was Patrick C. or Patrick W. is unknown.

Harry Hulihan played football for Rutland High School and admitted liking basketball "as a hobby," but baseball was his best sport. He was the ace pitcher for the high school nine and the local sandlot team, St. Peter's Athletic Association, earning a reputation as the state's top schoolboy hurler. Harry threw at least two no-hitters, against teams from Plattsburgh and Saranac Lake, New York. His exploits caught the attention of Connie Mack, who dispatched Ira Thomas, a former Athletics catcher from nearby Ballston Spa, New York, to scout the young lefthander. But after a brief tryout with the A's in the spring of 1919, Mack decided against signing Hulihan, feeling he was too raw and inexperienced.

Somewhat discouraged, Harry enrolled that fall at Middlebury College, which had already seen one great pitching talent, Ray Fisher, pass through its gates a decade earlier. Hulihan shattered Fisher's mound records and become one of the school's all-time greatest athletes. His most famous exploit came against Fordham

when he struck out twenty-four batters in a twelve-inning victory. Harry also starred for the football and basketball squads, and he even found time to be elected class president in his sophomore year. According to his yearbook, "Ike" Hulihan was known for his soft voice, persuasive charm, and coolness under fire in any situation, be it in the classroom or the women's dormitory.

During summers Hulihan pitched under a false name for a semipro team in Hartford. There he was spotted by John McGraw, manager of the New York Giants. After badgering Harry for two years, McGraw finally convinced him to sign after his junior year of 1922. Harry agreed to leave Middlebury early on the condition that he not be sent to the minors that season. For nearly two months he cooled his heels on the end of the Giant bench, picking up baseball acumen at the hands of his legendary manager, whom the rookie recalled years later as a "real toughie."

At the end of July 1922, the Giants, embroiled in a tense pennant race, had lost the services of ace pitcher Phil Douglas, who'd foolishly written a letter suggesting he'd take money to throw ball games, earning him a lifetime ban from Organized Baseball. With a huge hole in his rotation, McGraw turned to the league patsy, the cellar-dwelling Boston Braves. On July 30 the Bostonians, hard-pressed for cash and prospects, coughed up the pitcher McGraw felt he needed, righthander Hugh McQuillan. In return, the Giants parted with veteran pitcher Fred Toney, a cashier's check for $100,000, and top-prospect Harry Hulihan. Toney refused to report, so the Giants substituted pitcher Larry Benton.

Part of McGraw's rationale in trading Hulihan may have been to get him some seasoning elsewhere, then try to re-acquire him later. That was what happened with Benton, who returned to the Giants in 1927 (ironically in a trade for McQuillan) and won twenty-five games the following season. Hulihan initially protested the deal, but McGraw reminded him that he'd agreed only not to send Harry to the minors.

The 1922 Boston Braves were barely a cut above that level. After winning the World Series in the miracle season of 1914, the Braves had crashed and burned to the the league basement. At least Hulihan was put in the starting rotation for the last two months of the season. He performed quite well, posting a 2-3 record with a respectable 3.15 ERA and forcing his way into the Braves' plans for the next season.

At spring training in 1923, however, something snapped in Harry's left arm. At first the injury wasn't taken seriously, but the pain became too intense for him even to comb his hair. In desperation, the young lefthander decided on cor-

rective surgery, a radical step in a period in which sore arms were treated with ice water and burning liniment. A surgeon grafted a tendon from Harry's thigh into his left shoulder. Today it's popularly known as "Tommy John surgery," and it has successfully extended the careers of many pitchers. But for Harry Hulihan, solace came only as a medical pioneer. The operation succeeded in ending the pain, but he no longer could throw with any velocity. Several comeback attempts failed.

Fortunately Harry's studies provided the skills necessary to survive outside of baseball. He returned to Middlebury and earned his degree in 1924, then sold real estate in Florida for a time. In 1926 he began a successful career as a salesman for Aetna Life Insurance in New York City, following sports closely as a member of New York's Downtown Athletic Club. Harry married the former Dorothy Hightower in 1936 and raised two children. He returned to spend summers with relatives in Center Rutland, where he also lived out his retirement years. Neighbors remember him as a quiet man who could often be seen resting calmly on his porch, watching traffic whiz by on Route Four.

In this photograph of the Middlebury College baseball team, Harry Hulihan is the only player without a cap, perhaps to show off his unusual haircut. [Middlebury College Archives]

Harry Hulihan made it to the majors with the New York Giants in 1922. Though he was with the team for nearly two months, he didn't appear in a single game before his July 30 trade to the Boston Braves. [National Baseball Hall of Fame Library, Cooperstown, New York]

In 1977 Harry enjoyed one last day in the spotlight. Alert staffers at the *Rutland Herald* noted that a former big leaguer lived locally, and Harry was invited to throw out the ceremonial first pitch of the American Legion season at his old haunt, St. Peter's Field. Hulihan waxed nostalgic that day about his brief career, regaling bystanders with tales of a bygone era. A fan of contemporary baseball, he didn't begrudge current players their high salaries. As Harry put it, players in his day could "buy more then than you could today, what with all the taxes now." Though he regretted the injury that prematurely ended his career, he held no bitterness: "At least I was up in the majors and got to win a few games. A lot of other guys have tried out and never made it that far."

After a short illness, Harry Hulihan died on September 11, 1980. The annals of baseball history are filled with stories of sore-armed pitchers who failed to make it big, but Hulihan's saga remains noteworthy because of his inclusion in a critical trade and his role in the development of a surgical technique that's had a huge impact on baseball.

JOHN BENNETT

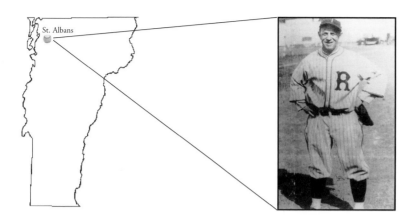

St. Albans

Bobby Murray

He Played Baseball the Old-Fashioned Way

In 1962 Bill Twomey was coaching a Little League team in Nashua, New Hampshire, when a sixty-eight-year-old man stepped down from the bleachers and asked if he could help. The man had an impish smile, twinkling blue eyes, and a simple philosophy: "Baseball is designed to be played a certain way—the old-fashioned way." That day the old-timer began a decade of involvement with the Nashua Little League. In recognition of his efforts he received the Service to Youth Award from the Nashua Boys Club in 1974, and the following year the Nashua Parks and Recreation Department gave him the Salute to Youth Award. After his death in 1979, the Nashua Little League named a field in his honor.

The old-timer's name was Bobby Murray, and his knack for teaching baseball was recognized by some of the sport's foremost authorities. "This guy was about as good an instructor of infield play as anyone I ever saw," says longtime Dartmouth baseball coach Tony Lupien, a former major leaguer who lives in Norwich, Vermont. Murray was so good, in fact, that Hall-of-Fame shortstop Pee Wee Reese once came to him for instruction. Unfortunately, current generations can't benefit from Murray's wisdom because an instructional book he wrote burned in a fire before he submitted it for publication. He was never able to bring himself to re-write it.

Robert Hayes Murray was born in St. Albans, Vermont, on the Fourth of July, 1894. At the time Murray lived there, St. Albans had a population exceeding 6,000, making it the fifth-largest city in Vermont. It was known

as the "Railroad City" because the Central Vermont Railway was headquartered there, and it was also the home of a pretty good baseball team featuring Ed Doheny, another Green Mountain Boy of Summer.

Bobby's father, John Murray, was a self-employed carpenter, and he and his wife, Julia, moved to Franklin, New Hampshire, when Bobby was still a toddler. As a young man Bobby became interested in Civil War history, and he visited regularly with the disabled and homeless Civil War veterans living at the Old Soldiers Home in Franklin. After attending prep school at Tilton Seminary and Westbrook Academy, Murray returned to Vermont and enrolled at Norwich University. During World War I he served in the Army, advancing to the rank of staff sergeant.

Murray tried his hand at boxing while stationed at Camp Devens, Masachusetts. He trained with Battling Levinsky, holder of the U.S. light-heavyweight championship until his twelve-round defeat by Gene Tunney at Madison Square Garden in 1922. Though Murray (5'6", 155 pounds) was no heavyweight himself, he could measure up to anyone when it came to toughness. "Bobby was the kind of guy," says Bill Twomey, "who could shake your hand and then hand you back your bones." After the war Murray focused his attention on baseball, and an unattributed clipping from his file at the National Baseball Library gives an indication of the type of player the lefthanded-hitting infielder was: "The fact is that the little Worcester player is really good, shining especially in the role of top man in the batting order. He hit for .285 last

118

season and he led the league in drawing bases on balls, which is his specialty. He also led it in getting hit by pitched balls, which is a useful but dangerous trait." In 1920 Murray was named the best shortstop in the Eastern League, and in 1921 he continued his climb towards the majors by playing Double-A ball (the top classification of that era) with Toledo.

Playing for Rochester in 1922, Bobby was involved in a freak accident that sowed the seeds for a lifetime friendship. After swinging two bats in the on-deck circle, Murray headed for the batter's box and innocently flipped the extra bat towards the dugout. Unfortunately, the bat struck a zealous twelve-year-old bat boy in the mouth, knocking out several teeth. Murray was so distraught that he paid the child's dental bill, then tracked his whereabouts over the years in case complications arose. The boy's name was Gabe Paul, and he went on to become president of the Cleveland Indians and New York Yankees.

Despite batting .296 the previous year with Rochester, Bobby found himself playing in a lower classification with the Nashville Vols in 1923. One of his teammates in Nashville was Lance Richbourg Sr., father of the Vermont artist whose painting of Larry Gardner graces the cover of this book. Another was a twenty-three-year-old outfielder who won Most Valuable Player

honors in the Southern Association that summer and went on to enjoy a Hall-of-Fame career. That player's name was Hazen Shirley Cuyler, better known as "Kiki" (pronounced "kie kie"), and Murray claimed that he was responsible for coming up with that nickname.

Murray Names a Hall of Famer

There are actually two stories of how Kiki Cuyler got his nickname, but either way Bobby Murray was involved. According to the most common version, for years Cuyler had been called "Cuy" by his teammates. At Nashville, when a flyball was hit to center field, the shortstop would call out "Cuy," signifying that Cuyler should make the catch, and the second baseman (Murray) would echo the call. Fans picked up the cry, and before long a writer tagged him with "Kiki."

Murray told a different story to Bill Twomey. According to Murray's version, Nashville's manager stuttered when he read the batting order aloud. When the team took the field, Murray, playing second base, would turn to Cuyler, playing center field, and yell out, "Hey, Ki—Ki—Ki—Cuyler," mimicking the manager. After the joke was repeated a few times, other players started referring to the future Hall of Famer as Kiki.

On September 23, 1923, Ossie Bluege, the Washington Senators' regular third baseman, shattered a bone in

Though he played only third base in the majors, Murray was adept at any infield position. [Murray Family Archives]

As Worcester's leadoff hitter in 1919-20, Bobby Murray specialized in reaching base by any means possible. [Murray Family Archives]

his right leg. It was the break Bobby Murray needed: hitting a career-high .307 at Nashville, he was ordered to report immediately to Griffith Stadium in Washington. The next day the Vermonter started for the Senators, playing third base and batting second, sandwiched between the pesky Nemo Leibold and hard-hitting Goose Goslin.

The opposing pitcher for the Chicago White Sox was righthander Charlie Robertson, who in 1922 had pitched the sixth perfect game in major league history in only his third big league start. On this day he was almost as good, shutting out the Senators 1-0 and holding Murray hitless in three official at-bats. Bobby had to wait until the next day for his first major league hit, a single.

Not until his third game, on September 26, 1923, did Bobby Murray understand the magnitude of what he'd accomplished in reaching the majors. As Chicago's lead-off hitter, Harry Hooper, prepared to step in, Murray turned towards the pitcher's mound from his position at third base and watched Walter Johnson warming up with his easy sidearm motion. Suddenly he realized he was standing on the same diamond as the greatest pitcher who ever lived. Years later Bobby admitted that it was the one time in his career that he felt chills running down his spine.

Murray played in each of Washington's last ten games of the 1923 season, batting .189 (seven singles in thirty-seven at-bats) with two runs scored and two RBIs. Despite playing out of his preferred positions in the middle infield, he didn't commit a single error.

Though he never returned to the majors, Murray continued to play professional baseball through 1937. All told, he played for ten different teams and managed four of them. During that time Bobby played with and against some of the great names in baseball history. The feat he remembered best came against Van Lingle Mungo, a temperamental fireballer who pitched for the Brooklyn Dodgers in the 1930s. "Mungo had us blanked and was working on a no-hitter," Murray said. "He would throw that big foot up in the air and that's all you would see and the ball would be by you. Well, he had us going into the ninth and I hit the ball off the fence, spoiling the no-hit, no-run effort. That Mungo didn't speak to me until about four years later."

During the '30s, actor Buster Keaton hired Murray as player-manager of his winter league club in Culver City, California. Keaton taught Murray his baggy-pants burlesque routines and even found him a role in a Hollywood movie. It was an obscure baseball film called "Slide Kelly Slide," and the director needed someone to play a background role as one of the sliding ballplayers. After receiving instructions on how to slide to produce the desired screen effect, Bobby expressed dissatisfaction that any film director would instruct his actors to deviate from proper sliding technique. Murray set up his own class on sliding for members of the cast, but in the end he reluctantly agreed to slide the way the director wanted him to.

Murray at Phillip Morris Sporting Goods in Nashua. Over the years he became a knowledgeable freshwater angler and could advise customers on fishing as well as baseball equipment. [Murray Family Archives]

This park memorializes Bobby Murray's contributions to youth baseball in the Nashua, New Hampshire, area. [Bill Twomey]

After his playing career Murray settled down in Nashua, where he lived for the last thirty-nine years of his life. He scouted at various times for the Detroit Tigers, Boston Braves, New York Yankees, and Kansas City Royals, and his diverse baseball experience included a stint in 1953 as business manager for a PONY League club in Corning, New York. From 1956 through 1959 he coached the baseball team at Providence College, and he also coached several semipro, American Legion, and Little League teams. After retiring from baseball Murray worked at Phillip Morris Sporting Goods in Nashua.

At the age of eighty-four, Bobby Murray was admitted to a Nashua hospital on January 2, 1979, and passed away two days later. In his final hours Bobby told Bill Twomey that a lot of old-timers had died bitter, but he could die knowing that he'd brought satisfaction to a lot of kids through baseball.

PAT O'CONNOR

After The Flood

(1928-1993)

On the morning of November 3, 1927, Ray Collins was driving his truck from his Colchester farm to Burlington to make a milk delivery and drop off his kids at school when a police officer stopped him at the Winooski Bridge. An early snowfall had melted beneath heavy rains, turning the Winooski River into a torrent, and the officer was concerned that the rushing waters might be damaging the bridge. Using his status as a local celebrity, Collins talked the officer into letting him pass, and the retired ballplayer thus became the last person to cross the Winooski Bridge before it was washed away.

With its economic infrastructure decimated by the Flood of 1927, the Green Mountain State plunged into depression two years before the stock market crash of 1929. Recovery was long and difficult—for the next half-century Vermont ranked among the poorest half-dozen states.

Mirroring Vermont's economic fortunes, the procession of Green Mountain Boys of Summer entered its own period of recession. In more than seven decades since the '27 Flood, only ten Vermonters have made it to the major leagues. The first were Steve Slayton in 1928 and Lou Polli in 1932, both of whom were gone from the majors by the time the first rope tow in the United States started hauling skiers up a hill outside Woodstock in 1933.

Birdie Tebbetts made his debut with the Detroit Tigers in 1936, the same year Vermonters voted against building a national parkway along the tops of the Green Mountains. When America declared war after the Japanese attacked Pearl Harbor in 1941, the Green Mountain State once again did its full duty—Slayton, Tebbetts, Walt Lanfranconi, Ralph Lapointe, and Ernie Johnson were among the 50,000 Vermonters who served their country.

Only Johnson was still active in the majors by the time WCAX in Burlington became the state's first television station in 1954, but one last flowering of Green Mountain baseball talent remained. Carlton Fisk reached the majors in 1969 while his brother Calvin was serving in Vietnam. When Pat Putnam joined Fisk as the only Vermonters in the major leagues in 1978, a couple guys named Ben Cohen and Jerry Greenfield had just opened an ice cream shop in a vacant gas station in Burlington. In 1981 Len Whitehouse joined Putnam on the Texas Rangers, and he and Mark Brown both finished their major league careers with the 1985 Minnesota Twins.

Fisk's stellar career finally ended on June 21, 1993, when he was handed his release by the Chicago White Sox. Since then not a single Vermonter has made the majors.

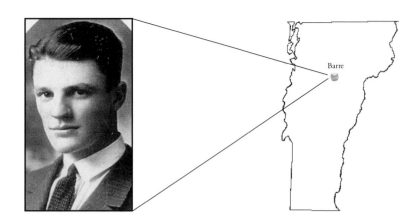

Barre

Steve Slayton

First of the Barre Pitchers

On an elevation just east of Barre's City Park stands the old Spaulding High School. Between 1915 and 1936, three future Green Mountain Boys of Summer attended school in the immense red-brick structure. The first to reach the majors was Steve Slayton, who pitched in three games for the Boston Red Sox in 1928. After a back injury cut short his professional career, Slayton eventually returned to Spaulding and became one of Vermont's most successful high school baseball coaches.

Foster Herbert Slayton was born on a farm in Barre on April 26, 1902. How he came to be called "Steve" is an odd story: as a youngster Foster was constantly expectorating, so his brother dubbed him "Steve" because it sounded like the noise he made when he spat. After graduating from Spaulding in 1920, Steve enrolled at Norwich University but was forced to withdraw in the spring of his freshman year when his father died unexpectedly. During the summer of 1924 he received his first taste of professional baseball with Waynesboro, Pennsylvania, of the Class-D Blue Ridge League, playing under the alias of Steven Foster to protect his amateur status. That fall he reentered college, this time at the University of New Hampshire.

At UNH Slayton joined the Kappa Sigma fraternity and was captain of the basketball team. He also captained the freshman baseball team in 1925, then earned three varsity letters in baseball under coach Hank Swasey. To this day he holds UNH career records for complete games (16) and innings pitched (206). His greatest performance

came in 1928, the year he led the Wildcats to an 11-8 record. That spring Notre Dame came to Durham with one of the top college teams in the country, but the twenty-six-year-old senior upset the Irish by pitching a three-hit shutout. The national press picked up the story, and following his June graduation Steve signed with the Red Sox and reported directly to Boston.

Slayton's manager with the Red Sox was Bill "Rough" Carrigan, the same hard and aggressive man who'd managed Larry Gardner and Ray Collins back when the BoSox were champions. After winning the World Series in 1916, Carrigan quit baseball at the peak of his success to become a banker in his hometown of Lewiston, Maine. He was persuaded to return in 1927, but in his absence the Sox had fallen on hard times. Carrigan managed the team for three years, 1927 through 1929, and finished last three straight times.

Joining the team in the middle of Carrigan's tenure, Steve made his big league debut at Fenway Park on July 21, 1928. Before an unusually large crowd of 17,000 on hand for "Ira Flagstead Day," Slayton pitched a scoreless ninth inning in a 5-1 loss to the Cleveland Indians. His next appearance came at Cleveland on July 25, and although the Red Sox lost both games of a doubleheader, 10-2 and 15-5, the *Boston Post* sung his praises: "Slayton, a rookie flinger from the University of New Hampshire, did the best job of hurling during the day's bombardment, holding the Indians to three hits after relieving Ed Morris in the first game. Slayton hurled four and two-thirds innings and exhibited a pretty curve and a burning fast ball that had the Indians popping them up."

Slayton's son, David, remembers his father mentioning that one of the hits he surrendered was a double to future Hall-of-Famer Charlie Gehringer of the Tigers. Sure enough, records confirm that at Detroit on July 28, in Slayton's third and final appearance in the majors, Gehringer doubled off him to knock in Marty McManus. To that point Steve had pitched well enough to stay with the Red Sox, giving up only six hits in seven innings for a 3.86 ERA. Why, then, was that Detroit game his last in the majors?

David Slayton remembers his father talking about a bizarre mix-up in that game. Carrigan had instructed the Red Sox to employ a shift against certain hitters, and Slayton was pitching when Rough visited the mound to give him some advice. Before the manager returned to the dugout, Slayton asked him, "No shift?" Carrigan, who was hard of hearing, misheard the question and thought instead that his rookie pitcher had made a wise comment. According to the story, Carrigan sent Slayton to Haverhill of the New England League to teach him a lesson. After the season the Red Sox released him.

As strange as that story sounds, newspaper accounts of the inning before Slayton was roughed up by Gehringer suggest that it might well be true. Steve entered with the bases loaded and only one out, certainly a time when a manager would want to have a word with his rookie pitcher. In this case the rookie worked out of the jam relatively unscathed, yielding a sacrifice fly before striking out Jack Warner to retire the side, but his arm was unable to rectify the damage his tongue had already caused.

By 1928 the St. Louis Cardinals had developed the first modern farm system, controlling 203 players on eight Cardinals-owned minor league teams. Figuring his odds of hooking on with a team were better in such a huge organization, Slayton attended a Cardinals tryout camp in 1929 and was one of six players signed from among a field of 150. That summer he developed back trouble and, in his own words, "lost my stuff in midseason." Slayton bounced from teams in Allentown to Waynesboro (where he'd started five years earlier) to Portland, Maine. His back pain was diagnosed as a problem with infected teeth, but it continued even after he had every tooth pulled.

Slayton attempted a comeback with Portland in 1930 but failed to finish out the season, retiring from professional baseball at the age of twenty-eight. Later that year he married Grace Lockwood of Dover, New Hampshire, who was still a UNH student. Six years later they had David, their only child. For years David held onto his father's baseball memorabilia, but he threw it away only one year before he was interviewed for this book. "Those scrapbooks hung around for seventy years, and I figured that was long enough," David said.

Somewhere there still exists a Fox Movietone News photograph of Steve Slayton posing with Babe Ruth and Lou Gehrig during a long-ago spring training in Florida. While on vacation a few years ago a relative saw it in an exhibit at Disney World, and David remembers his father mentioning it: "He was talking to Gehrig when Ruth sat down next to him. Photographers wanted to take [the two Yankees'] picture so he got up to leave, but Gehrig said, 'Sit down. You're alright just where you are.'"

After his playing career Slayton taught and coached for twelve years at Traip Academy in Kittery, Maine. During World War II he trained Air Force cadets at the University of Vermont, where he became acquainted with Larry Gardner. Though in his forties, Slayton ran seven-mile stints with the cadets three times a day and earned

After graduating from UNH in 1928, Slayton reported directly to the Boston Red Sox. [Slayton Family Archives]

Coach Slayton (lower right) and the Spaulding team celebrate their 5-1 victory over Burlington in the 1964 state championship game. [Aldrich Library, Barre]

extra money by pitching in semipro leagues. After the war Slayton remained in his native state and took a teaching post at St. Johnsbury Academy. In 1948 he joined the faculty of the Tilton School in New Hampshire, where he coached football and baseball.

Then in 1957 Slayton returned to Barre to coach the Spaulding High School baseball team. Over nine seasons he compiled a remarkable 115-22 record at Spaulding, leading the team to two undefeated seasons and four Vermont state titles before retiring in 1966. Still bothered by back problems, Steve moved to Raymond, New Hampshire, in 1980 to live with his son. After a brief illness, he died in Manchester's Elliott Hospital on December 20, 1984. Slayton was interred in Barre's Hope Cemetery, which is famous for its intricately carved granite grave markers. His final resting place is not far from that of Walt Lanfranconi, another Barre-born Green Mountain Boy of Summer.

On October 31, 1986, Steve Slayton was inducted posthumously into the University of New Hampshire's 100 Club Hall of Fame. His plaque hangs in the UNH fieldhouse, where a namesake grandson (Steve, not Foster) worked during his senior year at UNH in 1997.

JIM MACKAY & TOM SIMON

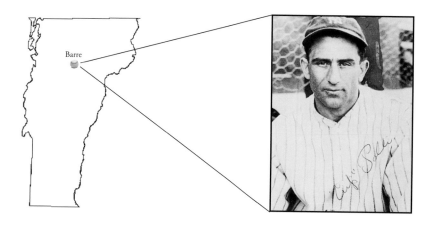

Crip Polli

The Oldest Living Major Leaguer

Total Baseball lists Lou "Crip" Polli's birthplace as Barre, but he actually wasn't born in Vermont—nor even the UnitedStates. The youngest of seven children, Louis Americo Polli was born on July 9, 1901, in Baveno, a little town on Lake Maggiore in the Italian Alps, near Italy's border with Switzerland. His unusual middle name, quite common in Barre for sons of Italian immigrants, hints at the circumstances under which the Pollis came to Barre and the pride they took in their new citizenship.

At the turn of the century Vermont quarries actively recruited skilled stonecutters from northern Italy, making them one of the few groups whose immigration was aggressively solicited. They were reputedly the best stonecutters in the world, descended from the men whose skills built Rome and supplied raw stone to Michelangelo. Louis' father, Battista, was one of that breed. He'd already emigrated to Barre at the time of Louis' birth, and the rest of the family joined him when Louis was only seven months old. The Pollis settled in a house at 44 Circle Street, where one of Lou's nephews lives to this day.

Barre was known for its radical politics during the era when Lou was growing up there. Some Italian granite workers joined labor unions and became active in the Socialist Party—they were even powerful enough to elect a socialist mayor. The Pollis, however, were apolitical—their only connection to the socialists, Lou recalls, was attending dances at the Socialist Hall on Granite Street. Lou remembers the adults throwing their coats in a pile on the floor and the children falling asleep on top of them.

As a kid Lou frequently tagged along behind his brothers. By the time he was thirteen he was competing in baseball against much older boys. Polli still remembers his first big break: "The team from Barre used to take a wagon to play its games, and the kids used to run behind the wagon all the way to Williamstown," he recalled. "Then one day the second baseman got sick, so they asked me to play. That meant I got to ride in the wagon on the way back, and didn't I feel like a big deal."

Lou attended Spaulding High School, but in those days the Spaulding baseball team lacked a coach. For away games Polli was placed in charge and given money to buy dinner for the team. Before long he transferred to a prep school with strong athletic teams, Goddard Seminary, located where Barre Auditorium is now. At Goddard Lou suffered a football injury that briefly put him on crutches, and his classmates branded him "Crip," short for "Cripple." He fully recovered from the injury but retains the nickname to this day. In fact, you're more likely to hear friends call him Crip than Lou.

Polli lettered in football and basketball at Goddard, but his best sport was baseball. During his senior year he attracted national attention by striking out twenty-eight batters in a ten-inning game against Cushing Academy on June 3, 1921, for which he was featured in *Ripley's Believe It Or Not*. During one five-game span that season Crip struck out 105 batters. Letters from colleges poured in, but he hid them from his parents. Crip had no interest in pursuing his education—all he wanted to do was play baseball.

Mary and Lou Polli's marriage in 1922 was controversial—it may have been the first between members of Barre's large Scottish and Italian communities—but it lasted nearly 70 years until death did them part. [Polli Family Archives]

The summer following his graduation from high school, Crip met Mary Catherine Smith after a baseball game at Gaysley Park in nearby Graniteville. A year later they married. The couple moved into a small house behind Mary's parents' home in Lower Graniteville, only a mile or so from the world-famous Rock of Ages Quarry. For the next several years, as Lou and Mary started a family, Lou worked during the week as a rigger in the quarry, climbing 150 feet to the tops of the derricks used to lift mammoth blocks of granite. On weekends he pitched for the Barre-Montpelier team in the Green Mountain League, distinguishing himself as the top pitcher in a semipro circuit that included former major league stars like Jeff Tesreau and Ray Fisher. Then in 1925 Lou began pitching on Saturdays and Sundays in the Boston Twilight League, earning up to $100 a game.

Polli finally got what he considers his real start in organized baseball in 1927 with Harrisburg of the New York-Penn League. He'd been discovered the previous summer

by Ben Hauser, his manager in the Boston Twilight League. Impressed by the lanky righthander's diverse repertoire of pitches—he threw a curve, sinker, knuckleball, and screwball to go along with a hard fastball—Hauser recommended Crip to the New York Yankees, for whom he worked as a part-time scout. In his first full season in the minors, Polli led the New York-Penn League in wins with eighteen and strikeouts with 109 while notching a sparkling 2.25 ERA. In 1928 he was promoted to the Yankees' top farm club, St. Paul of the American Association, where he slumped to 13-15 with a 3.53 ERA. But in his second season with St. Paul, Polli's twenty-two wins and 288 innings topped the Association.

Based on that performance, the Yankees invited Polli to his first big league spring training camp. It was a memorable experience: "There were twenty-six pitchers trying out for one job," Crip said. "It came down to me and Lefty Gomez." A future Hall of Famer, Gomez was coming off an 18-11 season with San Francisco in 1929. "He was seven years younger," Crip remarked, "so you knew damn well who would get the job." Still, Polli has marvelous memories of his thirty-one-day preseason barnstorm-

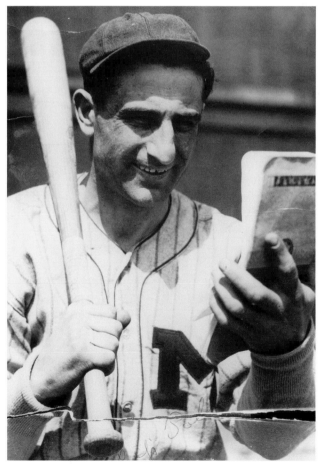

Impressive numbers: Polli compiled a record of 263-226 over 22 minor-league seasons. [Polli Family Archives]

ing tour with the Bronx Bombers, riding the rails on The Yankee Express and playing exhibition games all over the South.

Those Yankees were arguably the greatest team in baseball history, and Polli got to know many players who wound up in the Hall of Fame. His bridge partner, for example, was none other than Bill Dickey—and his frequent opponents were Lou and Eleanor Gehrig. "I roomed with Tony Lazzeri for a time," Polli said. "Earle Combs, too. But Lazzeri! He snored so hard that he kept me awake half the night. I'd go over and punch him in the arm to get him to stop. He did, but then he'd start up again and I'd lose more sleep." The teammate Polli is asked about most frequently is, of course, Babe Ruth: "He was full of hell, that guy, but I liked him. He was always nice to me. We'd shoot pool, and I played a lot of golf with him. We used to play at those Tom Thumb courses for a quarter a hole. He couldn't putt worth a damn. I took a lot of quarters from him."

After breaking free from the Yankees, Polli made his major league debut with the St. Louis Browns in 1932. [National Baseball Hall of Fame Library, Cooperstown, New York]

Did Prejudice Play a Part in Delaying Crip Polli's Baseball Career?

On April 15, 1920, two armed robbers shot and killed the paymaster and an armed guard for a shoe company in South Braintree, Massachusetts, absconding with $15,000. Italian immigrants Nicola Sacco and Bartolomeo Vanzetti, both admitted anarchists, were convicted of the murders. The ensuing national clamor over their executions called attention to the radical political views of some Italian-Americans, and baseball historians have speculated that prejudice might have played a part in causing Crip Polli's late start in organized ball. After all, Barre was infamous for its socialist mayor and its turn-of-the-century labor struggles. Could Polli have been branded simply by residence?

For his part, the ninety-eight-year-old Polli doesn't think so. At the time in question he had a wife and two kids to support, he says, and he earned more money working at the quarry and playing semipro ball on weekends than he ever could in the minors. Moreover, he actually did play organized baseball in 1922, albeit for only a brief time, winning three of four decisions for Montreal of the short-lived Eastern Canada League.

Polli was assigned to Louisville in 1930 after just missing out on making the Yankees. That was the first summer he brought his family to live with him during the season, and daughter Margaret remembers the culture shock she experienced in Kentucky. Even though Louisville won the American Association pennant, Polli suffered through a miserable 8-13 season, including a career-worst 5.82 ERA. To make things worse, he was sued after moving out of the first house he lived in and ended up having to pay rent on two houses. Then, to cap the terrible year, the Yankees released him.

But Polli's release may have been fortuitous. "Our catcher, Bill Dickey, later told me that the Yankee brass held me back because they didn't want me pitching for another big league team," Crip said. Now he had a chance to catch on with another organization—and that's what happened after he rebounded from his poor 1930 season to go 21-15 for the Milwaukee Brewers in 1931. On April 18, 1932, Polli pitched one inning for the St. Louis Browns in a 14-7 loss to Detroit, giving up a run on two hits and a walk. The next day he pitched again in a mop-up role as the Tigers won easily, 8-0. After those two appearances Crip pitched sparingly. Though he was with St. Louis for the entire season, he appeared in a total of just five games, pitching only seven innings.

At his own request Lou returned to Milwaukee in 1933, and the Pollis spent three more happy years in that baseball-crazy city. His most memorable day in a Brewer uniform came on September 7, 1935. The opposing pitcher was Lou Fette, a former St. Paul teammate who became a twenty-game winner as a Boston Braves rookie in 1937. Crip had told Fette that he'd throw

"Three Wops" was the newspaper caption on this photo of Polli (center) with Milwaukee teammates Lin Storti and George DeTore, both former major leaguers. [Polli Family Archives]

a no-hitter the next time he pitched against him, and that's exactly what he did.

In 1936-37 Crip played for the Montreal Royals, the team for which he pitched his second no-hitter on July 19, 1937. Living in Montreal was ideal, close enough to Vermont that he could come home on days off. But like his boyhood idol, Ty Cobb, Polli could be tough to handle—and his temper proved costly in 1937.

> I had a pretty good year and they had promised me a bonus. Then they wouldn't pay me. So I went to the offices, which were up on the second floor, and argued with those three Frenchmen who ran the team. [Editor's note: One of the three Frenchmen was Charles Trudeau, father of Canadian prime minister Pierre Trudeau.] I called them cheap Frenchmen, they said I'd never play for them again, and they punished me by sending me to Chattanooga.

Polli spent the next five seasons in the South, bouncing from Chattanooga to Knoxville to Jacksonville. Then in 1944 the forty-three-year-old led the International League in ERA with a 1.84 mark for Jersey City, earning a second shot at the majors. Used mostly in middle relief, Crip pitched thirty-six innings in nineteen games for the New York Giants, going 0-2 with a 4.54 ERA.

In 1945 Polli returned to Jersey City of the International League, ending his long career with a flourish in a minor key. His oldest daughter, Mary, had been suffering with tuberculosis for two years. On September 3, before Crip's last scheduled start of the season, he received news that Mary's condition had been diagnosed as terminal. Many men would have begged off that day, especially as the opponents were the fabled Newark Bears, on a fourteen-game winning streak. But Lou Polli, part of his mind numbed with the awful news, went out and pitched the game of his life. The forty-four-year-old veteran of twenty-two professional campaigns set down the

Bears inning after inning. When it was over he'd pitched his third minor league no-hitter. Polli never pitched another game in professional baseball.

Crip's heroic final performance made no difference to the inexorable march of his daughter's fate. Mary Polli died on November 5, 1945, in a sanatorium in Saranac Lake, New York, where Christy Mathewson had died two decades earlier. Following Mary's death, Lou went to Halifax, Nova Scotia, to manage a semipro team, then returned to Graniteville in 1947 and became the first constable for Barre Town, serving until 1970.

Polli was player-manager of the Lower Graniteville baseball team until about 1950, mostly playing shortstop but occasionally pitching. "Even at that point in his career he was by far the best pitcher I ever saw," said teammate Russell Ross. Polli also became involved in youth baseball. One of his favorite stories involved a group of Graniteville Little Leaguers:

Polli enjoyed a second major league stint with the New York Giants in 1944. [Polli Family Archives]

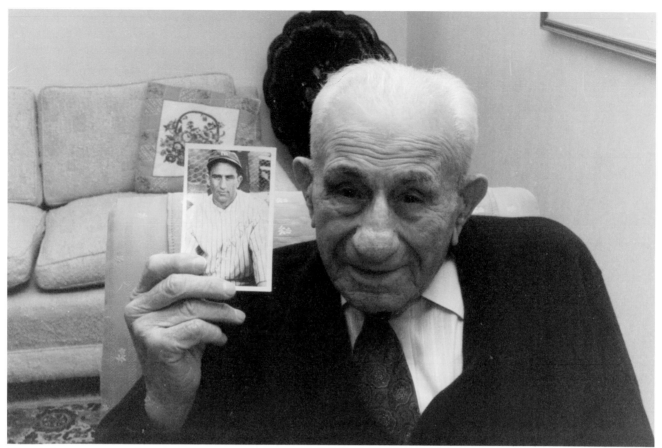

Though he never appeared in an official game for the Bronx Bombers, Polli has always considered himself a Yankee. [Polli Family Archives]

I instructed one youngster, who was seated on the bench, to follow another boy in the batting order. The kid who was up hit a home run, and when he started running around the bases, the second kid trotted behind him. When they got back to the bench I asked the second kid, "What were you doing?" And he said, "You told me to follow him, so I did." I nearly cracked up over that one, but I managed to hold back my laughter.

Over the years Polli took on the duties of town agent and tax collector. Daughter Margaret remembers him staying up late at night computing tax bills in his head, never using an adding machine. He remained in those offices until his retirement at age eighty in 1981. Crip still lived in the same house in Graniteville until 1996, when he moved in with Margaret in Barre.

Long-Lived Vermonters
Close readers may have noticed something unusual about the longevity of Green Mountain Boys of Summer: four of the thirty-four were thought to be the oldest living major leaguer at the time of their death. Tom Lynch died less than a week short of his ninety-fifth

birthday on March 28, 1955; Bert Abbey was ninety-two when he died on June 11, 1962; Ray Fisher was ninety-five when he died on November 3, 1982; and now Crip Polli is thought to be oldest, having been born on July 9, 1901.

But in Polli's case the claim is disputed. The official records say that Karl Swanson, a second baseman who played twenty-four games for the 1928-29 Chicago White Sox, was born on December 17, 1903, but Swanson claims he's three years older. "When I signed my contract with Chicago, I told them I was born in 1903," says Swanson. "I kind of cheated a little bit. Actually I was born December 19, 1900. That's on all my legal papers—my driver's license, the title to my home, everything. But the big league clubs never wanted to sign a player who was over twenty-four."

Polli was doing well until he slipped in the shower and fractured a hip in November 1997. He now lives at Woodridge Nursing Home, reading the *Burlington Free Press* and the *Montpelier Times-Argus* each day, turning first to the sports pages to see how his beloved Yankees did.

TOM SIMON

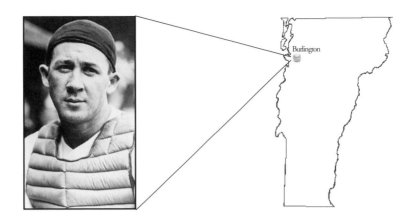

Birdie Tebbetts

The "Nashua Thrush" Was Hatched In Burlington

In a 1973 SABR survey, Birdie Tebbetts narrowly missed being chosen Vermont's greatest baseball player, finishing second to Larry Gardner by a mere handful of votes. In almost every respect, Tebbetts was a solid candidate: a lifetime .270 hitter, Birdie amassed exactly 1,000 hits in a career that spanned seventeen years, three of which were lost to military service. Perhaps what was lacking were strong Vermont ties—whereas Gardner spent nearly his entire life in the Green Mountains, Tebbetts left the state when he was only a couple months old.

But aside from being born here, Tebbetts had several other connections to the Green Mountain State. He nearly accepted a scholarship from Gardner to attend the University of Vermont—until the aspiring pre-med learned that afternoon laboratory sessions would conflict with baseball practice. Instead he chose Providence College at the behest of the scout who signed him to his first professional contract—none other than Vermont-born Jean Dubuc. But his fondest Vermont memory was of a 1948 barnstorming trip to Burlington, during which he met his future wife.

George Robert Tebbetts was born in Burlington on November 10, 1912. He was the third and final child of Charles and Elizabeth Ryan Tebbetts, and his round, freckled face and flaming red hair reflected his mother's Irish heritage. George's most distinguishing characteristic, though, was his unusually high-pitched voice. As a toddler he acquired the nickname "Birdie" after an aunt observed that his voice sounded like a bird chirping.

The Tebbetts family lived in a brick Federal-style house that still stands on King Street. Birdie's father, Charles Tebbetts, first appeared in the *Burlington City Directory* in 1911. At the time he worked as a shipping clerk for Swift & Company, a wholesaler of meats and provisions located at the corner of Maple and Battery streets. That's why the family was living in Vermont when Birdie was born, but Charles was originally from New Hampshire, having grown up on a farm near Dover. Within a couple months of Birdie's birth, Swift promoted Charles to salesman and transferred him back to his native state. The family settled in Nashua, but tragedy struck one year later when Charles died, leaving Mary to raise three children on her own. "We were very poor," Tebbetts recalled.

When Birdie was eight he had the fortune of meeting Francis Parnell Murphy, owner of Nashua's biggest industry, the Thom McAn Shoe Company, and later governor of New Hampshire. Murphy sponsored the Nashua Millionaires, an independent baseball team composed of ex-professionals and collegiate All-Americans, and Birdie served as the team's mascot. "Murphy happened to take a liking to me," Tebbetts said. "Having no father of my own, I guess I adopted him in my mind as a father. He helped me in a number of ways, and no man in my life has ever exerted a more powerful influence on me." One obvious perk was that Tebbetts never had to pay for a pair of shoes.

That stint as mascot for the Millionaires was also responsible for Tebbetts becoming a catcher. His idol on the team was Clyde Sukeforth, best-known today as the man whom Branch Rickey assigned to scout Jackie Robinson for the Brooklyn Dodgers. Sukey was also a pretty good backstop who went on to enjoy a ten-year career in the majors with Cincinnati and Brooklyn, and Birdie imitated his moves behind the plate. Tebbetts became so adept, in fact, that it became a standard pregame attraction for the youngster to warm up Nashua's starting pitcher.

Birdie grew up to be a star athlete at Nashua High School, playing football, basketball, and especially baseball. By his senior year of 1930 he'd received scholarship offers from numerous colleges (one was a six-year scholarship from UVM that included medical school) and professional bids from major league clubs. The man who signed Lou Gehrig, in fact—legendary New York Yankees scout Paul Krichell—told Birdie's mother that the Yankees considered her son the best amateur prospect in the country. Imagine the money he could command if he were in that position today!

Tebbetts eventually chose to sign with the Detroit Tigers after being scouted by Dubuc and approved by the team's manager, future Hall-of-Famer Bucky Harris.

Tebbetts was signed to a Detroit Tigers contract by Green Mountain Boy of Summer Jean Dubuc. [National Baseball Hall of Fame Library, Cooperstown, New York]

"I got a bonus that was sufficient to wipe out all our family debts," Birdie said. Better yet, the Tigers agreed to pay his way through any college in the country. Birdie narrowed his choice to Holy Cross and Providence, but it took two stars of the deadball era to help make his final decision. "I was actually leaning towards Holy Cross, which was coached by Jack Barry, the old Philadelphia A's shortstop," Tebbetts said. "But Dubuc had offered to pay my way down to New York so I could work out with the Tigers at Yankee Stadium, and when Barry got wind of it he threatened to have my amateur status revoked." The old Tiger righthander mentioned this to Birdie, who became so angry that he chose Providence. "In my first game for Providence I tripled to beat Holy Cross," Tebbetts said. "It was one of the highlights of my baseball career."

Each summer, following the end of the college baseball season, Birdie played for East Douglas in the Blackstone Valley League, a high-level semipro circuit consisting mostly of teams from New England mill towns. Though supposedly amateur, teams spared no expense in attracting the best talent available. It wasn't uncommon for major leaguers who had off-days in Boston to sign on for important games. That's how Tebbetts in the span of one week found himself catching future Hall-of-Famers Lefty Grove and Carl Hubbell, both in the prime of their careers.

Birdie Tebbetts graduated from Providence College with a degree in philosophy in 1934, the year Detroit purchased future Hall-of-Fame catcher Mickey Cochrane from the Philadelphia A's. With the veteran backstop installed as player-manager, the Tigers ran away with their first American League pennant since 1909. The following year Cochrane led the Tigers to another pennant and a World Series victory over the Chicago Cubs, giving Detroit its first championship ever. With Cochrane a fixture behind the plate, clearly there was no need for Tebbetts in Detroit.

Birdie spent three seasons in the minors before receiving a call-up to the Tigers in September 1936. In 1937 he made the team out of spring training, but the season was in its infancy when he and three others received notice that they were being sent to Toledo following an afternoon game with the Yankees. The others watched the game from the grandstand, but Tebbetts elected to remain in uniform in case he was needed. In the fourteenth inning Birdie was pressed into duty as a pinch hitter. He delivered a game-winning double into the right-field corner, and after that he didn't leave the majors for another sixteen years.

On May 25, 1937, an opening in Detroit's starting lineup suddenly appeared when Cochrane's skull was frac-

Tebbetts is at far right in this photo of the Birdie Tebbetts All-Stars taken at Centennial Field on October 12, 1948. [Tony Lupien]

tured by a pitch from Bump Hadley of the Yankees. Rookie Rudy York was thrown into the catching breach and responded with sixty-eight home runs and 230 RBIs over the next two seasons, but his defense was awful. By 1939 Cochrane's replacement as manager, Del Baker, had seen enough. He installed Tebbetts as Detroit's regular catcher and Birdie batted a respectable .261 in 106 games.

In 1940 Baker shifted Hank Greenberg to left field to open up a regular spot for York at first base. The pair combined to hit seventy-four home runs as the Tigers finished a whisker ahead of the Indians and Yankees in one of the closest pennant races ever. After batting .294 for the regular season, Tebbetts went hitless in eleven World Series at-bats, even though the Tigers were stealing Cincinnati catcher Jimmie Wilson's signs. "We knew every pitch the Reds were throwing against us," Birdie said. "The screwiest part of it was that it didn't do us a damn bit of good." With solid pitching from Paul Derringer and Bucky Walters, Cincinnati edged out the Tigers in a seven-game series.

Tebbetts caught for the American League in the 1941 and 1942 All-Star Games, but military service during World War II took him out of baseball for the next three seasons. Birdie batted only .243 on his return in 1946 and continued to struggle in 1947, batting .094 as of May 20. On that date the Tigers traded him to the Red Sox for Hal Wagner, a catcher nearing the end of a twelve-year career. The swap proved a bargain for Boston.

Tebbetts batted .299 for the remainder of 1947, lifting his average for the year to .267. Reminiscent of the vengeance he inflicted on Holy Cross, Birdie managed to hit nearly .400 against Detroit.

He was Boston's regular catcher again in 1948 and made the American League All-Star Team. After 154 games that season, the Red Sox and Cleveland ended up tied at 96-58, necessitating a one-game play-off. On October 4, 1948, the Indians beat Denny Galehouse at Fenway Park, preventing the Red Sox from joining the Braves in an all-Boston World Series.

Birdie Meets His Mate in Vermont

Following the 1948 season Birdie Tebbetts barnstormed throughout New England with a team of his own composition. The Birdie Tebbetts Major League All-Stars featured Snuffy Stirnweiss and Spec Shea of the Yankees, Vic Wertz of the Tigers, Eddie Pellegrini of the Browns, Carl Sheib and Joe Coleman of the Athletics, Vern Stephens and Jimmy Piersall of the Red Sox, and Chicago White Sox first baseman Tony Lupien, a Massachusetts native who made his home in Springfield, Vermont.

On Columbus Day the team came to Burlington's Centennial Field to play an aggregation managed by Larry Gardner and composed mostly of players from Burlington's amateur Suburban League. The local squad was beefed up by the addition of St. Louis Cardinals infielder Ralph Lapointe of Winooski, and the two teams exchanged pitchers and catchers to make the game more interesting. A crowd of over 4,500 packed Centennial to see the Tebbetts All-Stars cruise to an 8-4 victory. Appropriately, the game's top performances were turned in by players with Vermont connections: Lupien was 4-for-5 with a triple and three RBIs, while Lapointe paced the locals with two singles and a stolen base.

The game was staged for the benefit of a local charity, and afterwards a banquet was held at the Hotel Vermont. Birdie was chatting with Stephen Hartnett, proprietor of a Burlington restaurant, when he noticed a beautiful brunette about twenty feet away. "Boy, that's a good-looking girl," Tebbetts said to his companion. "I sure would like to meet her." Hartnett called the woman over and said, "Mr. Tebbetts, I'd like you to meet my daughter Mary." At the time Mary Hartnett was working as a secretary to Vermont Governor Ernest Gibson, who was unable to attend the banquet and sent Mary in his place.

Stephen Hartnett was active in the Burlington Elks Club, and at her father's request Mary wrote to Tebbetts and asked what he'd charge to give a speech to the Elks at their winter sports banquet. Tebbetts replied to Mr. Hartnett that his usual fee was $350, but he'd donate the money back to the Elks if he could get a date with his daughter. Mary wrote back that "the fee is too high

and his daughter is not interested," but Birdie persisted. "That winter I drove up from Nashua through those mountains and spoke at that banquet," Tebbetts said. The effort paid off. Birdie married Mary Hartnett on October 28, 1950.

A thirty-seven-year-old Tebbetts batted .310 with a career-high eight home runs for the Red Sox in 1950, but despite the increased production he caught just seventy-four games—only one more than his back-up, twenty-eight-year-old Matt Batts. During a postseason banquet, Birdie told reporters that the reason he'd played so little was that one or two "juvenile delinquents and moronic malcontents" on the Boston pitching staff didn't want him catching them. The Red Sox didn't appreciate Birdie's candor. Though weak behind the plate, they sold Tebbetts to Cleveland. Over the next two seasons he spelled perennial all-star Jim Hegan, a superb defensive catcher.

Tebbetts knew he was nearing the end of his playing days, but he wasn't sure what he wanted to do next. Earlier in his career he'd considered farming, even taking postgraduate courses in agriculture at the University of New Hampshire in 1941. The war halted his studies, however, and he switched to selling insurance as an off-season activity, working as an associate for the Paul Sadler Agency in Nashua. But following the 1952 season he decided to accept an offer from the Indians to manage their Triple-A farm team in Indianapolis. Sports writers predicted that before long he'd be managing in the majors.

Those predictions came true one year later when a strange set of circumstances led to his hiring by the Cincinnati Redlegs (during the McCarthy era the team preferred not to be called the Reds). The Redlegs didn't have a Triple-A affiliate, so Cincinnati's general manager, Gabe Paul, made a deal with his cross-state counterpart in Cleveland, Hank Greenberg. The Redlegs agreed to send prospects to Tebbetts at Indianapolis if the Indians would help stock Cincinnati's Double-A team at Tulsa. Greenberg asked the Redlegs to send reports on his players from Tulsa's manager, Joe Schultz, so Paul requested Tebbetts' reports on the Redlegs prospects. "When I got them, I was amazed," Paul said. "Birdie's reports were the most complete I'd ever seen."

Frustrated by Cincinnati's fourth consecutive sixth-place finish in 1953, Paul decided to fire manager Rogers Hornsby. Initially he'd hoped to hire Al Lopez, but when the Cleveland manager announced his decision to remain with the Indians, Paul asked Greenberg for permission to hire Tebbetts. Not wanting to stand in the way of his old teammate, Greenberg acquiesced, and on September 28, 1953, Birdie Tebbetts became Cincinnati's

Tebbetts and his bride, the former Mary Hartnett of Burlington, pose after their wedding ceremony in Boston. [National Baseball Hall of Fame Library, Cooperstown, New York]

Tebbetts (perched on the bat rack) is pictured with the sluggers who helped his Redlegs tie a National League record with 221 home runs in 1956: (from left to right) Frank Robinson, Ed Bailey, Wally Post, Ted Kluszewski, and Gus Bell. [National Baseball Hall of Fame Library, Cooperstown, New York]

fifth manager in seven years. To this day he is the only Vermonter ever to manage in the major leagues.

The Redlegs experienced slight improvement in their first two seasons under Tebbetts, finishing in fifth place both years. Then in 1956 the Redlegs stayed in the race until the last day of the season, ending up with a 91-63 record, two games behind Brooklyn and one behind Milwaukee. It was the first time Cincinnati had finished in the first division in eleven years. Tebbetts was voted National League Manager of the Year.

Cincinnati finally appeared to be on the verge of a pennant, but the Redlegs finished a disappointing fourth in both of the next two seasons. Paul and Tebbetts fell under heavy criticism. Finally Birdie decided to quit, as Paul confirmed years later.

Nobody believes me when I say Birdie quit. They still think I fired him. Absolutely not. I tried to get him to stay. He was a nervous wreck and he looked bad.

He came to me and said, "Why don't you pay me off and let me go home?" I talked him out of it. Rumors began to fly and I told the reporters that what we needed were new players, not a new manager. And I meant it.

Three weeks later, he came to me again, requesting to leave. This time I thought it would be the best thing for his health, so I accepted his resignation. But he positively was not going to get fired. He could have stayed at Cincinnati as long as he wanted to. The way he looked, I didn't think he'd ever manage again.

In fact, neither did Tebbetts. At the press conference announcing his resignation, he told reporters he was through with managing.

Birdie landed an executive position with the Milwaukee Braves, but he missed the excitement of being in the dugout. When the team fired Chuck Dressen in September 1961, Tebbetts returned to managing for the last month of the season. Despite talented players like Hank Aaron, Eddie Mathews, Joe Adcock, Warren Spahn, and

Lew Burdette, the Braves finished fourth. Ironically, they'd won the pennant in 1958 when Tebbetts last managed the Reds, and in 1961 the Reds won when he was managing the Braves.

During the 1962 World Series Birdie accepted an offer to manage the Indians from Gabe Paul, who'd moved on from Cincinnati to become general manager at Cleveland. In his return to the A.L., Birdie guided a young Cleveland team to a fifth-place tie in 1963. By that point he'd been smoking three packs a day for the last twenty-five years, and his weight had ballooned to 238 pounds.

In Tucson on April 1, 1964, just as spring training was ending, Tebbetts suffered a heart attack. The fifty-two-year-old underwent bypass surgery at the Mayo Clinic, and it was reported that he was probably out for the season. Miraculously, he returned to the Indians on July 4, remaining with the team until he was fired on August 19,1966. In ten seasons as a manager, he'd compiled a record of 748-705 (.515).

Though he never again managed in the majors, Tebbetts worked in professional baseball as a scout and minor league manager for the New York Mets, New York Yankees, and Baltimore Orioles until his retirement in 1992. Settling down in Holmes Beach, Florida, in his eighties, Birdie helped out with the Anna Maria Island Little League.

Birdie Tebbetts died on March 25, 1999. "I'd like to be remembered as a good father and a good citizen," he told *The Bradenton Herald* a month before his death, "but I am a baseball guy. That's all I am. That's all I ever was. That's all I ever want to be."

TOM SIMON

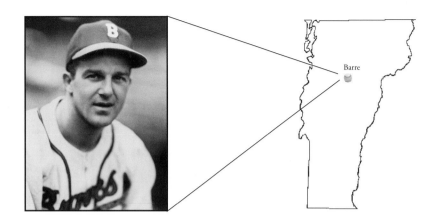

Walt Lanfranconi

Last of the Barre Pitchers

Walter Oswald Lanfranconi was born in Barre on November 9, 1916, around the time fellow Barre-born pitchers Steve Slayton and Lou Polli were entering high school. Lanfranconi's father, Stefano, had been a stone cutter in Switzerland, not far from the town in northern Italy where Battista Polli (Lou's father) had engaged in the same trade. Like Polli, Stefano Lanfranconi emigrated to Vermont to find work in Barre's granite industry.

After five years of cutting stone in the Green Mountains, Stefano moved his family back to the Swiss Alps when Walter was eighteen months old. Why he returned to Switzerland isn't entirely clear—by some accounts he was homesick, but by others he inherited property on the Swiss-Italian border. Whatever the case, Stefano came back to Barre after two years in Switzerland. Walt, meanwhile, remained in the Alps with his mother, attending kindergarten and primary school there. It wasn't until the future big leaguer was six that he and his mother returned to Vermont.

In the baseball hotbed that was Barre in the 1920s and '30s, Walt took to America's national pastime at the relatively late age of thirteen. He was small for an athlete (he grew to be only 5'7" and 155 pounds), but at Spaulding High School he became known as the "Boy Wonder" of the Granite River Valley, lettering in baseball, basketball, and track. Walt's pitching caught the attention of Stuffy McInnis, then scouting for the Washington Senators. Walt received a letter from Washington owner Clark Griffith instructing him to report to

Fenway Park when the Senators were in Boston. As the story goes, Washington manager Bucky Harris took a quick look at the diminutive Vermonter and sent him home, saying, "I don't want any drugstore pitchers."

After three years at Spaulding High School, Walt transferred to Montpelier Seminary for his senior year of 1937. Before the school year was over he caught on with the Burlington Cardinals of Vermont's famous Northern League. Walt's manager at Burlington was Ray Fisher, another Green Mountain Boy of Summer, but Fisher released him after only three games. Walt got even. Pitching for the rival Montpelier Senators on the day of his high-school graduation, Walt hurled a one-hit masterpiece against Fisher's flock before a packed crowd that included many big league scouts.

One of them, former major leaguer and UVM athletic director Clyde Engle, signed Lanfranconi to a contract with the Toronto Maple Leafs of the Double-A International league. Walt appeared in only one game for Toronto in 1937, allowing ten runs in only four innings. After the Maple Leafs sent him to the Canadian-American League for a brief apprenticeship, Walt returned to Toronto in 1938 and remained for the next four seasons. During spring training in 1939 he enjoyed his greatest baseball thrill to that point, pitching in an exhibition contest against the Boston Red Sox. For several innings Walt mowed through a star-studded lineup featuring Jimmie Foxx, Joe Cronin, Bobby Doerr, and a rookie named Ted Williams. He gave up just two singles, both to Doerr.

Walt Lanfranconi (in the back row at right) was the youngest player on Barre's strong Knights of Columbus team. [Lanfranconi Family Archives]

The 1940 season proved to be the shortest of Walt's professional career. In just his fourth appearance he suffered severe elbow pain and was sent to Dr. George Bennett of the Johns Hopkins Hospital in Baltimore. The diagnosis: bone chips had grown onto the nerves in his elbow, and even with surgery his chances were one-in-100 of ever pitching again. "I can't pitch as it is," Walt told Dr. Bennett, "so what have I got to lose?" The surgery was performed on June 3, 1940. Walt was placed on the voluntarily retired list.

Overcoming the odds, Walt returned to the Maple Leafs in 1941 and was even named Opening Day starter by manager Tony Lazzeri, the former Yankee great. Walt's selection irked teammate Vallie "Chief" Eaves, who felt that he was the best pitcher on the Toronto staff. When Lazzeri announced that Walt would open the season, Eaves picked up a pair of scissors and started towards Walt, saying, "It's all your fault. I'm going to pitch today." After Walt fended him off, Eaves went after Lazzeri before the Toronto players chased him out of the clubhouse.

After winning his first five starts in 1941, Walt suddenly found himself relegated to the bullpen when Lazzeri was replaced as manager by Lena Blackburne. Best-remembered as the discover of Delaware River mud for rubbing the gloss off new baseballs, Blackburne was known to be eccentric. While managing the Chicago White Sox in 1929, for example, he engaged in a savage fistfight with one of his own players, Art Shires. Walt's season turned upside down after Blackburne's arrival. He lost fifteen of his last eighteen decisions and, not surprisingly, grew to dislike his new manager. On one occasion Blackburne called on Walt before he'd had a chance to throw a single warm-up pitch. Entering with the bases loaded and no outs, he struck out the first batter and made the next two pop up to end the game.

When Walt got to the clubhouse, Blackburne said, "That's the luckiest relief pitching I have ever seen."

At the end of the season Blackburne announced that he was returning to the Philadelphia Athletics as a coach the following season. Curiously, he asked Walt if he wanted to join him on the A's or be sold to the Chicago Cubs. Without hesitation Walt chose the latter, arriving in Chicago during the waning days of the 1941 season as the Cubs were sputtering to a sixth-place finish. In his major league debut on September 12, Lanfranconi started against the Cincinnati Reds and suffered a 2-0 setback to Cincinnati ace Bucky Walters. Walt's fortunes that day may have been doomed from the start—Cubs manager Jimmie Wilson fielded an experimental lineup consisting entirely of rookies. The Barre native appeared in only one more game that fall, pitching a single inning of relief.

The following year the Cubs held spring training at Catalina Island off the coast of California, but Walt wasn't there long before he was farmed out to the Milwaukee Brewers. His new manager was Charlie Grimm, the popular player-manager of the Cubs back in the '20s and '30s. Pitching both as a starter and reliever, Lanfranconi became Grimm's workhorse, finishing with a 15-13 record in a career-high forty-two appearances.

Lanfranconi spent parts of five seasons with the Toronto Maple Leafs. [Lanfranconi Family Archives]

With a strong season behind him, Walt looked forward to re-joining the Cubs in 1943.

But with World War II raging in Europe, fate had something else in store. Walt spent the next three years on the front lines in Europe, earning two battle stars with the 12th Armored Division. Even after VE day Walt stayed on with the occupation forces. Playing baseball for his company team, the Vermonter broke his leg sliding into second base on July 28, 1945. That injury put an abrupt end to his European playing activities, though he continued to manage the company team.

After forty-five months in military service, Walt arrived home in Barre in February 1946, just in time to leave for spring training with the Milwaukee Brewers. Though his leg still bothered him, he picked up where he'd left off nearly four years earlier by winning five of his first six decisions. Then came another brush with injury that nearly ended Walt's baseball career. While fielding grounders at third base during batting practice, he was hit by a line drive that cracked his right shin bone. Walt struggled after returning too soon, finishing with an 8-10 record. Now hampered by two leg injuries, Lanfranconi left at the end of the season thinking he was through with baseball.

When he arrived in Vermont Walt told his fiancee, Eda Dindo, that he'd decided to give up baseball. She insisted that he give it one more chance. That winter Milwaukee sold his contract to the Boston Braves. In mid-February 1947, six weeks after their wedding, Walt and Eda took the train from Boston to Fort Lauderdale for spring training. The only other player on board was a second-year pitcher named Warren Spahn, who at that point had just eight major league wins under his belt. Spahn, of course, went on to 355 additional victories to become the winningest southpaw in history. Walt and Warren became close friends and ended up rooming together on road trips.

Once in camp, Walt made an immediate impression by socking a home run in batting practice against Mort Cooper. He also pitched well during the exhibition season, and after his third outing word reached the *Barre Times*: "Boston sports writers were loud in their praise of the pitching performance given by Walter Lanfranconi of Barre in the [three] hitless innings he pitched against the Philadelphia Athletics on Monday." Gene Mack, cartoonist and writer for the *Boston Globe*, featured a caricature history of Lanfranconi's progress in baseball from his start upward with Toronto to his present hopes with Boston.

When the Braves broke camp in early April, Walt was with them as they barnstormed north. Any doubt that he'd make the team was erased after his memorable de-

Walt made his major league debut with the Chicago Cubs on September 12, 1941. [Lanfranconi Family Archives]

but in Boston. Before re-locating to Milwaukee in 1953, the Braves played an annual three-game series against the Red Sox just prior to opening the regular season. The winner wound up with bragging rights, no matter which team did better during the regular season. During the 1947 intercity series, Walt Lanfranconi became a household name in Boston.

On a raw Sunday afternoon, the Sox and Braves battled for four hours to a 7-7 tie in sixteen innings before 30,884 "too thrilled to be cold" customers at Fenway Park. The game featured titanic homeruns by Ted Williams and Rudy York off Spahn and a miraculous performance by a rookie pitcher. Relieving Spahn in the seventh, Lanfranconi held the Sox scoreless over the next six innings. Comments about Walt's heroics appeared in newspapers for the next week. In the *Boston Globe*, Bob Holbrook wrote:

> Walter Lanfranconi, who was in more hot water than a fish in Warm Springs, went in and pitched amazing baseball, retiring the Red Sox two innings in a row when the bases were choked and no one was out. He agreed that this was as

harrowing an experience as he ever hopes to encounter. When he returned to the bench after retiring the Sox the entire team rose and greeted him with encouragement and praise. Lanfranconi [has] clinched a position with the Braves.

The Braves opened the regular season at Ebbets Field on April 15, 1947. On that historic day, dressed in a Dodger uniform with number "42" on the back, a Georgia-born black man named Jackie Robinson made his major league debut. Playing first base, a position he wasn't accustomed to, Robinson went hitless in four at-bats, but the Dodgers triumphed 5-3, primarily through the hitting of center fielder "Pistol Pete" Reiser and the Braves' erratic defensive play. Walt made his first appearance of the season, coming in to pitch one inning of scoreless relief, allowing no hits and fanning two. He missed pitching to Robinson by one inning.

The 1947 season progressed with Walt pitching both long and short relief. Four times he was thrust into a starting role, and on the second of those occasions he was particularly successful. In the midst of a three-game losing streak, the Braves needed a starter for the second game of a July 4th doubleheader in Philadelphia. After Johnny Sain, stalwart of the Boston mound corps, won the first game, 10-3, Walt pitched a brilliant four-hitter in the nightcap, winning 7-1. It was his only complete game in the major leagues. According to Mike Gillooly of the *Boston Evening American*, Walt "had his own fielding to thank for stopping the damaging Phillies. On three occasions, he broke the backs of the Phils with lightning grabs of their smashes in a nifty exhibition of the correct way to win your own ball games."

Some major leaguers hit the ball so hard it's nearly impossible to field. Walt learned that lesson one afternoon against the St. Louis Cardinals. His first time facing Stan Musial, winner of seven N.L. batting crowns, Walt struck him out using his newly-devel-

oped change-up. Musial headed back to the dugout, bat in hand, yelling, "You better not throw that pitch to me again." A couple innings later Stan The Man returned to the plate. After fooling Musial the first time, Walt thought another change-up was in order. Musial drilled it between Walt's legs and into center field. After rounding first base, Musial cupped his hands and yelled, "You're lucky your center fielder didn't have to field three balls."

During offseasons Lanfranconi trained with this baseball carved from Vermont granite. [Stan Hamlet]

Walt Lanfranconi Day

At 7 a.m. on Sunday, September 7, 1947, a round-trip excursion train, "complete with diner and air-conditioned coaches," pulled out of Depot Square in Barre. With 200 local baseball fans aboard, the train made its way on the Central Vermont and Boston & Maine railroads to Boston's North Station. It was Walt Lanfranconi Day, and the 200 fans were headed to Braves Field in time for pregame ceremonies, joining another 300 who'd driven from Barre.

Larry Gardner and Vermont Governor Ernest Gibson were on hand to present Walt with a new, cherry red Oldsmobile convertible purchased for the occasion by hometown contributions. The Braves' opponents were the Phillies, whose shortstop, Vermont native Ralph Lapointe, also participated in the pregame festivities. After the presentation, all of the Braves relievers climbed aboard and Walt circled the field while the Braves troubadours played the popular ditty "In My Merry Oldsmobile."

The game that followed was anti-climactic. The Phillies shut out the Braves, 2-0, on a Blix Donnelly three-hitter. Walt didn't pitch. But it was an outstanding day nonetheless, and Walt sent the following letter to the *Barre Times*:

To you my friends of Barre and surrounding communities who, on September 7 at Braves Field, held a day in my honor, I wish to express my deepest appreciation.

This honor to me was more than can be expressed, for such occasions as these are held once only in a lifetime. To see such a large delegation present on "my" day was in itself a great honor indeed. Never had I imagined that such a day would ever be held for me.

I can indeed say this was without a doubt one of the finest events of my life, and one that will never be forgotten. To the person, or persons, whose idea it was to have this occasion, I wish to express my deepest thanks. Words of appreciation cannot be written. They would only be a small part of expressing the feelings which I have had since that day.

Last but not least, to each and every individual who made it possible for this day to be such a success, to all of you my friends, I can only say that this was one of the happiest days of my life.

September 7, 1947, was Walt Lanfranconi Day at Braves Field. From left to right: Vermont Governor Ernest Gibson, Lanfranconi, Larry Gardner, and Ralph Lapointe. [Lanfranconi Family Archives]

The day after the 1947 season ended, Walt and Eda Lanfranconi drove home to Barre in their new convertible. With a record of 86-68, Boston finished in third place, eight games behind the pennant-winning Dodgers and three behind second-place St. Louis. It was the Braves' second consecutive first-division finish, the first time they'd accomplished that feat since 1934. Clearly better times were just around the corner. As for Walt's personal statistics, he saw action in thirty-six games and pitched sixty-four innings. His record was 4-4 and he recorded one save. His 2.95 ERA was the lowest to that point of his professional career.

Though hardly the league's best pitcher, Walt figured he deserved a raise for 1948. The Braves owners, Perini, Rugo, and Maney (the "Three Steam Shovels" of heavy-construction fame), put forth several offers, each calling for more than the minimum salary of $5,000. Walt refused each offer. The owners responded by selling him and disgruntled shortstop Dick Culler to the Los Angeles Angels of the Pacific Coast League. The Boston media was unsympathetic to Walt's plight. One scribe wrote:

Walt Lanfranconi figured that being a big leaguer called for a bank president's pay . . . That's been the trouble with the Lanfranconis of the major leagues in this inflationary period. None of them looked at the other side of the picture: the six weeks away from snow and ice and cold at the close of winter; the three-hour working day; the travel about the country; the six-month working stint; or the hike in their speaking fees— sums for appearing at civic and sports events as "orators."

That's the reason Walt was sent down to the Pacific Coast League. That's the reason Dick Culler, always a hold-out, departed from Boston's pleasant atmosphere. They placed too high a value on their services.

The tirade concluded with a comparison to another player with Vermont ties: "It could be that Lanfranconi will be back in a year or so—just as Tony Lupien earned another try at the big top after two great seasons on the coast. But we'll bet when he does come back he'll weigh the money question much more carefully."

Alas, Lanfranconi never did return to the majors. While the Braves were winning a pennant in 1948, Walt spent the season as a reliever in the P.C.L. After languishing in the minors through the 1952 season, he returned to Barre and bought an Esso filling station on Washington Street, running it until his retirement in 1978. Eda worked part-time in Dario Giannoni's Jewelry Store and at Homer Fitts Company, a furniture store. The Lanfranconis raised two children, Stephen, born in 1948, and Carol Ann, born in 1954.

Walt's interests were typical Vermont: hunting, fishing, and golf. He was a member of the Barre Country Club, the Mutuo Soccorso, the American Legion, and St. Monica Church. Walt was seventy when he died of a heart attack on August 18, 1986.

STAN HAMLET

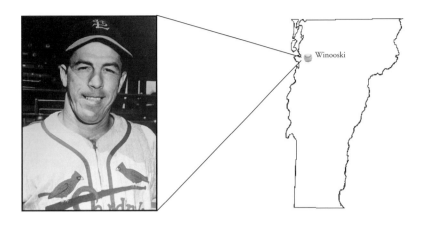

Ralph Lapointe

He Lived In Deeds, Not Years

Less than a mile from Interstate 89's Winooski exit is a shady lane called Lapointe Street. Until his untimely death of cancer at the age of forty-five, Ralph Lapointe, one of the most beloved of the Green Mountain Boys of Summer, lived in a suburban-style ranchhouse at 3 Lapointe Street. Though his major league career was unremarkable, Lapointe's achievements in coaching and civic affairs, coupled with his outgoing personality, made him a legend in his hometown. He was president of the Winooski Little League and a member of the parks commission and the committee responsible for building the current Winooski High School.

Raoul Robert Lapointe was born in Winooski on January 8, 1922. The old mill town on the banks of the Winooski River was the home of a sizable French-Canadian population, and the young Lapointe grew up speaking both French and English. He preferred the anglicized Ralph to Raoul, however, and the former name is listed on both his wedding license and passport (though army documents and his UVM diploma both use the latter name). As a kid, though, he was just as often called "Chick," and his brother George, whom longtime Winooski residents claim was an even better athlete than Ralph, was known as "Zum." Former Northern Leaguer Lennie Merullo remembers that when he and Zum played for the Burlington Cardinals in 1937, Ralph Lapointe served as the team's batboy.

A speedy infielder whose best position was shortstop, Ralph starred in baseball, football, and basketball at Winooski High School and Vermont Junior College. After playing baseball during the summer of 1941 for the St. Johnsbury Senators of the Twin-State League, Lapointe enrolled at the University of Vermont that fall and played halfback on UVM's freshman football team. That year he also played freshman basketball and baseball, batting third in the order and covering shortstop.

Ralph and Zum Lapointe spent the summer of 1942 playing for the South Portland Shipbuilding Corporation in the Western Maine League. Returning to campus in the fall, Ralph enjoyed one of the greatest seasons in UVM football history. With the "Gold Dust Twins," Lapointe and Norm Beaulieu, in the backfield, Vermont went 4-3 and Lapointe scored sixty-seven of the team's 127 points, setting a new school record for scoring and finishing third in the East in that category. After receiving honorable mention on the *Boston Post* and Associated Press Little All-America teams, Ralph capped off a memorable fall by marrying Cathryn Maroney on Thanksgiving Day. Backfield-mate Beaulieu served as best man.

Lapointe used his extraordinary athleticism to make UVM's varsity basketball team as a sophomore. Ironically, he never got a chance to play varsity baseball for Vermont. With the outbreak of World War II, the army inducted fifty-five UVM students who were members of the enlisted reserve corps. One of them was Lapointe, who was ordered to report to Fort Devens on February 19, 1943. After basic training, PFC Raoul Lapointe was

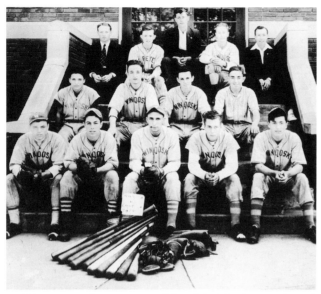

Ralph Lapointe (front row, second from left) helped Winooski High School post an 8-4 record in 1938. [Lapointe Family Archives]

average for the year to .308, good enough for a berth on *The Sporting News* Rookie All-Star Team. Lapointe shared that honor with future Hall-of-Famers Jackie Robinson and Yogi Berra, and two ex-Northern Leaguers—Sam Mele, a former Burlington Cardinal, and Bill McCahan, formerly of the Bennington Generals. The future looked promising for the twenty-six-year-old Lapointe, but in spring training 1948 Philadelphia acquired slick-fielding shortstop Eddie Miller from the Cincinnati Reds. With Lapointe suddenly expendable, the Phillies sent him and $20,000 to the St. Louis Cardinals on April 7, 1948, for first baseman Dick Sisler.

The move from the cellar-dwelling Phillies to the perenially-contending Cards was far less appealing than it sounded. Ralph found himself trapped behind All-Star shortstop Marty Marion and Hall-of-Fame second baseman Red Schoendienst. Relegated to a utility role, Lapointe appeared in eighty-seven games in 1948 and batted just .225. In 1949 the Cardinals sent him to Rochester of the International League, where he moved to third base and batted .273 as the Red Wings' leadoff hitter. Just before the 1950 season Lapointe was sold to

sent to Haverford College in Pennsylvania for specialized training as a linguist. For the next three years he served in that capacity, also playing baseball and basketball under the alias "Joe Moss" while at Camp Ritchie, Maryland. Meanwhile Beaulieu was shot down over Belgium and spent the rest of the war in a German POW camp. He managed to survive the ordeal but lost touch with Lapointe over the ensuing years.

On February 23, 1946, the day of his discharge from the army, Ralph Lapointe signed a contract to play professional baseball with the Philadelphia Phillies. He chose the Phillies over the Boston Braves, Detroit Tigers, and the San Francisco 49ers of the All-America Football Conference. The Phillies sent Lapointe to Wilmington of the Interstate League, where he batted .320, helping the Blue Rocks to a first-place finish and earning a spot as a first-team All-Star.

After spending the offseason taking classes at UVM and serving as an assistant to football coach Fuzzy Evans, Ralph impressed Philadelphia manager Ben Chapman with his hustling, hard-nosed style of play. Lapointe made the Phillies out of spring training in 1947 and began the season as the starting shortstop. But he got off to a slow start and on May 14 was demoted to the International League's Baltimore Orioles, for whom he hit a home run in his first at-bat. In another game he committed six errors (believed to be a league record) before homering with two outs in the ninth inning to give Baltimore a 6-5 victory over Rochester.

On August 12 Lapointe was recalled to Philadelphia. He hit .340 for the remainder of the season, raising his

Lapointe started the 1947 season as Philadelphia's regular shortstop. [Lapointe Family Archives]

In Montreal on June 22, 1947, 150 Vermonters attended Ralph Lapointe Day, presenting the Baltimore shortstop with a watch and money. Ralph received a big hand from the Montreal fans when he accepted the gifts in French. [Lapointe Family Archives]

the Toronto Maple Leafs, a Phillies farm club. After finishing out the 1951 season with the Tulsa Oilers, Lapointe retired from professional baseball.

For many ballplayers forced to give up early on once-bright major league aspirations, life is all downhill. Not so for Lapointe. His best years lay ahead, as his native Vermont proved the perfect place for his talents to blossom. On December 15, 1951, UVM athletic director Larry Gardner selected Lapointe as his successor as baseball coach. Gardner's decision proved to be one of his most inspired. Lapointe's enthusiasm, competitiveness, and ability to inspire others made him one of the top college coaches in the country.

Lapointe was an immediate success. His first squad enjoyed Vermont's best season in eleven years, and in 1953 he guided the Catamounts to their first state championship since World War II. The 1953 state title was the first of eleven consecutive Vermont championships Lapointe brought to UVM. In 1955 the Cats went 13-10, their

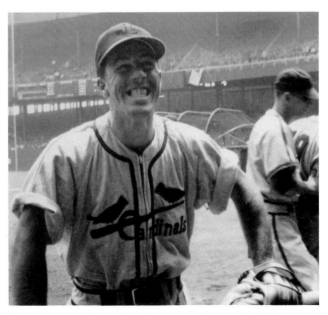

Lapointe mugs for a friend's camera during the 1948 season. [Lapointe Family Archives]

Lapointe's combativeness made him popular with teammates and fans. [Lapointe Family Archives]

league as a whole was not as healthy and disbanded just days before the 1956 season opener. Ralph Lapointe's career as a player was over.

As Burlington was losing its minor league team, the local college squad was enjoying its most successful season in decades. Lapointe's Catamounts were a New England powerhouse in 1956, posting an 18-6 record that was the best in the region. UVM came into the regular season finale at Centennial Field needing a win against Boston University to secure the school's first-ever berth in the NCAA District I Playoffs. Behind spectacular pitching from Jack Lamabe, a hard-throwing sophomore who went on to a seven-year career in the majors, UVM battled B.U. to a 1-1 tie through eight innings, only to lose, 2-1, on a broken-bat single in the ninth.

That memorable contest would have been the end of UVM's season, but the Catamounts received a second chance when Colby College withdrew from the District tournament due to conflicts with final exams (a decision that ignited violent protests on the Colby campus). Determined to make the most of the opportunity, the Catamounts easily disposed of UMass, 8-1, to advance to the title game. Just one win away from the College World Series, Vermont

most wins to that point under Lapointe and their winningest season in eighteen years. Vermont fans looked forward to even greater success in 1956, but before that happened, they were finally treated to a chance to see Ralph Lapointe play baseball.

Burlington's new professional team, the Athletics of Quebec's Class-C Provincial League, was the city's first entry into the organized minor leagues since 1907. The A's started their debut season poorly and spent most of the spring in the second division, but a series of personnel changes strengthened the team considerably. The most popular move was the June signing of Lapointe, who joined the A's after UVM's season ended. Ralph provided consistent play at third base and strong leadership in the clubhouse and dugout.

Burlington finished the season one game over .500, barely earning a spot in the Provincial League playoffs. After shocking the first-place St. John Cardinals in the first round of the playoffs, the A's lost the championship to the Quebec Braves, four games to one. Burlington also finished second to Quebec in attendance, but the

Larry Gardner (left) and Ralph Lapointe (right) present the first annual Larry Gardner Award to Bobby Cronin, UVM's most valuable player in 1965. [Gardner Family Archives]

Kit and Ralph Lapointe accept an award from friend Baxter Cummings at a UVM sports banquet. A portrait of Lapointe now hangs in the lobby of Patrick Gymnasium. [Lapointe Family Archives]

suffered a heartbreaking season closer, losing a rain-shortened, five-inning contest to New Hampshire, 2-0.

Ralph Lapointe led the Catamounts for eleven more wonderful seasons. His 1962 squad won twenty-one games and earned Ralph another trip to the NCAA District Play-offs, where Vermont again finished a disappointing second. In 1967, his final year at the helm, the Vermont Sportscasters & Sportswriters Association awarded him an engraved silver bowl for "outstanding contribution to Vermont sports through the years," and he was named NCAA Region I College Baseball Coach of the Year. In sixteen years, his teams posted a 216-127 record, never suffered a losing season, and won thirteen state championships and two Yankee Conference crowns. Lapointe sent eight players into professional baseball. More importantly, he had a positive impact on the lives of hundreds.

After an agonizing two-year battle with cancer, Ralph Lapointe died on September 13, 1967. "Ralph loved people and people loved him," the *Burlington Free Press* editorialized the next day. "There was nothing false about him at all. Everything was straight, honest, and sincere."

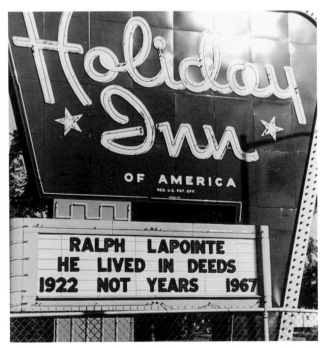

Lapointe was revered in the Burlington area. [Lapointe Family Archives]

Two months after Lapointe's untimely death, Centennial Field's clubhouse and locker-room facilities were dedicated to the memory of the beloved Vermont coach.

DOMINICK DENARO

The Ralph Lapointe Field House

The years following Ralph Lapointe's death were lean ones at Centennial Field. Faced with serious budgetary problems, UVM discontinued its varsity baseball program after the 1971 season, ending an eighty-four-year association with the sport and leaving the sixty-six-year-old ballpark without its home team. The field rapidly fell into disrepair, and the Ralph Lapointe Field House was taken over by the school's plumbing department.

Baseball returned as a club sport in 1976 and was reinstated to varsity status two years later, but the plumbing department maintained control over the facility.

Over the years, the exterior sign identifying the building as the Ralph Lapointe Field House was removed, and the bronze plaque honoring Ralph's accomplishments was covered with a punch clock and time cards. Nearly a decade passed without anything done to return the building to its original purpose.

In 1987 Ralph's wife, Kit, enlisted the aid of one of his former players, Martin Johnson, to have the Field House restored to its proper place of honor. A massive letter-writing campaign followed, and the university was inundated with emotional demands that Ralph's memory be properly observed. UVM responded fittingly, and the Lapointe Field House was re-dedicated on June 4, 1988. It stands today as a proud tribute not only to the man whose name it bears, but also to the loyal ballplayers who insisted that his memory never be forgotten.

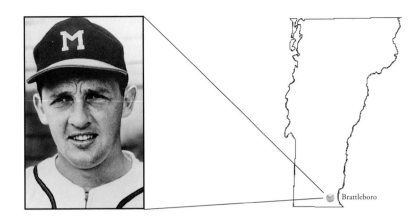

Ernie Johnson

From Brattleboro to Broadcasting

A right-handed relief pitcher whose major league career spanned the entire decade of the 1950s, Ernie Johnson retired with a lifetime record of 40-23 and an ERA of 3.77 in 273 games. "Maybe not the stuff of Cooperstown," said Hall-of-Famer Eddie Mathews, a former teammate, "but damn it, the man could pitch." Johnson's even greater claim to fame, however, came as a television broadcaster for the Atlanta Braves.

The youngest of three children, Ernest Thorwald Johnson was born in Brattleboro on June 16, 1924. His father, Thorwald, and his mother, Alina "Inkie" Ingeborg, had emigrated from Sweden in the early 1900s. They were lured to Brattleboro by the Estey Organ Company, a world-famous manufacturer of pipe organs. With many Swedes among its 500 employees, Estey was one of the biggest employers in Vermont around the turn of the century, and the neighborhood where Ernie Johnson grew up, just up the bank from the Estey factory, was known as Esteyville. Ernie's father worked at Estey for forty-five years, and also delivered newspapers on Sundays during the Great Depression.

Ernie recalls that he sometimes went along on those delivery runs "just to be with my father and read the sports page." The children of Esteyville were crazy for sports, and Ernie's first paying job was caddying at the local golf course. "A caddie received thirty-five cents for nine holes and sixty cents for eighteen," Johnson remembers. He occasionally played a round when he was not caddying, but for the most part his free time was spent in neighborhood games of baseball, football, or basketball, depending on the season. "We played pick-up baseball games over on the hospital grounds and neighborhood teams at Oak Grove School," Johnson remembers. "We also played baseball and basketball teams at Austine School for the Deaf. I became friends with several of the deaf students."

Growing up in Vermont, Ernie never played Little League baseball. In fact, the Little League field in Brattleboro wasn't built until 1952, ten years after he'd made his professional debut. Ernie's first taste of organized sports came in high school. He always had above-average size and was a good all-around athlete, but most felt that his best sport was basketball. His father installed a hoop outside their house on Pleasant Street, and Johnson recalls that he and his friends played even in the snow. Even after he chose baseball as his profession, Ernie stayed in shape during winters by playing semipro basketball in Vermont and professional basketball in Connecticut.

According to most accounts, Johnson was merely an average baseball player until 1942, his senior year at Brattleboro High School. He actually lost his first game that season, 8-1 to a strong team from Greenfield, Massachusetts, but only one of the runs was earned. Ernie bounced back with a win in his next start, taking a shutout two outs into the ninth inning before yielding a two-run homer.

Ernie Johnson's next three games comprise one of the most unusual pitching streaks in the history of Vermont high school baseball. On May 8 he pitched a one-hit shut-

151

out against Springfield. In his next game, against Bellows Falls on May 13, he pitched another one-hitter, this time taking a no-hitter into the ninth inning before giving up a single. Then on May 20 he took another no-hitter into the ninth inning in a game against Deerfield, Massachusetts. Again his no-hit bid was spoiled, this time by a pair of hits with one out, but he struck out twenty in what was probably the best game of his high school career.

For the 1942 season, Johnson pitched all but two of Brattleboro's games, averaging twelve strikeouts, compiling a 6-3 record, a 1.09 ERA, a .409 batting average, and leading the team with thirteen RBIs. At the time, though, almost nobody thought he was a potential major leaguer. When asked about it years later, one of his teammates replied, "It never entered my mind or any of our other teammates' minds. Baseball players from Brattleboro, Vermont, just don't make it to the major leagues."

One man thought differently. Ray Draghetti, Johnson's coach at Brattleboro High School, believed

his 6' 4", 180-lb. pitcher had the size and talent to make the majors. Following Johnson's graduation, Draghetti took him to Boston for a couple of tryouts, as described in Bob Dubuque's article in the June 19, 1942, edition of the *Brattleboro Reformer*:

We haven't been asleep, but just careful in not reporting that Ernie Johnson was down in Boston for a few days trying out with the Red Sox. It got pretty well noised around, but we wanted to wait until the kid got home again to find out what the story was.

Ray Draghetti, who took Ernie to Boston yesterday to work out with the Braves, said the Sox were interested in the Brattleboro High School star and let him read the fine print on a contract, which he did not sign. The Sox wanted Ernie to stay home and put on some beef this summer and go south with them on a farm team in the winter. However, it would appear to be a summer wasted here since there is little prospect of semi-pro ball. That's the story to date.

Johnson (front row, center) was a star pitcher for Brattleboro High School in 1942. [Dana Sprague]

One week after the tryouts, Casey Stengel's Boston Braves gave Ernie the choice of traveling with the big league club and throwing batting practice or signing a contract and reporting directly to the minors. He chose the former, and within ten days he was 100 miles from home, pitching batting practice to a team that included future Hall-of-Famers Paul Waner and Ernie Lombardi. After nearly three weeks of traveling with the Braves, Ernie signed a minor league contract and was sent to Hartford of the Eastern League, for whom he made his professional debut on August 9, 1942. He pitched in only eight games that summer, posting a 2-2 record and a 2.84 ERA, but one game stands out in his memory: "My mom was a homemaker, a great mom. She went to Hartford once to watch me pitch and I gave up a three-run homer. The fans started booing. She turned to some of them and proudly said, 'That's my boy.' They slumped down in their seats quietly."

That, of course, was the era of World War II, and Ernie was drafted into the United States Marine Corps before the 1943 season. He participated in the Okinawa invasion and was discharged as a staff sergeant in February 1946. Ernie then returned to Brattleboro. While attending a high school basketball game that winter he first noticed Lois Denhard, a cheerleader whom he married one year later. "When we first met, she asked me what I did. I said, 'Play baseball,' and she said, 'No, really, what do you do for a living?' After she saw my first minor league check, she asked again."

The next several years were like a rollercoaster ride for the Johnsons. After only one inning of work with Hartford in 1946, Ernie was demoted to Pawtucket of the New England League. Though he pitched adequately, as attested by his 3.95 ERA, Johnson was 4-7, one of only two losing records in his fourteen years as a professional pitcher. He returned to Hartford and posted winning records in 1947 and 1948, and in 1949 he earned a promotion to the Braves' Triple-A affiliate, the Milwaukee Brewers of the American Association. After only eleven innings, however, the Braves demoted him to Class-A Denver. Undaunted, Johnson became one of the best pitchers in the Western League, and his 15-5 record and 2.37 ERA earned him a place on the all-star team.

The Boston Braves invited Ernie Johnson to spring training as a non-roster player in 1950. After he gave up a home run to Ted Williams in an exhibition game, Johnson remembers manager Billy Southworth saying, "Don't worry, kid, he's hit 'em off better pitchers than you." The resilient Vermonter surprised everyone by breaking camp with the big league club. For the first time he was earning what he describes as "real money"—$5,000 a year. Johnson made his major league debut in Philadelphia on April 28,

1950. Though he pitched in only sixteen games, he managed to hang on with the Braves for most of the season. Johnson was 2-0, but his 6.97 ERA accounts for his late-season demotion to Hartford.

The Braves sent Johnson to the minors again in 1951, this time to Milwaukee, but he refused to become discouraged. He went 15-4, led the American Association in ERA (2.62) and winning percentage (.789), and pitched the Brewers to the Governors' Cup and a Junior World Series victory over the Montreal Royals. Including his five post-season victories, Ernie Johnson was a twenty-game winner in 1951. He started the 1952 season with Boston, and this time he was in the majors to stay. Bothered by a sore arm, Ernie pitched mostly in relief and went 6-3 for the Braves. He also received ten starting assignments and pitched a shutout in one of them—one of only three complete games he pitched in the major leagues.

Before the 1953 season, the Braves left Boston, where they were always less popular than the Red Sox, and headed west for Milwaukee, where Ernie had played minor league ball just two years earlier. It was the first change of cities for a major league franchise in a half-century, and the Braves' success guaranteed that it wouldn't be the last. From 1953 to 1957, in the major league city with the smallest population, the Braves averaged 2.1 million in attendance, almost doubling their nearest competitor.

Happy Days in Milwaukee
Ernie Johnson remembers the euphoria of those early years in Milwaukee:

I have been in baseball for more than three decades, and I have never seen anything remotely close to Milwaukee in the '50s. They were wild, incredible years. Nobody cared in Boston whether we lived or died. Then, in Milwaukee, the town went bananas. We couldn't buy a thing—fans would give us everything free. The players were treated like royalty. Every day was a feast.

The news of the shift had come in spring training down in Bradenton. When we went north to Milwaukee, they had a huge parade and we went downtown. When we got there, I'll never forget how the people put up a Christmas tree—in April—inside the Schroeder Hotel. They were so beautiful. They said that since we'd missed Christmas with them, they wanted to celebrate it with us now. So there were hundreds of presents under the tree—shaving kits, toiletries, radios, appliances. Just ga-ga from the first day.

It was like a small town. Some of us lived five minutes from the park. In those first few years we'd go around town, and even when we tried, we couldn't pay for what we bought—the sponsors wouldn't let us.

Ernie got off to a poor start to the 1953 season—so poor, in fact, that he thought he might be headed back to the minors. But things turned around, and in one stretch of seven days he received credit for three victories. Johnson became a mainstay in the bullpen of a great Milwaukee pitching staff. His thirty-five relief appearances led the team, and his 2.67 ERA was second on the staff to Warren Spahn's league-leading 2.10. Ernie followed up that performance in 1954 by posting a 2.81 ERA in forty games, establishing himself as one of the premier relief pitchers in baseball.

Towards the end of the 1954 season the citizens of Brattleboro planned a special day in Ernie's honor. In the sports pages of the *Reformer*, Vic Harrison wrote the following under the title "Toast for a Great Guy":

> Figuratively speaking, Brattleboro will raise its glass high sometime the first part of next month to toast one of its sons who left town eight years ago to follow his chosen profession of baseball and has become Vermont's only major leaguer.
>
> Ernie Johnson's popularity, and the high esteem in which his townspeople hold him, was never more evident than at the kickoff meeting Tuesday night. It seemed to this scribe

as though everybody wanted to do everything to make the day not only a success, but one that will stand out as a time when the whole town cooperated to make it absolutely "the most." And since then the willing and hard-working co-chairmen, Charlie LaRosa and Bob Manning, tell us that they are having no trouble getting all the help they need. People are flocking to them in droves—all wanting to do something for Ernie.

> Thus a spark that a gangly Brattleboro kid lit years ago, when he was not only a potentially great athlete, but a darn nice youngster to boot, has turned into a brightly burning flame for one of the finest gentlemen and sportsmen that we'll ever have the pleasure to know.

> And just as though Charlie Grimm knew something was in the wind, he ups and starts Ernie against the Redlegs the day after we had our meeting. And Ernie came through in fine style, winning his sixth [editor's note: actually his fifth] game.

Though the New York Yankees were the dominant team of the '50s, the Milwaukee Braves, with players like Mathews, Spahn, and Henry Aaron, more than held their own. The Braves won the National League pen-

Returning to Brattleboro for a special "Welcome Home Dinner" after the 1957 World Series, Ernie was billed as "Brattleboro's Own World Series Hero." [Ernie Johnson]

nant in 1957 and met the Yankees in the World Series. Ernie Johnson remembers the thrill of pitching in Yankee Stadium: "I remember walking to the mound and all I could think of was, 'Son, you have made it. You have finally made it.' God, I was so happy. I was walking with the ghosts of Ruth and Gehrig—me, just a kid who had lived and died baseball all his life."

The Braves won the 1957 World Series in seven games, and Ernie played a major role. Pitching in three games, he gave up only two hits and one run in seven innings, striking out eight and walking only one. The run he gave up was a homer off the foul pole by Hank Bauer that proved to be the winning run in Game Six, but when asked if he thought it was a cheap shot, Johnson replied with characteristic modesty: "There was nothing cheap about that home run. He hit it so hard it may have bent the pole."

The 1958 season was Ernie's last as a player in Milwaukee. Pitching in only fifteen games, he once again had a winning record (3-1), but his ERA ballooned to 8.10. Before the season was over, the Braves, who were on their way to another World Series match-up against the Yankees, placed the thirty-three-year-old Johnson on waivers. He remembered it distinctly:

When the Braves got waivers on me in August, I guess the race was pretty well settled and nobody wanted to pay the $20,000 to claim me along with the salary. Then the Braves were very decent with me and let it be known that I could make my deal or stay with their chain, as I pleased. I know there were stories that I tried to land with the Giants and other National League clubs, but that isn't so. The first man to call me when I was free was Richards and I didn't look further.

The Richards to whom Ernie referred was Paul Richards, manager of the Baltimore Orioles. Johnson spent his final year in the majors with Baltimore in 1959. He pitched respectably, compiling a 4-1 record and a 4.11 ERA, but the Orioles released him at the end of the season. He signed on with the Cleveland Indians, but arm troubles plagued him in the spring. "They offered to send me to the minors to work things out, but I knew it was time to call it quits," Johnson said.

Ernie returned to Milwaukee to host a television show called "Play Ball," in which he and a guest sat around talking baseball and drinking milk. He also handled the commentary on twenty Braves telecasts and did some speaking on the banquet circuit, but his main job was selling life insurance for Northwestern Mutual. "I thought I'd be selling insurance the rest of my life," he recalled. But in 1962 the Braves hired him as administrative assistant to President John McHale. "Being in the front office had always been my ambition," Ernie

Johnson's fifty-two-year association with the Braves is the longest of any person in the organization. [Ernie Johnson]

said. "From the time I broke into baseball, that was what I wanted to do rather than managing or coaching."

Ernie's job eventually evolved into that of a full-time broadcaster, and he's been announcing Braves games ever since. He moved with the club to Atlanta in 1965 and was named Georgia Broadcaster of the Year in 1977, 1983, and 1986. He also received three television Emmys. Ernie retired as a full-time announcer at the end of the 1989 season.

His popularity with Braves fans was never more evident than on September 2, 1989, when the Braves honored him on "Ernie Johnson Day." The attendance exceeded 42,000, making it the largest crowd for a Braves home game that season. During the pre-game ceremony, Johnson received a forty-eight-inch television set from his fellow broadcasters, a satellite dish and annual use of a condominium in Florida from TBS, and an automobile from the Braves. He also received proclamations from the Brattleboro selectmen and the governors of Vermont and Georgia. "It was fabulous," Ernie said. "We are still in a state of shock. It was the

Ted Turner and Jimmy Carter were present to honor Brattleboro's only big leaguer on Ernie Johnson Day, September 2, 1989, at Atlanta's Municipal Stadium. [Ernie Johnson]

greatest day I have ever had, and it is something Lois and the whole family will never forget."

Ernie is retired now, living in Alpharetta, Georgia, and spending lots of time with his wife, three children (daughters Dawn and Chris are teachers, and Ernie Jr., following in his father's footsteps, is a sportscaster for TBS), and five grandchildren. Until recently he called approximately thirty games per year on Sports South Network and substituted occasionally on TBS. In more than three decades of broadcasting, Johnson worked more than 4,100 games, and through it all maintained his grace and gentle humor. For all of the home runs hit by Hank Aaron and knuckle balls thrown by Phil Niekro, nobody has spread more goodwill for "America's Team" than Ernie Johnson.

"I love baseball," Ernie says, "and I think it shows."

DANA SPRAGUE

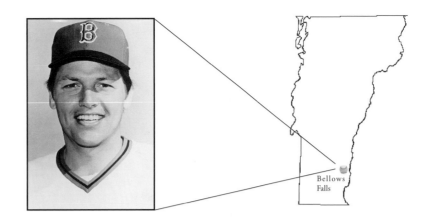

Bellows
Falls

Carlton Fisk

From Charlestown to Cooperstown

Born in Bellows Falls, Vermont, on December 26, 1947, Carlton Fisk embodies traditional New England values like pride, ruggedness, and individuality. That was what Boston Red Sox public relations director Dick Bresciani was trying to capture in 1997 when he wrote that Fisk was a "native of Vermont" on his original plaque for the Red Sox Hall of Fame.

Ironically, the greatest baseball player ever born in Vermont—and the man responsible for perhaps the most dramatic moment in New England sports history—doesn't consider himself a Vermonter. Fisk grew up on the other side of the Connecticut River in Charlestown, New Hampshire, a town of less than 1,000 inhabitants—it just so happened that Bellows Falls had the nearest hospital. So in a display of traditional New England stubbornness, Fisk insisted that his plaque be re-cast (at a cost of $3,000 to the Red Sox) to delete the Vermont reference and reflect that he was raised in New Hampshire.

Fisk did play American Legion baseball in Vermont for Post Five in the town of his birth, and for years a simple white sign with an "X" marked the spot at the Bellows Falls field where one of his blasts landed. In fact, in his first at bat for Bellows Falls back in 1965, Fisk crushed a home run at Cooperstown's famous Doubleday Field, on the site where baseball was supposedly invented. In storybook fashion, he'll return to Cooperstown on July 23, 2000, for his induction into the National Baseball Hall of Fame.

Carlton Ernest Fisk inherited his extraordinary work ethic and athletic talent from his parents. His father, Cecil,

worked for years as an engineer in the tool-and-dye industry in Springfield, Vermont. A job like that would be enough for most people, but Cecil also worked the Fisk family farm. Often he dismounted from the tractor, raced to a local tennis match, soundly defeated his opponent, then returned to the farm to resume his chores. In addition to tennis, Cecil also was a superb basketball player. Carlton's mother, Leona, was famous in her own right as a champion candlepin bowler. Certainly the gene for coordination ran deep in the Fisk family.

The Fisks of Charlestown established an athletic dynasty. Carlton's older brother, Calvin, his younger brothers, Conrad and Cedric, and his sisters, Janet and June, all exhibited unusual athletic prowess. In fact, the son who is destined for the Hall of Fame was not considered the most talented of the progeny. Carlton was chubby as a youngster, which is how and when he acquired his well-known nickname, Pudge. "If you saw him as an eighth grader, you would not believe he could accomplish the things he has," said Ralph Silva, his high-school coach. But Carlton was strong, and Coach Silva honed that strength by implementing weight training long before it became commonplace.

Beginning in 1962, when Calvin and Carlton first attended Charlestown High School together, and continuing through 1972, when June graduated from the newly regionalized Fall Mountain School District, the Fisks could be counted on to appear in post-season playoffs. Along with Calvin, Conrad, and Cedric, Carlton

Cecil Fisk's only comment was that Carlton had missed four free throws.

Cecil wasn't being harsh or overbearing—he simply understood that to excel as an athlete, mental toughness was essential. Cecil's philosophy on child-rearing was simple: "I expected them to do as well as they could, whatever they did." Cecil and Leona Fisk sat behind the bench during basketball games but never said a word to Coach Silva, criticized his strategy, nor let on if they disagreed with how their sons were handled. "No Hall of Famer ever had a better start than Fisk," said Bellows Falls American Legion coach Tim Ryan, "and it was because of his parents."

Because of the northern New England weather, Carlton Fisk's high-school baseball career consisted of no more than sixteen games a season. Before early-season practice, he and his teammates often had to shovel off the Charlestown High School baseball field, which was shaded from direct sunlight. Sometimes the

Carlton's chubby physique as a child earned him the nickname "Pudge." [Fisk Family Archives]

formed the nucleus of a dominant Charlestown presence in basketball, baseball, and soccer. Early on, though, Pudge's greatest accomplishments came on the hardwood. "Fisk could have made it in basketball," said Coach Silva. "He was that tough."

After developing his hoop talent in his grandfather's barn, Carlton went on to some legendary high school performances. In a 1963 regional playoff game at the Boston Garden, for example, he made such an impression in a victory over Winooski, Vermont (led by Ralph Lapointe's son, Dave), that Walter Brown, owner of the Celtics, leaned over to a local reporter and said, "You have got to tell me—who is that kid?" That same year, playing against Hopkinton in the New Hampshire Class-M semifinals, the 6' 2" Fisk scored forty points and yanked down thirty-nine rebounds—even though the opposition included players who were 6' 10", 6' 8", and 6' 3". When he fouled out with a minute left, Fisk received a standing ovation from the Portsmouth crowd. Charlestown lost by two points, and an oft-told story is that after his son's memorable performance,

Fisk starred in soccer and basketball as well as baseball at Charlestown High School. [Fisk Family Archives]

team simply practiced in the nearby Fisk cornfield. "I'd let them practice for as long as they wanted, long after we would have otherwise gone home," said Coach Silva. "Of course, they don't do that anymore."

Carlton demanded that practice be taken seriously—on one occasion he punched out a teammate for goofing off. The competitive nature of those practices resulted in Carlton's first experience as a catcher. During batting practice, with Carlton manning third base and Calvin behind the plate, a foul pop drew both of their attention. With the entire team yelling "Fisk!" both attempted to make the catch, and the resulting collision made Calvin look like a hockey player (only one of the two teeth retrieved could be saved). Because the catcher's mask no longer fit over his swollen jaw, catching responsibilities fell to Carlton. (In typical Fisk fashion, Calvin played the next day, only in left field.)

Calvin, Carlton, and Conrad all pitched for the Charlestown team, which went 49-3 during Carlton's high-school career. One of those losses came in the Class-M state championship against a strong team from Woodsville. Despite striking out fourteen, Carlton was a victim of his own aggressiveness. With one out and the winning run on third, the Woodsville batter laid down a perfect squeeze bunt that hugged the third-base line. Not hearing his teammates' cries of "Let it go foul!" Carlton leaped off the mound, picked up the ball, and threw across his body, making an amazing play to nail the batter at first as the winning run scored.

Because of the short high-school season, American Legion baseball takes on special importance in New England. Carlton played for Claremont in his first year of eligibility, but in 1965 he switched to Bellows Falls Post Five, which had won the Vermont State Championship the previous year. The switch was a positive one for Fisk—Bellows Falls was closer than Claremont and more of a sports town. In one game, so the story goes, Carlton was at the plate and behind in the count, fooled by two consecutive curveballs. When the catcher called for a fastball and was emphatically shaken off by the pitcher, the manager called time and approached the mound. "There's no way I'm throwing him a fastball," the hurler said. But the manager insisted that he throw what the catcher called, and Fisk hit the next pitch (a fastball) on a line over the center-field fence.

Though he played in less than 100 games as an amateur, Fisk gained the attention of professional scouts. One thought he had potential but told Coach Ryan that his bat wasn't quick enough—his power was mostly to right field. Ryan's response was typically self-effacing: "He'll get better coaches in the minors who can teach him to hit to left." But despite his success in baseball

(or, more accurately, his all-around athletic success, as he was named Charlestown High's most valuable player in soccer and basketball as well), Carlton accepted a basketball scholarship to the University of New Hampshire.

The decision to attend UNH was made easier by the presence in Durham of his older brother, Calvin, who was captain of the soccer team and an All-Yankee Conference sweeper. But soon Calvin was drafted by both the Baltimore Orioles and the military. He was twenty-five by the time he returned from Vietnam, too old (according to the Baltimore front office) to embark on a career in professional baseball. Carlton's younger brother Conrad, considered the best pitcher of the Fisk clan, later signed with the Montreal Expos. He was undefeated and threw a no-hitter in the playoffs during his senior year of high school, but an arm injury ended his career prematurely. Cedric, whose scholastic batting average was higher than that of any of his older brothers, didn't pursue athletics beyond high school.

During the winter of 1965-66, Carlton led the UNH freshman basketball team to an undefeated season. While at UNH he also met his future wife, Linda Foust, a na-

Fisk struggled through his first experience as a member of a losing team in Waterloo, Iowa, during his first year of pro ball. [Fisk Family Archives]

Carlton Fisk and Larry Gardner, the two greatest baseball players ever born in Vermont, break bread together at a 1972 hotstove banquet at the Ethan Allen Club in Burlington. [Gardner Family Archives]

tive of Manchester, New Hampshire. Then, in January 1966, the Boston Red Sox drafted him in the first round. Fisk was at first suspicious, suspecting that he was the token New Englander the Red Sox had taken to pacify local fans. He ended up signing mainly because he realized "I could never be a six-foot-two power forward and play for the Celtics."

Carlton Fisk's baseball career almost came to an end at Waterloo, Iowa, Boston's entry-level team in the Class-A Midwest League. Despite batting .338 with twelve home runs in sixty-two games, he was despondent. Pudge's letters home show that the source of most of his frustration was the team's losing record. The Waterloo Hawks finished 56-68, 26.5 games behind the league-leading Cedar Rapids Cardinals. Losing was new and intolerable to Fisk.

But he persisted and in September 1969 the Red Sox called him up from Double-A Pittsfield. The twenty-one-year-old Fisk made his major league debut in the first game of a doubleheader against the Baltimore Orioles on September 18. His cup of coffee turned bitter—

in two games he went 0-for-5 with two strikeouts—and Bill Liston wrote in the *Herald-Traveler*, "The word on Fisk is that he needs a year of Triple A ball, especially to enable him to handle breaking pitches with the bat."

That year of Triple-A ball became one year with Double-A Pawtucket in 1970 and another with Triple-A Louisville in 1971, but Fisk remained upbeat and continued to improve. At Louisville his manager was Darrell Johnson, whom he credited for making him a major leaguer. "Johnson taught me to think about all the important facets of the catcher's role, the things that help pitchers in various ways and those that let your teammates know you want to win," he told an interviewer in 1973. Johnson also helped Fisk improve his hitting. "When I put the equipment on, my job is defense: to get the other team out, help the pitchers get the batters, help the fielders—to run the game," Fisk said. "Once I take the equipment off, however, I stop thinking defense and start thinking offense." That new concentration resulted in a .263 average at Louisville, thirty-four points higher than his average the previous season at Pawtucket.

Despite his excellent play (.313 with two home runs) in fourteen games with Boston at the end of the 1971 season, Carlton Fisk was only the third-string catcher for the Red Sox in 1972. The starter was Duane Josephson, who'd batted .245 with ten home runs in '71 after coming to Boston in a trade with the White Sox. Bob Montgomery was the back-up. But when Josephson was injured in the second game of the season and rival baserunners were running at will on Montgomery, Fisk became a regular in Boston.

From the start, Carlton was a slugger. By June 15 the twenty-four-year-old rookie had collected thirty-two hits, twenty for extra bases. His average was .278 and his slugging percentage was .574. His confidence rose with his slugging average, which stood at .628 by July 12. He was beginning to attract attention. "Fisk is rapidly gain-ing the reputation of being the Johnny Bench of the American League," wrote one sportswriter. In July Earl Weaver selected him to represent the A.L. in the All-Star Game in Atlanta. Fisk replaced Bill Freehan in the sixth inning and suddenly found himself playing against Hank Aaron and Willie Mays, whose bubble-gum cards he'd collected back in Charlestown.

For the 1972 season, Fisk caught 131 games and batted .293 with twenty-two home runs. His accomplishments earned him selection as the American League's Rookie of the Year, the first player ever to receive the honor by unanimous vote. He also won the Gold Glove for A.L. catchers and finished fourth in balloting for the A.L.'s Most Valuable Player. In a testament to the times, Pudge's salary reportedly rose from $18,000 to $30,000, which was considered "as big a pay raise as any player in the game."

*Though injuries slowed him several times during his career, Fisk's toughness and competitiveness showed in his defensive work. Here he defends home plate against Roy Howell of the Toronto Blue Jays. [*Toronto Star *photo, courtesy of the National Baseball Hall of Fame Library, Cooperstown, New York.]*

The Red Sox had been searching for a quality receiver ever since the Birdie Tebbetts/Sammy White era of 1948-59. In Fisk they finally had a tough, productive, intelligent, and dependable backstop. "If you play against him, you hate him," said manager Eddie Kasko, "but if you play with him and want to win, you love him. He plays as if he were on the Crusades."

The dreaded sophomore jinx caught up to Carlton Fisk in the second half of the 1973 season. Batting .303 on June 23, he hit only .228 in July, .198 in August, and .186 in September. The extended slump was nothing compared to challenges soon to come. At Municipal Stadium on June 28, 1974, the Red Sox and Indians were deadlocked at 1-1 with two outs in the bottom of the ninth inning when Cleveland's Leron Lee rounded third and crashed into the fully-extended Fisk, who was reaching for a high relay throw from shortstop Mario Guerrero. Pudge tore ligaments in his left knee. "My career was supposed to be over," he recalled. "I was supposed to walk with a limp and have chronic back problems the rest of my life."

But Fisk returned in 1975, and the long, lonely hours spent in rehabilitation made a lasting impression on him. Though for years the knee injury hampered his ability to throw out baserunners, he feels that it may have been a blessing. "In some ways, hurting my knee was one of the best things ever to happen to my off-season psyche," Fisk said while still an active player. "Now, everything I do is programmed toward getting ready to play baseball. Before, winter was just a time to have fun hacking around the basketball court." His obsession with conditioning was the secret to his twenty-two-year career in the majors. Though injuries continued to plague him—in all, he spent over five-and-one-half seasons on the disabled list—he always managed to return, allowing him to catch in 2,229 games, the most in major league history. "More than the home runs, it's the longevity that stands out as his greatest achievement," says high-school coach Silva.

After coming back from the 1974 knee surgery, Fisk was hit by a pitched ball in spring training and broke his forearm. Returning to a standing ovation on June 23, 1975, Pudge hit .331 over the remainder of the season to lead the Red Sox to the A.L. East title. Fisk batted .417 against the Oakland A's in the League Championship Series, but his greatest heroics were yet to come.

The Greatest Game Ever Played

Game Six of the 1975 World Series—a must-win game for the Boston Red Sox, down three-games-to-two to the Cincinnati Reds—was a wild, seesaw affair. The Red Sox jumped out to a 3-0 lead on Fred Lynn's three-run homer in the first inning, but the Reds came back and took a 6-3 lead into the eighth, when Bernie

Carbo's pinch-hit, three-run homer tied the game. In the ninth inning the Red Sox failed to score despite loading the bases with no outs, and the game headed into extra innings with the score knotted at six.

It was 12:33 a.m. by the time Carlton Fisk stepped to the plate to lead off the bottom half of the twelfth against Pat Darcy, the eighth Reds pitcher of the night. On Darcy's second pitch, Fisk lofted a high shot down the left-field line. Millions of television viewers watched Fisk wave wildly as he made his way down the first-base line, willing the ball to stay fair. When it glanced off the foul pole—a fair ball—John Kiley, the Fenway Park organist, launched into Handel's "Hallelujah Chorus" as the native Vermonter circled the bases in triumph. The home run touched off a celebration throughout the region—in Fisk's native Bellows Falls, church bells rang out in the early-morning stillness.

Many consider Fisk's game-winning blast the exclamation point on the greatest baseball game ever played. In Game Seven, however, current Vermont resident Bill Lee couldn't hold on to another 3-0 lead, and the Reds took the series with a 4-3 victory. The Red Sox were once again denied their first World Series championship since Green Mountain Boy of Summer Jean Dubuc pinch hit for the victorious Bosox in the 1918 fall classic.

"Hallelujah!" Fisk touches home plate after his game-winning home run in Game Six of the 1975 World Series. [National Baseball Hall of Fame Library, Cooperstown, New York]

Carlton Fisk was named to the A.L. All-Star team seven times during his nine-year tenure in Boston, but by 1980 he questioned whether the Red Sox still valued his service. [National Baseball Hall of Fame Library, Cooperstown, New York]

Following their heart-breaking loss in the 1975 World Series, the Red Sox remained competitive but repeatedly lost out to the New York Yankees or Baltimore Orioles. During one pennant race when his team was battling Boston, Baltimore manager Earl Weaver said, "The guy they'd hate to lose most, even more than [Jim] Rice, is Fisk." In determining Fisk's importance, consider that in 1980 the Sox were 68-44 when he was behind the plate, 15-33 when he wasn't. Yet after the 1980 season Fisk was questioning whether the Red Sox front office really wanted him. Contract negotiations proceeded slowly, then general manager Haywood Sullivan blundered by failing to mail Fisk's contract on time, making him a free agent.

The Red Sox offered Carlton a guaranteed $2 million plus incentives. The perenially non-contending Chicago White Sox, for whom Fisk's acquisition would create instant credibility, offered $3.5 million. Nevertheless, the decision to leave Boston was difficult. After the Red Sox traded Rick Burleson, Butch Hobson, and Fred Lynn to the California Angels that winter, however, Fisk questioned Boston's commitment to winning. Conversely, the White Sox, with new owners Eddie Einhorn and Jerry Reinsdorf, were improving. Fisk decided to sign with Chicago.

In 1983 the White Sox made their first appearance in the postseason since 1959, and many credited Fisk's work with young pitchers Steve Trout, Britt Burns, and Richard Dotson as the key. Pudge averaged 125 games for Chicago through 1985, when he hit thirty-seven home runs with 107 RBIs. But that year his honeymoon with the White Sox front office ended with a salary dispute, and subsequent re-signings in 1987, 1991, and 1993 were about as smooth as Vermont dirt roads during mud season.

At an age when most players are capable of nothing more than an occasional appearance at a fantasy camp or old-timers' game, Fisk continued his quest for personal goals. In Kansas City on August 9, 1990, he hit his 349th home run as a catcher, setting a major league record. His son Casey was there. "I had goosebumps when he hugged his boy at home plate," said White Sox manager Jeff Torborg. "That's a big emotional thing right there. It meant so much to those two and that family."

In 1993 Fisk caught his 2,226th game, surpassing Bob Boone as the all-time leader. Then, on June 21, the White Sox released him. The next day, Carlton and Linda Fisk sent a simple but heartfelt message to the Boston faithful. They hired a plane to tow a banner reading, "IT ALL

Fisk spent thirteen years in Chicago and finished his career with the White Sox, with whom he set all-time records for games caught and home runs by a catcher. [National Baseball Hall of Fame Library, Cooperstown, New York]

STARTED HERE. THANKS BOSTON FANS. PUDGE FISK." They sent a similar message across the sky over Comiskey Park.

Among the dozen Hall-of-Fame catchers for whom numbers are available (complete statistics don't exist for Negro Leaguer Josh Gibson), Carlton Fisk ranks first in total games caught, putouts, at-bats, hits, and doubles; second in total home runs and runs scored; third in RBI; and tied for fourth in fielding percentage. Fisk's stolen bases for modern Hall-of-Fame catchers are second to none. He was an eleven-time All-Star. The White Sox retired his number 72 in 1997, the same year he was elected to the Red Sox Hall of Fame. Fisk's election to the National Baseball Hall of Fame was almost a bygone conclusion, but it was made official in January 2000.

After some delay, Fisk provided the answer to a difficult question by announcing that he will wear a Red Sox cap into the Hall, even though he spent thirteen years with the White Sox and only nine full seasons with the Red Sox. "I would like to say that this has always been my favorite hat, and I will be wearing this hat probably for the rest of my career," said the man who currently works as special assistant to Red Sox general manager Dan Duquette. At that same press conference, Duquette told a surprised Fisk that the team had decided to retire his number 27. "I didn't think I met the criteria," said Fisk. "It gives me goose bumps to think about it. I didn't think it was at all possible." In the past, the Red Sox have stated that they will retire a number only for a player who is in the Hall, spent more than ten years with the team, and finished his career in Boston.

Fisk will always be remembered for his dramatic home run in the '75 Series, but the incident that best represents how he played the game came on an otherwise unmemorable night in 1989 when Deion Sanders, then a rookie with the New York Yankees, failed to run out an infield grounder. The next time "Neon Deion" came to the plate, Fisk growled, "Listen to me, you #%*^. Next time run it out."

Even though Sanders played for the opposition, and the hated Yankees at that, he'd violated the Fisk Code of Baseball Ethics. Thou shalt hustle. Thou shalt run it out. To Fisk, the proper way to play the game was always important—with passion, preparation, integrity, and respect. He acquired those values on the farm in Charlestown, and they propelled him all the way to Cooperstown.

BRIAN STEVENS

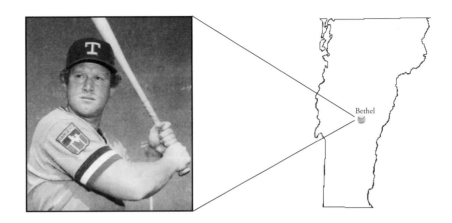

Pat Putnam

From Shelburne Little League to A.L. Rookie of the Year

From his start in the Shelburne Little League, Pat Putnam developed into a left-handed power hitter who played first base and designated hitter for eight years in the major leagues. Though he enjoyed several fine seasons in the majors, the former first-round draft choice, Minor League Player of the Year, and A.L. Rookie of the Year never quite achieved the stardom many had predicted for him. After finishing his career in baseball with two seasons in Japan, Putnam returned to Fort Myers, Florida, where he'd moved as a child.

Patrick Edward Putnam was born in Bethel, Vermont, on December 3, 1953. Though the tiny Windsor County village has a population of only 1,000, it's the birthplace of two Green Mountain Boys of Summer. Amazingly, even though their births were separated by eighty-four years, they're related. The first was Harry Burrell, who pitched for St. Louis of the American Association in 1891 (see pp. 19-20). Pat Putnam's mother's maiden name was Marguerite Burrell, and it turns out that she's a member of Harry's extended family.

Pat grew up in Shelburne, Vermont, a suburb of Burlington. His father, Robert, worked as a salesman in a Burlington hardware store and coached Pat in the Shelburne Little League. Robert was transferred to South Florida when Pat was only eight years old. The Putnams settled in Fort Myers, where the climate allowed Pat to play baseball throughout the year.

After graduating from Fort Myers High School in 1972, Pat attended Miami Dade North Junior College on a baseball scholarship. Following his second year at the junior college he was drafted by the New York Mets, but instead of signing he accepted a scholarship from South Alabama University. Pat's coach at SAU was former major league all-star Eddie "The Brat" Stanky, who'd managed in the majors with the St. Louis Cardinals and Chicago White Sox. Putnam played only one year for Stanky—the Texas Rangers selected him in the first round of the secondary phase of the June 1975 draft, and this time he was offered terms that he couldn't refuse.

Pat Putnam began his professional career with two years in Class A under Wayne Terwilliger, a tough ex-Marine who'd played second base in the majors throughout the 1950s. Though the fifty-year-old "Twig" had been in baseball for most of his life, he was nonetheless astounded by Putnam's performance at Asheville during the summer of 1976. After the season Terwilliger said, "I have never managed anyone like him. He's the best."

According to *The Sporting News*, Putnam was the "most prolific offensive player in the [Western Carolina League's] history." He batted .361, hit twenty-four home runs, and drove in 142 runs—an average of one per game—to become the WCL's first triple-crown winner. Pat led the WCL in no less than ten offensive departments that season, and he even managed to lead the league's first basemen with a .993 fielding percentage. For his exploits he was named TSN's Minor League Player of the Year, the first Class-A player to earn that honor since Johnny Vander Meer in 1936.

Texas rewarded Pat with a huge promotion to Triple-A in 1977, and the twenty-three-year-old Vermonter proved that he belonged by hitting .301 for Tucson. Impressed, the Rangers called him up to the majors in September. Appearing in eleven games, Pat batted .308 with four doubles among his eight hits as Texas finished a surprising second in the A.L. West. Unfortunately, Putnam had no chance for a starting position in Texas because the Rangers had Mike Hargrove at first base and Richie Zisk at designated hitter. Returning to the Pacific Coast League in 1978, Pat again performed well enough to receive a late-season call-up. This time he batted just .152.

Putnam made the Rangers out of spring training in 1979 after Hargrove and Zisk were traded during the offseason, but still his path to regular playing time was blocked. Only after early-season injuries to Oscar Gamble and Mike Jorgenson did a position open up for him, and he responded by hitting .277 with a team-leading eighteen homers. "It's kind of incredible when you look back and see the things that had to happen, and did happen, for me to be where I am right now," he said at the end of the season. Putnam qualified as a rookie because he hadn't exceeded 130 at-bats during his two previous stints with the Rangers, and both *The Sporting News* and Topps baseball cards named him 1979 A.L. Rookie of the Year. No less an authority than Earl Weaver predicted Pat would eventually win an MVP award.

With his prominence came increased attention from the press, and in its issue of June 7, 1980, *The Sporting News* stated that "Putnam belongs on any all-whacko list for his proclivities of eating dog biscuits, imitating Shamu the Whale in the whirlpool and assorted other eccentricities." Though he says he'd just as soon not tell the world about it, the soft-spoken Putnam doesn't deny eating dog biscuits.

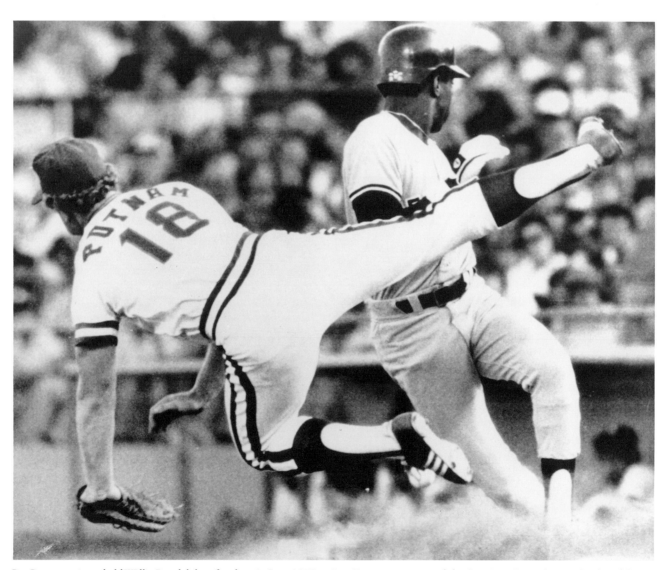

Pat Putnam tries to hold Willie Randolph at first base in June 1979 action. Putnam was named the American League's 1979 Rookie of the Year by The Sporting News *and Topps baseball cards. [AP photo, courtesy of the National Baseball Hall of Fame Library, Cooperstown, New York]*

Like two other Green Mountain Boys of Summer of his era, Putnam finished his major league career with the Minnesota Twins. [National Baseball Hall of Fame Library, Cooperstown, New York]

Pat Putnam wasn't the only Green Mountain Boy of Summer on those Texas Rangers. In September 1981 pitcher Len Whitehouse made his major league debut with that club, and he remembers meeting fellow Vermonter Putnam. "There were always baseball cards in the locker room, and I'd read on the back of a card that Putnam was from Bethel," says Whitehouse. "He said he was born there and that was about it, but still we sort of bonded."

Putnam's next three seasons with the Rangers weren't as productive as his rookie year, but still he put up decent numbers. Don Zimmer, who took over the reigns as Texas manager in 1981, said, "When you talk about Pat Putnam, you have to talk about potential. He's got the power and the talent to do a lot of things with the bat." But Putnam never became the big RBI man Zimmer had hoped for, and eventually he lost his starting position to Dave Hostetler. On December 21, 1982, Pat was traded to the Seattle Mariners for pitcher Ron Musselman.

The Mariners lost 102 games and finished last in the A.L. West in 1983, but nobody could blame Putnam. Given an opportunity to play regularly, Pat batted .269,

led the Mariners in home runs with nineteen and RBIs with sixty-seven (career highs in both categories), and was chosen the team's MVP by his teammates. Putnam considers that award and his Rookie of the Year honors as his greatest achievements in baseball. But despite coming off his best season in the majors, Putnam lost his job as the Mariners' regular first baseman in 1984 to Seattle native Ken Phelps. It appeared to be a break for Putnam when Phelps broke a finger in the first week of the season, but the Mariners called up Alvin Davis from the minors and gave him the starting assignment.

Davis set or tied team records for most RBI, game-winning RBI, walks, intentional walks, and home runs by a rookie. He was named to the A.L. All-Star team and received the A.L. Rookie of the Year award, becoming the only Mariner to win a major award in the first dozen years of the franchise. On his return Phelps was used as Seattle's primary left-handed designated hitter, making Putnam expendable, especially considering his slow start (a .200 batting average and just two home runs in 155 at-bats). A falling-out with manager Del Crandall didn't help matters. On August 29, 1984, Putnam was sold to the Minnesota Twins.

Pat's short stint in Minneapolis is best forgotten. He batted a miserable .079 in eleven games before injuring ligaments in his fingers. In February 1985 he signed as a free agent with the Kansas City Royals. Spring training in Fort Myers was a homecoming for him, and he was optimistic about his chances of making the team. "I know the opportunity is here," he said. "I know I can still hit." Putnam proved it by blasting a game-winning, three-run homer in an early exhibition, but he was left off the Opening Day roster and spent the entire '85 season with Kansas City's Triple-A affiliate in Omaha.

The next stop in Putnam's career was the Land of the Rising Sun, where the muscular 6' 1", 214-pound redhead stood out among his Japanese teammates. Playing for the Nippon Ham Fighters, the *gaijin* (foreigner) slugged thirty-seven homers and batted .266 over the 1986-87 seasons. Pat's final stint as a professional baseball player was in 1989-90 with the Fort Myers Sun Sox of the Senior Professional Baseball Association, a short-lived winter league for retired players thirty-five and older.

Still a bachelor, Putnam resides in Fort Myers, his hometown of the last thirty-five years, where he owns a business called Home Environment Center, specializing in air and water purification. In language befitting a native Vermonter, Putnam explained that he went into the business because "air and water are two things we use every day, and it seems to make sense that they should be as clean as possible."

JEFF PURTELL

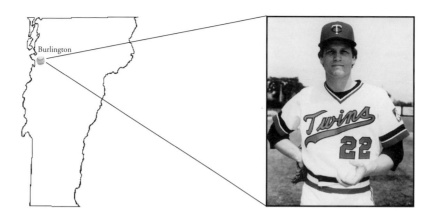

Len Whitehouse

The Vulture

Len Whitehouse's baseball career effectively illustrates the difficulties modern Vermonters face in reaching the major leagues. Whereas nearly all of his competitors hailed from warmer climates, where they could play 100 games in a season, Whitehouse was lucky to play sixteen. "I'd thrown more snowballs than baseballs," the pitcher says. But through perseverance, luck, and the fact that he threw left-handed, Whitehouse managed to reach the majors and hang on for one full season and parts of three others, compiling a 9-4 lifetime record. "There were all sorts of little things that had to happen, and they did," Len said, "but only because I was The Vulture, hanging around waiting for roadkill. When it came, I picked it up."

Leonard Joseph Whitehouse was born in Burlington on September 10, 1957. His father was an I.N.S. accountant, his mother worked at General Electric's armament factory, and his brother, Pat, was already twelve years old. The Whitehouse family moved from George Street to South Union Street and eventually out to the New North End, where Len played his first organized baseball. He threw so hard his Little League coaches made him a pitcher, and in one six-inning game he got all eighteen outs by strikeout. "I probably walked half as many as I struck out, though," Len acknowledged.

As a freshman at Burlington High School, Whitehouse tried out for the varsity baseball team but was cut by Orrie Jay, in the last year of his celebrated coaching career at B.H.S. Len made the team as a sophomore but

was mostly just a pinch-hitter, and it wasn't until his senior year of 1975 that he became a regular starter. Even then he was not the Seahorses' best pitcher. "I would think I was the second pitcher," Len said, "though I don't know if anybody else would." He fared better in American Legion baseball, where he threw the last nine-inning no-hitter in Vermont—games were shortened to seven innings the next year—but scouts still ignored the 5' 9", 135-pound lefty.

After graduating from high school, Whitehouse got a job selling shoes at Sears on Shelburne Road. Then, during the summer of 1976, he received the first of many breaks that helped him reach the major leagues. On a motorcycle trip to California, Len called home from Chicago and learned that he'd been invited to a Pittsburgh Pirates tryout camp in Connecticut. He drove back east for the tryout, and afterwards Branch Rickey III took him aside. "You're not ready yet for the professional ranks so I can't help you out there," Rickey said, "but if you want a good league with good competition, I can tell you who to call."

The name was Claire Wilkins, and she ran the Pinellas County Winter League in Clearwater, Florida. Whitehouse called her, set up a tryout for himself and his friend Scott Moody, a B.H.S. second baseman, and both made the team. The two players rented an apartment together, but only a few weeks later Moody returned to Vermont. Len didn't have enough money to pay the rent on his own, so after he was evicted he tried sleeping on Clearwater

168

Len Whitehouse (middle row, second from left) got his start in Burlington's New North End Little League. [Len Whitehouse]

Clearwater Beach. "A lady police officer came along and said, 'You can't stay here,'" Len said. "I told her I didn't have any place to go, and she said, 'Well, I can tell you where you might be able to get away with this. You know where the causeway is to Tampa? You can pull your car under the bridge.'"

For three weeks Whitehouse slept under the bridge in his '72 Corolla. He gave his parents the number of a nearby pay phone and told them to call him every day at a certain time. "I'd go over there and act like it was my apartment they were calling so they wouldn't worry," Len says. Finally an older couple took him in for the last two months of the season. Whitehouse pitched well enough to appear in the all-star game, in which he struck out five batters in two innings. "After the game I waited around, figuring the scouts we're gonna be all over me," Len said. "Well, nobody showed up. I should have known better. I was 135 pounds, maybe even lighter after sleeping under the bridge."

The season ended just before Thanksgiving, and Whitehouse went home to Vermont thinking about going back to school. Then in early December he received a call from Joe Branzell, a Texas Rangers scout, asking him if he'd like to play professional baseball. Len signed the contract at the Burlington airport on Christmas Day, after which Branzell immediately flew out. "As my signing bonus, I got a keychain and a year-old yearbook," Len said.

When Whitehouse arrived at spring training, Dick Such, the Rangers' minor league pitching coach, asked him to throw the great curveball they'd signed him for. There was some confusion when Len admitted that his curveball wasn't all that good, but he pitched well enough overall to put the rocky introduction behind him. The

Rangers sent him to their Single-A team in Asheville, North Carolina.

The Rangers also administered a psychological test called the Athletic Motivational Profile to all of their players. Whitehouse's report said:

> You have little, if any, respect for coaches and find it difficult to value coaching as a contributor to your athletic development. You resent demands placed upon you by the coach and may be uncooperative with the team captain. This attitude could be reflected in extreme independence.

"That pretty well summed up my attitude towards coaching," Len said, "but they couldn't get rid of me because I had a good work ethic. 'The kid loves baseball, he just loves it,' I'm sure that's what they were saying."

After a rough start in Asheville and demotion to a rookie league his first year, Len began a steady ascent of the Rangers' minor-league ladder. During his second season in Double A, his manager, Wayne Terwilliger, called him into the office and said, "You're getting called up to Charleston. They had an injury up there and they need

Whitehouse wasn't even the best pitcher on the Burlington High School team, but he eventually became the second B.H.S. left-hander to reach the majors (the first was Ray Collins). [Len Whitehouse]

Sporting a Japanese flag bandana, fu manchu, and shades, Whitehouse mugs for the camera with some Asheville teammates before a pro wrestling promotion in 1978. [Len Whitehouse]

somebody to fill a spot." Whitehouse drove all day and night to Columbus, Ohio, where Charleston was playing. When he got there he knocked on the door of Charleston's manager, Tommy Burgess, and said, "Hi, Mr. Burgess, I'm Len Whitehouse and I just got called up from Tulsa." Burgess didn't know anything about it, so he called Joe Klein, the Rangers' minor-league director. It turned out that there was a miscommunication about how badly hurt the other player was, but since Whitehouse was there they decided to put the player on the ten-day disabled list. Len won three games in the ten days and spent the rest of that season at Triple A.

The next year Whitehouse played the entire season at Triple A and put up his best statistics yet, earning a promotion to the Texas Rangers on September 1, 1981. "I flew in that same day, picked up my equipment, got dressed, went out on the field, and into the bullpen," Len remembered. "I'm sitting back, thinking, Aah, this is great. What a great place. This is *big*. I figured I was gonna have a few days to sit back, relax, and get used to what was going on." Then the bullpen phone rang.

Though it was only the second inning, the Toronto Blue Jays were pummeling starting pitcher Danny Darwin, so Texas manager Don Zimmer was calling for Whitehouse. Len remembers the game distinctly:

I was a little nervous and walked the first guy, then I struck out the next guy for the second out of the inning. Then Lloyd Moseby came up. I got two strikes on him real quick, fastballs, and I thought, Well, this is a great time to show Zimmer the stuff I got, being lefty against lefty. I hung an 0-2 slider, a mortal sin, and he hits it out of the park. That was it. I came right out of the game.

Len didn't pitch again until the last day of the season, when none of the veteran pitchers wanted the assignment. He started against the California Angels and got blasted. "I didn't walk people, I just got crushed," Len remembered. "They were hitting rockets. My confidence was shot."

Whitehouse returned to Triple A in 1982 and had the worst year of his baseball life. In his last start of the season he got knocked out in the second inning. Heading back to the clubhouse, he took off his glove and threw it into the stands. "I quit the game, then and there," Len said. "Fifteen minutes later they brought my glove back—some guy returned it. But when I got back to the Denver airport, my luggage was there but my baseball bag with all my equipment never showed up. I figured that was yet another omen." When he got home to Burlington, Len called his agent. "Tell Texas to trade me or release me," he said.

On November 1, 1982, the Texas Rangers traded Len Whitehouse to the Minnesota Twins for pitcher John Pacella. "My dad read it in the *Burlington Free Press*—that's how I found out about it," Len said. At that time he reached a turning point—the player who had "little, if any, respect for coaches" decided to seek some advice. Len went to see Jim Brewer, the old Los Angeles Dodgers relief pitcher who was coaching at Oral Roberts University. "The first day he watched me throw for ten min-

Whitehouse had the worst year of his career with the Denver Bears in 1982. [Len Whitehouse]

utes, then I said, 'Well, what do you think?' He said, 'I can help you, if you can do one thing: forget everything you know about pitching.'" In six weeks with Brewer, Len learned the mechanics of pitching and went from throwing eighty-eight m.p.h. on a good day, eighty-five on average, to throwing ninety-four tops, ninety-two on average. He also gained the ability to place the ball exactly where he wanted.

At spring training that year, Whitehouse was playing an exhibition game in Dunedin when he ran into a woman he hadn't seen in seven years—Claire Wilkins. "Hey, Claire, you'll never guess what happened to me," Len said. "I know, you've made it to the major leagues," said Wilkins, "but how do you think you got started?" She then told him how he came to be signed.

A week after the all-star game in Clearwater in 1976, Joe Branzell, the scout, had asked Wilkins, "Hey, Claire, who was the lefthander who pitched in that game?" Wilkins knew Branzell was pursuing another southpaw who was attracting attention, not Whitehouse. She was also aware that Len wanted to play professionally so badly that he'd lived under a bridge, however, so she gave the scout Len's name and phone number.

"Branzell called me on the phone, set it up, flew up here on Christmas Day to sign this prospect with a great curveball, and ran into me," Len said. "That's why they wanted to see my curveball at spring training. I was a mistake. But it was all sorts of mistakes—opportunities—that allowed me to get to the big leagues."

Whitehouse made the Minnesota Twins out of spring training in 1983, the only year he was with a major league team from start to finish. It was a storybook season for the twenty-six-year-old reliever:

> I remember my first appearance in Yankee Stadium. It was a Friday night and I knew Channel 11 would be carrying the game. We get Channel 11 here in New England and everybody's a Yankee hater—at least everybody in my family—so I knew they'd be watching. I was nervous about that as I walked in, and it's a long way from those monuments to the mound. Ron Davis had loaded the bases for me with two outs in the ninth, and they brought in Lou Piniella to pinch hit. I popped him up and got the save. I was a Red Sox fan growing up—I didn't like the Yankees either—so that was probably the highlight of my career.

Len developed a knack for entering games just before the Twins rallied for come-from-behind wins—which is how he earned his unusual nickname. "They started calling me 'The Vulture' because every time I went in I'd get a victory," he said. "Kent Hrbek used to tell [manager Billy] Gardner just to get me warming up, because every time I toed the rubber, even in the bullpen, we started scoring." Len ended up winning seven of eight decisions that season.

In 1983 Kent Hrbek dubbed Whitehouse "The Vulture" for his habit of scavenging wins from other pitchers. [Len Whitehouse]

He was also leading the American League with sixty appearances with a month left in the season, and was up throwing in probably another fifty games that he never got into. "I always had a rubber arm so I didn't worry about it, but it took its toll," Len said. One day in early September the Twins were playing at Fenway Park when Whitehouse approached pitching coach Johnny Podres and said, "Pods, my arm is dead. Do you mind if I take the day off?" Podres said, "You want a day off, Len, you got it." Whitehouse didn't pitch again the rest of the season.

He also didn't make the club the next year out of spring training. Coming off a 7-1 season with sixty appearances, he didn't even get to pitch in spring training—the Twins just sent him right down to the minors. Eventually he was recalled and put up even better statistics in 1984 than he had in his rookie season, but towards the end of the year he was sent down again to make room for Curt Wardle, who supposedly threw ninety-five m.p.h.

Whitehouse again failed to make the big league club in 1985, but when screwball pitcher Tom Klawitter struggled with his control, Len was recalled three weeks into the season. "I had hurt my arm at Toledo trying to prove everybody wrong by throwing the living heck out of the ball," Whitehouse said. "By the time they called me up I wasn't breaking ninety anymore, and I couldn't throw day after day. In the one game I remem-

Len Whitehouse and family enjoy a Minnesota Twins fantasy camp in 1996. [Len Whitehouse]

ber from '85, I loaded the bases and gave up a grand slam to Ken Singleton, and that was the end of my major league career."

After a couple years in the minors, Whitehouse returned to Vermont, earned his real-estate license, and worked for Hickok and Boardman. "I was terrible," he said. "Just like in baseball, I was a set-up man, not a closer. If anybody had any doubt in their mind that this might not be the house they wanted, I'd show them ten more." Whitehouse sold real estate until 1990, when he went into the autobody business for two years with his brother-in-law. At that point he was working two jobs, doing autobody repairs during the day and teaching pitching clinics at the Baseball Academy until 11 p.m. Eventually he handed over the moonlighting position to Jim Neidlinger, another retired major league pitcher who has settled in Burlington.

Whitehouse currently works as an upholsterer at St. Michael's College. For several years he served as pitching coach at St. Mike's but gave it up when his third daughter was born. Recently he's returned to coaching at the University of Vermont, and he's also been involved with a Minnesota Twins fantasy camp. The camp is like a mini-spring training, and on the last day the pros play a game against the campers. Whitehouse doesn't pitch in those games, however, because of something that happened during the first year he went:

When I pitch I have to go all-or-nothing—I can't throw BP. I have to throw the ball as hard as I can or I can't throw strikes. I get in there and the first two guys I punch out on seven pitches. These are people who haven't played baseball in twenty years, and my pitches are still in the eighties, so they're screaming, "Slow it down." I slow it down and the next thing you know, I'm walking people left and right.

Then up comes this left-handed guy from Warren, a fellow Vermonter who never played any baseball. He's had a great week and he's all excited and ready to hit, and he gets up there and I plunk him right in the middle of the back with a good fastball. He starts walking down to first base and I said, "You don't want to do that. You came here to hit, so get back in there." So he gets back in there and I smash him right in the same spot with another fastball. He ended up taking his base that time. That was that. I never pitched at fantasy camp again.

Still, Whitehouse has enjoyed the overall experience. "The other pros are all bigger names than me, guys like Harmon Killebrew, Tony Oliva, Butch Wynegar, Bert Blyleven," Len said. "It's a fantasy camp for me. I get to hang around with the big shots and act like one, but really I'm just like the campers, having a great time talking to all those guys."

Tom Simon

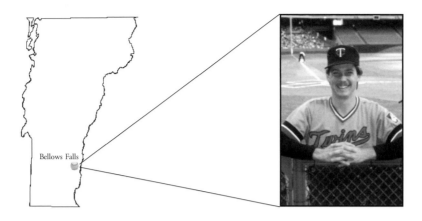

Mark Brown

Two Good Cups of Coffee

If there'd been a maternity ward on the New Hampshire side of the Connecticut River south of Claremont, we would have at least two fewer subjects for this book. That wasn't the case, however, so on July 13, 1959, Mark Anthony Brown, like Carlton Fisk before him, was born in the hospital at Bellows Falls. Crossing the river would be a theme in the lives of all members of the Brown family. For example, Mark's father, who worked his way up from mechanic to management with St. Johnsbury Trucking, commuted mainly to Vermont hubs like Bellows Falls and White River Junction. Though Mark went to school in New Hampshire, he played organized sports in Vermont.

Mark Brown comes from a family that's well-known in local baseball circles. Some say his older brother, Frank, was a better pitcher than Mark. "I was always in his shadow," said Mark, "and up there I probably always will be." Dave, the youngest of the three brothers, was drafted in 1988 by the Baltimore Orioles and pitched one year in the New York-Penn League for Erie, where his pitching coach was Mark. "Dave was wild," observed his coach. "When he came into the game, everybody would see me go for the Tums." Mom was their number one fan and dad their first pitching coach (his philosophy was "grip it and rip it," according to Mark). Even Mark's uncles were involved in baseball, serving as umpires.

Mark Brown followed the precedent of Carlton Fisk—born in Bellows Falls, raised in New Hampshire. And in the small world of Vermont baseball, it should come as

no surprise that the two players had a connection before they took their games to the highest level.

"Border Vermonters" Meet

Back in 1965, when Mark Brown was in grammar school, he served as Carlton Fisk's batboy for the championship Bellows Falls American Legion team. Mark's uncles umpired Fisk's games, so they brought the six-year-old to the field with them and charged him with retrieving the bats. Did the two future major leaguers ever speak? Brown doesn't think so. "I was a little kid," he said. "To me [Fisk] looked like a giant."

Brown does credit Fisk for opening doors. "It all started with Pudge Fisk," Brown said. "Here he was, some big old hick from the Twin States, playing for Bellows Falls Legion Post Five. Then he gets to the Vermont State Championship, and everyone saw the guy and said, 'Wow! There are actually some guys who can play.' That gave guys like myself an opportunity."

But did the two Bellows Falls "natives" ever meet in the majors? Their careers overlapped chronologically, after all, and both were in the American League. The answer, as Brown tells it, is yes and no. Yes, Brown was with the Twins in 1985 when they played Fisk's White Sox at Comiskey Park. And no, he couldn't get up the courage to approach Fisk.

"Logistics got in the way," Brown said. "[Fisk] wouldn't come out of batting practice until late, so it was hard to see him. He was always kind of tough to approach—kind of standoffish and a very tough guy. A

Nine-year-old Mark Brown poses before heading off to a Little League game in Bellows Falls. Mark's entire family was active in the local baseball scene while he was growing up. [Mark Brown]

nice guy once you get a chance to know him, but he won't let you in, that type of guy. A typical New Englander. I should have tried to break down the barrier and say hi, but I didn't do it."

It was clear from the start that Mark Brown would turn out to be an exceptional baseball player. While he was still a teenager his fastball was clocked at eighty-eight m.p.h. During the first of his two seasons playing for American Legion Post Five (the same team he'd served as batboy), the team would have won a state championship, claims Mark, if his brother Frank hadn't hurt his arm. After two years at Fall Mountain High School, Mark spent his junior and senior years at the Loomis-Chaffee School in Windsor, Connecticut. In two seasons in the New England Prep School League, Brown pitched eighty innings, allowed thirty hits, struck out 157 batters, and was 8-2 with a school record 1.35 ERA. He also pitched a no-hitter during his senior year of 1977.

Following his freshman year at the University of Massachusetts, Mark joined the semipro Saxtons River [Vermont] Pirates. The team compiled a 33-6 record in the Twin-State League during the summer of 1978, then went 38-11 after jumping to the newly revived Northern League in '79. Brown pitched some gems for the Pirates: a no-hitter and fifteen strikeouts against the Burlington A's; a one-hitter against Hartford, New York; a seventeen-strikeout performance against the Burlington Expos; eighteen more strikeouts in a win over Essex; and seventeen k's again, this time against the A's. Two-thirds of the way through the '78 season, Brown's numbers were as impressive as his prep school stats: a 7-2 record and 108 strikeouts in fifty-five innings pitched.

In Brown's two losses he allowed a grand total of one earned run, and even that he did with style. The date was July 11, 1978, and the Pirates were taking on the Brattleboro Maples in a night game at Brattleboro's Stolte

Mark uncorks a pitch during his senior year at the Loomis-Chaffee School in Windsor, Connecticut. [Mark Brown]

Mark Brown pitches for Saxtons River against the Brattleboro Maples in one of his last Northern League appearances before he was drafted by Baltimore. In fact, the newspaper caption that appeared with the photo was headlined "An Oriole." [Mark Brown]

still speaks reverently about Burlington's Centennial Field, and the Brattleboro field where chickenwire screens protect the dugouts still makes him chuckle. Brown has also constructed a hypothetical ballpark in his mind, a catch-all place to capture memories of baseball in Vermont:

> I remember, in the summer time, just playing. There'd be one piece of fence in center field, then there'd be a cow pasture in right, then where you warmed up off the bench there'd be another cow pasture, there'd be cow corn growing. Or, behind the backstop, if you lost the ball, it was probably in a tree pit.
>
> All those fields, all those places. Everybody was into it. Even if there were only fifty people there and they had to pass the hat to pay the umpire, they were into it. It was such a good time, such a good bunch of guys to play with. It would be neat to get all those old guys together, maybe play some old men's softball.

Despite finishing his junior year at UMass with a disappointing 4-6 record, Brown was selected early in the sixth round of the 1980 draft. He met with scouts at his home in North Walpole and took all of five minutes to accept Baltimore's initial offer of $7,500. Then it was off to rookie league in Bluefield, West Virginia, and soon thereafter to Class-A ball in Miami. After ten appearances, all starts, his ERA stood at 4.73—almost a full run higher than it would be at any other stop in his minor league career.

Eventually Brown returned to New Hampshire after the Orioles shut him down for the rest of the season due to a sore shoulder. The injury—tendinitis, officially—was slow to heal, forcing him to miss the first part of the 1981 season. "It's kind of a bummer," Brown said, looking back. "You're twenty-one years old, it's your first full year of pro ball, and you're on the disabled list." The injury taught him to be a better all-around pitcher, even if it tempered his velocity. His newfound knowledge helped him rise rapidly through the minors.

Each time Brown was promoted he lowered his ERA. The best example is 1982, when Brown went from A to AA to AAA while his ERA dipped from 3.10 to 2.09 to 1.42. By 1983 he'd earned a spot on Baltimore's forty-man roster and his first invitation to major league spring training. After being assigned to the Orioles' top farm team in Rochester, New York, Brown suffered a torn labrum and missed parts of June, July, and August. The next year he returned to Rochester and enjoyed an eventful summer. First he got engaged. He also pitched well in forty-four games. Then on August 9, 1984, Mark Anthony Brown became the thirty-fourth and, to this date, last Vermonter to play in the major leagues.

The first big league batter Brown faced, Julio Franco, smashed a line drive off his knee. To add insult to injury,

Field. Pitted against Brown was Dave Klenda, a former Tidewater Tide who'd joined the Maples the previous week after seven years in the minors, and for eight innings the two pitchers matched zeroes. Saxtons River had managed a couple of singles, but Brown was no-hitting the Maples. Three outs later, Klenda closed out his line: nine innings, two hits, zero runs, twelve strikeouts, and four walks. In the bottom half of the inning, Brattleboro's Pete Campbell stepped to the plate with one out and hit a towering home run to win the game.

As time passed, the legend of that night grew, and so, according to Mark Brown, did its legacy: a revival of interest in the local hardball circuit. "It was such a big night for baseball," Brown said. "[The fans] saw that it was really good baseball, not some beer league, with good pitching, good hitting, and good fielding. And the game was such a thriller." The *Rutland Herald* called Campbell's game-winner a "story-book finish to a fine ball game." Officially, the *Brattleboro Reformer* spoke in more muted prose, citing a "dramatic end to a well-played contest." Off the record, though, reporter Ken Campbell took on a more excitable tone, according to Saxtons River coach Dave Moore. "He told me it was the best game he'd ever seen," Moore said. Of course Campbell would say that—it was his own son who hit the home run!

Other Brown memories revolve around places. The man may have played in major league ballparks, but he the hit went for an infield single, and, worst of all, it came on what Brown thought was a good pitch. "I threw him a real nasty slider on the outside corner and he took it right off my kneecap. [The ball] trickled over to first base. I hobbled over there and just watched him run to first, and he was safe." Brown pitched on and was hit hard. He gave up another hit, Cal Ripken made an error, and a 4-4 tie was suddenly a 6-4 deficit. "I had my first appearance, my first loss, and my first sore knee," Brown said. "I finished the inning, then [manager] Joe Altobelli took me out. He thought I might hurt my knee more by throwing for another few innings."

"It was alright, it wasn't really hurt bad," Brown said. "It was funny, I got to the clubhouse and I remember Mike Flanagan coming up to me, patting me on the back, saying, 'Oh yeah, welcome to the big leagues, even the outs here are hard.'" Brown says those words from a fellow New Hampshire resident meant a lot to him, as did the treatment he received during each of his five summers in the Baltimore chain. "They were a great organization," he says. "When I went well, they promoted me; when I was hurt, they put me on the disabled list; when I got to the big leagues they were good to me, they gave me a shot."

Mark Brown pitched well for Baltimore over the last couple months of the '84 season. In nine games he gave up fewer hits than innings pitched and struck out more batters than he walked. To cap it off, he picked up his first—and, as it turned out, only—big league win on the last day of the season, striking out Red Sox slugger Jim Rice for his final out. Then Brown and his teammates set off on a three-week, fifteen-game barnstorming tour of Japan, playing five games against the Yomiuri Giants, another five against the Hiroshima Carp, and four more against regional all-star teams. "In Japan we played on a couple of skin fields," Brown said, referring to all-dirt, no-grass infields. "It was just like Vermont—you could pick up boulders."

The following spring the Orioles, satisfied that they'd seen what Brown could do and in need of more balance in their bullpen, traded him to the Minnesota Twins for lefthander Brad Havens. Baltimore's pitching staff was talented (second in the A.L. in ERA in 1984) and extravagantly deep, whereas Minnesota's bullpen had closer Ron Davis and a lot of problems. Best of all for Brown, the Twins' new manager, Ray Miller, had been the Orioles' pitching coach. Here was a chance to establish himself with an emerging team with good hitting, good defense, and little pitching.

Brown pitched well at Triple-A Toledo, where he was first assigned by the Twins. The parent club, meanwhile, continued to get shelled. By late June, when Brown was called up, Minnesota's team ERA was a league-worst 4.84.

Brown drove all night to get to Minneapolis and the Twins' infamous indoor stadium. "I couldn't wait to get there. 'Gotta get to the Metrodome,' I kept saying." This time the Bellows Falls native decided to take some serious stock of his situation. "It kind of struck me: small town boy makes it to the big leagues. Here I am again!"

A Conspiracy Against Vermonters?

In a cruel twist of baseball fate, when the Minnesota Twins recalled Mark Brown from the minors in 1985, the pitcher he replaced was fellow Vermonter Len Whitehouse. It was a remarkable coincidence, especially considering that only three of the close to 1,000 players active in 1985 hailed from the Green Mountains. Was there some quota on Green Mountain Boys in the major leagues?

Brown remembers the circumstances clearly. "Lenny Whitehouse met me at the clubhouse, and he told me he was being sent down, and it would be really helpful if he didn't have to close out the lease and lose all this money if I would just move into his apartment," Brown said. "So that's how I got the chance to meet him. I said, 'I hate to meet you under these circumstances,' and Whitehouse said, 'That's all right.'"

Brown earned the only win of his major league career with the Baltimore Orioles at Fenway Park on September 30, 1984. [Mark Brown]

For his part, Whitehouse has blocked it out of his memory: "I don't remember anything from '85 except giving up a grand slam. It was a bad year for me. But the way I understand it, the guy who replaced me when I was sent down was Mark Brown, and not only did he take my job, he also took my apartment. I was only there for a week so I don't even remember where I was living."

Brown got bombed in his first outing and after two weeks his ERA stood at 11.57. By August he'd almost halved it to 6.89, but by then it was too late. Brown was sent back to Toledo, his roster spot taken by the talented but oft-suspended drug offender, Steve Howe. Back with the Mudhens, Brown was united with Len Whitehouse, the two Green Mountain Boys of Summer playing together for the first time. To his credit, Brown pitched admirably. His ERA was 2.94, he reduced his walks-to-innings-pitched ratio to an all-time low, and his arm felt great. Unfortunately, no one seemed to care.

Brown went to spring training in 1986 hoping to get one more shot, but he was immediately sent down to Toledo. Then he got released. Brown went home, thinking, Who's going to pick up a twenty-seven-year-old reliever three weeks into the season? The surprising answer was Baltimore. Brown played out the year at Double-A Charlotte, where he'd pitched so well five years earlier as an up-and-coming prospect. Now he was heading the other direction. "My low point came when I got put on the disabled list and I wasn't even hurt," Brown said.

He returned to Rochester and played in an adult league for a couple of seasons, intending to play first base exclusively but eventually giving in and pitching a few games. Mark enjoyed playing with his brother Dave for the first time but ended up hurting his shoulder.

After his pitching career ended, Brown coached in the New York-Penn league with the Erie Orioles. [Mark Brown]

Today Brown lives in the Kansas City, Missouri, area with his wife and three daughters. He remains an active instructor and mentor for young ball players as the youth pastor and athletic director for his church. He also instructs at Mac-N-Seitz, an indoor facility run by fellow major leaguers Mike McFarlane and Kevin Seitzer. He talks about wanting to share his love for the game, and about how maybe he can help kids realize their dreams, or better yet, get a good education thanks to sports.

In the end, *Total Baseball* shows that Mark Brown had but a single major league win. To some that may seem sad, but a dozen years later it doesn't seem to bother the man himself. "I only got a couple cups of coffee," the Vermonter said, breaking into a wide smile. "But they were good cups."

JEREMY ROSENBERG

Flatlanders of Summer

Three of Vermont's Finest Non-Native Major Leaguers

For a player to become a Green Mountain Boy of Summer, *Total Baseball* had to list him as having been born in Vermont. As previously discussed, *Total Baseball* is not infallible. Our research led to the determination that three players traditionally included in this elite group were born outside of Vermont's borders. The inclusion of two of those players (Arlington Pond and Crip Polli) in *Green Mountain Boys of Summer* reflects their significant contributions to Vermont baseball, despite their misfortune of having really been born "away."

Yet there is an impressive—and growing—list of players who are without question "flatlanders" by birth, but who have been claimed by Vermont and Vermont baseball at some time in their lives. Documenting all of them would be an impossible task, but some of the players stand out for their their success on the diamond and long-standing commitment to the state. In the end, three men—Tony Lupien, Bill Lee, and Mike Rochford—merit notice in any Vermont baseball book.

Though the paths of the three players were different, their ties to Vermont are strong. Unlike several Green Mountain Boys of Summer who moved out of state before they began their baseball careers, Mike Rochford moved here very young and developed his skills in-state. In fact, he and Len Whitehouse are the only players from Vermont high schools to play in the majors in the last forty years. Tony Lupien and Bill Lee, on the other hand, fell in love with Vermont and settled here as adults after successful major league careers. They both became teachers of the game, passing their knowledge to a new generation of players.

Tony Lupien

Ivy League Leader

Tony Lupien has led what can be considered the quintessential New England baseball life. Born in 1917 in Chelmsford, Massachusetts, Ulysses John Lupien, Jr., known as "Tony" or "Lupe," grew up in a baseball family. His father had played semipro baseball to help fund his Harvard education, and he passed along his expertise to his four sons. Though he was never very big, growing to 5' 8", Ulysses, Jr., excelled in baseball and the other sports he tried.

When he followed his father and two of his brothers to Harvard, Tony played quarterback on the freshman football team and first base on the baseball team. His exploits on the diamond caught the eye of Billy Evans, director of the Red Sox farm system. Evans offered to cover Tony's tuition at Harvard until graduation on two conditions: first, that Tony play baseball after getting his degree; and, second, that he give up playing football. Tony had a lot of potential in football, so it wasn't an easy decision, but once he made it he never looked back.

Tony was ready to sign when the Red Sox contacted him shortly after his graduation in 1939. He reported to the Scranton Miners to begin what turned out to be a quick climb through the minor leagues. At the end of the 1940 season Boston promoted him to the majors, and he trained with the team in the spring of 1941. The legendary Jimmie Foxx held onto his spot for that year, but by 1942 it was clear he was on his way out. "You don't succeed a player like Foxx," Lupien said. "I only followed him at first base."

Tony started slowly in Boston, but he became a solid player both in the field and at the plate. Perhaps his biggest drawback was a lack of power—he finished his career with only eighteen home runs in six seasons—and he was traded to Philadelphia in 1944 despite good numbers in other areas of the game. After one season with the Phillies, Lupien enlisted in the Navy for a short time at the end of World War II, then returned to find that Philadelphia had sold his contract to the minor-league Hollywood Stars.

Lupien fought the trade, eventually filing a lawsuit when his attempts at informal resolution failed. Years later he co-authored *The Imperfect Diamond,* a book that expresses his dissatisfaction with how major league baseball is run. But while his case was pending, Tony excelled on the field for Hollywood, capturing the Pacific Coast League's MVP award in 1947. His performance earned him a promotion to the Chicago White Sox, for whom he played every inning of the 1948 season, his final year in the majors.

After a few years without baseball, Tony began coaching the Jamestown, New York, PONY League team in the summer. His winter job, as coach of the Middlebury College basketball team, began what is now a "half-century love affair" with Vermont. Tony found stability in 1956 when Red Rolfe hired him as the baseball and freshman basketball coach at Dartmouth College. Respected as one of "the outstanding teachers at Dartmouth," Tony never recruited and stressed teamwork and values to his players. Nonetheless, his 313 wins and four EIBL championships attest to his teams' competitive excellence. Lupien retired to his Norwich, Vermont, home in 1977.

Tony Lupien's experiences in baseball are best summed up by Tony himself—it has been "a gypsy life for many years, a life of hardship, but a wonderful life."

PAT O'CONNOR

Bill Lee

A Lefty in the Kingdom

Although born, raised, and educated in California, Bill Lee has called Craftsbury, Vermont, home since 1988. Lee moved to friendly territory, because his stellar pitching for the Boston Red Sox and Montreal Expos had made him a local favorite long before he decided to settle in the Green Mountains.

After playing for the national powerhouse University of Southern California baseball program in the mid-1960s, Lee embarked on a successful fourteen-year major league career. He reached the top of his game in the mid-1970s, compiling three straight seventeen-win seasons for the Boston Red Sox. He started Game Seven of the classic 1975 World Series against the Reds, taking a 3-2 lead into the seventh inning before being relieved. In all, Lee won 119 games before he left the majors in 1982 at the age of thirty-six.

Despite his success, Lee is remembered as well, if not better, for his maverick ways than his pitching. Known as the "Spaceman" for his independence of thought, whimsical humor, and global concern, Lee became a hero to many people in the post-Vietnam 1970s, but he often clashed with team management and the baseball establishment. The Red Sox traded him to Montreal in 1978 after he feuded with manager Don Zimmer, calling Zimmer a "gerbil" among other things.

Lee's four-year stay with the Expos was also tempestuous, and his release after an altercation with the manager there ended his major league career. Bill Lee was by no means done playing baseball, however, and the night after he was cut by Montreal, he suited up and played in a Quebec Senior League game. He played in Canada for six more years, eventually settling in Monkton, New Brunswick.

Lee was a natural for the new baseball fantasy camp industry. In 1987 the developers of the first Red Sox fantasy camp, John and Steward Savage of Rutland, drove all the way to Monkton to persuade Lee to attend. "I said sure," Lee explains. "I was flattered. I decided my professional career was over. [Wife] Pam and I wouldn't go to Venezuela for winter ball; instead we would go to the fantasy camp and then to Vermont. We had been thinking about living in Vermont anyway."

After making temporary living arrangements during their first year in the Green Mountains, the Lees found their own piece of Vermont. "Scott Reed was at that first fantasy camp. He had a spot of land he would sell us in Craftsbury. It was on a hill looking across to the Common. It was gorgeous, the most beautiful place I had ever seen. We could hear the bells ringing on the Common in the mornings. 'This is it,' we said, and the rest is history."

Bill Lee is now in his fifties, but he remains first and foremost a ballplayer, a barnstormer on the move to senior tournaments, fantasy camps, exhibitions, and so forth throughout the year. He will go almost anywhere to play, instruct, or speak about the game. "I've got to get to Albania," he says. "I want to play baseball in all the Communist countries." Bill Lee is still the Spaceman, but now he is a Vermont treasure too.

KARL LINDHOLM

Mike Rochford

A Vermonter But By Birth

If not for his father's short-term transfer to New Hampshire, Michael Joseph Rochford would not only be a Green Mountain Boy of Summer, but one of the rare modern players who actually grew up and developed his game in Vermont. Though the state cannot claim him as a native, Rochford is truly a product of Vermont baseball.

Rochford's family returned from Salem, New Hampshire, shortly after Mike was born in 1963. They settled in South Burlington, which soon developed one of the best baseball programs in the state, and Mike prospered on teams that regularly contended for state titles at the Little League and Babe Ruth levels. By the time he reached high school, the left-hander had grown to 6' 3" (he eventually reached 6' 4" and 205 pounds).

Rochford loomed large in sports all three seasons at South Burlington High School. In fall he quarterbacked the football team and was Vermont's Player of the Year as a senior. In winter he was a four-year starter on the basketball team and helped the Rebels reach the state semifinals as a senior. In spring, of course, he starred as a pitcher and first baseman, and he finished off his astonishing senior-year exploits by shutting down Rutland 4-2 with thirteen strikeouts in the state title game. Mike finished the year 10-0 with a 0.20 ERA.

Numbers like that usually attract attention, but Rochford went undrafted. He played with the Burlington Expos that summer, then headed south to Santa Fe Community College in Gainesville, Florida, a junior college baseball powerhouse. The move paid off in January 1982,

when he was selected by the Boston Red Sox in the first round of the secondary draft. The Red Sox signed him after he completed the 1982 spring season at Santa Fe.

Mike excelled at Elmira in the New York-Penn League in 1982, then at Winston-Salem in the Single-A Carolina League the following year. His jump to Triple-A Pawtucket in 1984 resulted in his first losing record, but a short demotion to Double-A New Britain got him back on track, and he performed well at Pawtucket for the 1986-87 seasons.

Mike pitched well for the PawSox in 1988, also, and in September he finally got the call to the majors, coming out of the bullpen to face left-handed hitters during Boston's successful pennant run. He began 1989 back in Pawtucket, but on Boston's forty-man roster. The Red Sox recalled him in mid-season, and he pitched in four games out of the bullpen.

With Boston's pitching staff depleted in 1990, Mike had a shot at making the starting rotation. Early in the season he took the mound against Detroit. Unfortunately, the Tigers pounded him, and he pitched in only one more game before being sent back to Pawtucket. His major league career was over just as it seemed it was beginning, but Rochford never became bitter about how things turned out—he was grateful for the opportunity he was given.

After winding up his professional baseball career in Japan, Mike found a new profession that still allowed him to use his athletic talent—teaching golf. He is currently the head pro at a country club in Boca Raton, Florida.

BRUCE BOSLEY

Green Mountain Boys of Summer Cumulative Statistics

Position Players

Player	Years Played	G	Avg.	Sllg %	AB	Hits	HR	RBI	R	BB	SO
F. Mann	1882-87	577	.262	.383	2,277	597	12		388	163	41
F. Olin	1884-85	49	.316	.379	177	56	1		29	13	
T. Lynch	1884-85	42	.258	.358	159	41			20	19	8
D. Hazelton	1902	7	.130	.130	23	3				2	
A. McConnell	1908-11	409	.264	.319	1,506	398	3	119	200	107	
L. Gardner	1908-24	1,922	.289	.385	6,684	1,931	27	929	867	654	282
H. Stafford	1916	1	.000	.000	1	0	0	0	0	0	0
E. Bowman	1920	2	.000	.000	1	0	0	0	1	1	0
B. Murray	1923	10	.179	.205	39	7	0	0	2	0	1
B. Tebbetts	1936-52	1,162	.270	.358	3,705	1,000	38	469	357	389	261
R. Lapointe	1947-48	143	.266	.296	433	115	1	30	60	34	9
C. Fisk	1969, 1971-93	2,499	.269	.457	8,756	2,356	376	1,330	1,276	849	1,385
P. Putnam	1977-84	677	.255	.408	1,989	508	63	255	223	144	260
Totals		7,500	.272	.401	25,750	7,012	521	3,132	3,423	2,376	2,247

Pitchers

Player	Years Played	W	L	Pct.	ERA	G	GS	CG	IP	H	BB	SO
H. Porter	1884-89	96	107	.473	3.70	207	206	201	1,793.1	1,893	466	659
L. Viau	1888-92	83	77	.519	3.33	178	162	146	1,442.0	1,441	526	554
H. Burrell	1891	5	2	.714	4.81	7	4	3	43.0	51	21	19
B. Abbey	1892-96	22	40	.355	4.52	79	66	52	568.0	688	192	161
A. Pond	1895-98	35	19	.648	3.45	69	57	46	496.0	517	150	156
E. Doheny	1895-1903	75	83	.475	3.75	183	168	140	1,392.2	1,412	665	567
F. Dupee	1901	0	1	.000	∞	1	1	0	0.0	0	3	0
J. Dubuc	1908-19	86	76	.531	3.04	258	150	101	1,444.1	1,290	577	438
R. Collins	1909-15	84	62	.575	2.51	199	150	90	1,345.0	1,251	271	513
C. Evans	1909-10	1	4	.200	4.96	17	4	1	52.2	53	41	23
R. Fisher	1910-20	100	94	.515	2.82	278	208	110	1,755.2	1,667	481	680
B. Smith	1913-15	1	0	1.000	4.31	17	4	1	52.2	53	41	23
G. Leclair	1914-15	8	10	.444	3.36	55	19	12	236.0	222	61	91
D. Keefe	1917-22	9	17	.346	4.15	97	27	12	353.2	403	113	126
H. Hulihan	1922	2	3	.400	3.15	7	6	2	40.0	40	26	16
S. Slayton	1928	0	0	.000	3.86	3	0	0	7.0	6	3	2
L. Polli	1932, 1944	0	2	.000	4.68	24	0	0	42.1	55	23	11
W. Lanfranconi	1941, 1947	4	5	.444	2.96	38	5	1	70.0	72	29	19
E. Johnson	1950-59	40	23	.635	3.77	273	19	3	574.2	587	231	319
L. Whitehouse	1981, 1983-85	9	4	.692	4.68	97	1	0	115.1	119	65	68
M. Brown	1984-85	1	2	.333	5.12	15	0	0	38.2	43	14	15
Totals		661	631	.512	3.38	2,100	1,254	920	11,845.8	11,851	3,979	4,347

Vermont High School Players in the Major League Draft

Player	Year	Round	ML Team	Hometown	Position	High School (College)
Robert Danaher	1967	32	Houston	Montpelier	RHP	Montpelier H.S.
Daniel DeMichele	1967	2*	NY (NL)	Cranston, RI	OF	Vermont Academy
Don Picard	1968	10	St. Louis	Winooski	LHP	Winooski H.S. (Lyndon State College)
Harmon Bove	1968	27	Houston	Burlington	C	Burlington H.S.
Michael McDonald	1968	49	Kansas City	Rutland	C-1B	Vermont Academy
John Luman	1968	6*	Oakland	Burlington	RHP-OF	Burlington H.S. (Vermont Technical College)
David Lapointe	1969	49	Montreal	Winooski	SS	Winooski H.S./VT Academy (University of Vermont)
Gary Smith	1971	10	Houston	Gilman	LHP	Concord H.S.
Kevin Carney	1972	24	Montreal	Burlington	C	Burlington H.S. (Rollins College)
Kevin Carney	1973	4*	California			
Gerry Greene	1974	31	Montreal	Essex Jct.	C	Essex H.S. (University of Massachusetts)
Dale Halvorson	1975	5	Montreal	Essex Jct.	LHP	Essex H.S. (U.S. Naval Academy)
Delbert Stacy	1978	48	Cleveland	Rutland	RHP	Rutland H.S.
Jon Soderberg	1979	13	Chicago (AL)	Essex Jct.	RHP	Essex H.S. (Lousiana State University)
Bob Valliant	1980	6	Montreal	Wells River	LHP	Oxbow Union H.S.
Ken Martin	1980	11	NY (AL)	Waterbury	RHP	Burlington H.S.
Bill Currier	1981	6	Philadelphia	Essex Jct.	OF	Essex H.S. (University of Vermont)
Jeff Greene	1981	19	Los Angeles	Essex Jct.	SS	Essex H.S. (University of Vermont)
Mike Rochford	1982	1*	Boston	S. Burlington	LHP	S. Burlington H.S. (Santa Fe Community College)
Gary Parmenter	1983	1*	Chicago (NL)	Bennington	RHP	Mt. Anthony Union H.S. (University of South Carolina)
Scott Morse	1986	5	Texas	Saxtons River	RHP	Bellows Falls H.S. (University of Maine)
Matt Raleigh	1992	14	Montreal	Swanton	IF	Missisquoi Union H.S. (Western Carolina)
Matt Murphy	1993	28	Milwaukee	Woodstock	LHP	Woodstock H.S. (University of Vermont)
Bill Vielleux	1993	48	Chicago (NL)	White River Jct.	SS	Hartford Union H.S.
Eric Leblanc	1996	33	Cincinnati	North Troy	LHP	North Country Union H.S. (College of St. Rose)
Chris Richard	1998	38	Montreal	Burlington	OF	Burlington H.S. (Norwalk CT Tech)
Chris Richard	1999	45	Montreal			

*indicates January draft, secondary phase; all others selected in June draft, regular phase

Index

Hemming, George, 29
Henricksen, Olaf, 82
Herrmann, Garry, 49, 92
Herzog, Buck, 106
Higgins, Bob, 58-59
Hilltop Park (N.Y.), 60, 88
Hiroshima Carp, 177
Hoblitzell, Dick, 67
Hobson, Butch, 163
Hockey, 52, 54, 55, 95
Hoey, Jack, 58
Hoffer, Wizard, 29-30
Holloway, Sterling, 114
Hollywood Stars, 180
Holy Cross, College of the, 50, 58, 74, 134
Holyoke, Mass. (team), 13, 87
Hooper, Harry, 48, 61-62, 67-68, 69, 81, 82, 120
Hoosick Falls, N.Y., 83
Hopkinton, N.H. (team), 158
Hornsby, Rogers, 136
Hostetler, Dave, 167
Howarth, Oberlin, 36
Howe, Irwin M., 85
Howe, Steve, 178
Howell, Roy, *161*
Hrbek, Kent, 171, *172*
Hubbard, Jesse, 79
Hubbell, Carl, 134
Hulihan, Dorothy Hightower, 116
Hulihan, Harry, **115-17**, *115-17*
Hulihan, Patrick C., 115
Hulihan, Patrick W., 115
Huntington Avenue Grounds (Boston), 60, 76

Imperfect Diamond, The (book), 180
Indianapolis, Ind. (team), 136
Intercity Park (Barre-Montpelier), 73
International League, 11, 48, 49, 102, 104, 113, 131, 139, 146
Interstate League, 59, 73, 146
Iowa State League, 20
Ira Flagstead Day, 125
Ireland, 10, 109
Irwin, Arthur, 88
Italy, 128

Jackson, Joe, 64
Jacksonville, Fla. (team), 131
Jamestown, N.Y. (team), 180
Jamieson, Charlie, 65
Japan, baseball in, 93, 165, 167, 177, 182
Jay, Orrie, 168
Jennings, Hugh, 29, 30, 71
Jersey City, N.J. (team), 131
John, Tommy, 116
John Morrills (team), 23
Johnson, Aline "Inkie" Ingeborg, 151
Johnson, Ben, 85
Johnson, Chris, 156
Johnson, Darrell, 160
Johnson, Dawn, 156
Johnson, Eric "Hootie," 86
Johnson, Ernie, 123, **151-56**, *151-52, 154-56*
Johnson, Ernie Jr., 156
Johnson, Lois Denhard, 153
Johnson, Martin, 150
Johnson, Walter, 38, 52, 78, 91, 120
Johnstown, Pa. (team), 42-43

Joliet, Ill. (team), 19
Jones & Lamson Mill (Springfield, Vt.), 77
Jones & Lamson Mill (Windsor, Vt.), 3
Jones, Davy, 102
Jorgenson, Mike, 166
Josephson, Duane, 161
Judge, Joe, 113

Kaese, Harold, 106
Kake Walk, 72
Kaline, Al, 82
Kansas City Athletics, 111
Kansas City Cowboys, 14
Kansas City Royals, 121, 167
Kasko, Eddie, 162
Katoll, John, 37
Kauff, Benny, 105
Kaufmann, Ewing, 111
Keating, Ray, *90*
Keaton, Buster, 120
Keefe, Charles, 109
Keefe, Charles Jr., 109
Keefe, Dave, 45, 98, **109-111**, *109, 111*
Keefe, Mary, 109
Keeler, Willie, 29, 30, 60
Keenan, Jim, 15
Kelley, Joe, 29, *30*
Kelly, George, 105
Kendall's Spavin Cure, 55
Kennedy, John F., 95
Kerr, Dickie, 92
Kiley, John, 162
Killebrew, Harmon, 173
Kimball, Bud, 110
Kimball Union Academy, 39
King, Stanley, 66
Kinsella, Larry, 23
Kinsella, W. P., 103
Klawitter, Tom, 172
Klein, Joe, 170
Klenda, Dave, 176
Kluszewski, Ted, *139*
Knoxville, Tenn. (team), 110, 131
Konetchy, Ed, 102
Krichell, Paul, 54, 134
Kuhn, Bowie, 96

LaClaire, George. *See* Leclair, George
LaCrosse, Wis. (Team), 101
Lajoie, Napoleon, 31, 86
Lake, Fred, 59, 75
Landgraf, Ernest, 54
Landis, Kenesaw Mountain, 54, 92-93
Lane, F. C., 52
Lanfranconi, Carol Ann, 144
Lanfranconi, Eda Dindo, 141, 143-44
Lanfranconi, Stefano, 139
Lanfranconi, Stephen, 144
Lanfranconi, Walt, 123, 127, **139-44**, *139-41, 143*
Lange, Frank, 98
Lapointe, Catherine Maroney, 145, 149
Lapointe, Ralph, 21, 123, 135, 136, 142, *143*, **145-50**, *145-49*, 158
Lapointe, Zum (George), 145
Lapointe Field House (Burlington, Vt.), 150
Laporte, Frank, 60
Lardner, Ring, 61

LaRosa, Charlie, 154
Lawson, Bob ("Doc"), 41
Lazzeri, Tony, 130, 140
Leclair, George, 85, **100-102**, *100-101*
Leclair, Georges III, 102
Lee, Bill, 162, 179, **181**, *181*
Lee, Leron, 162
Lefler, Wade, 114
Leibold, Nemo, 120
Leonard, Dutch, 79
Levinsky, "Battling," 118
Lewis, Duffy, 62, 69-70, 82, 114
Lincoln Park (Enosburg Falls, Vt.), 59
Little League Baseball, 118, 121, 131-32, 138, 145, 151, 168, *169, 175*, 182
Little Rock, Ark. (team), 102
Lobert, Hans, 105
Lombardi, Ernie, 153
Long Point (Ferrisburgh, Vt.), 93, *93*
Loomis-Chaffee School (Ct.), 175, *175*
Lopez, Al, 136
Lord, Harry, 48, 60, 61
Los Angeles, Cal., 114
Los Angeles Angels, 143-44
Louisville, Ky. (team), 130, 160
Louisville Colonels, 17, 35
Lower Graniteville, Vt. (team), 131
Luddington Mariners, 49
Lupien, Tony, 118, 135, 136, 143, 179, **180**, *180*
Lush, Billy, 88
Lutzke, Rube, 65
Lynch, Ann Reilly, 10
Lynch, Anne Margaret, 11
Lynch, Bartholomew, 10
Lynch, George, 11
Lynch, Mary Agnes Batterbury, 11
Lynch, Thomas J., 10
Lynch, Thomas James, **10-12**, *10-11*, 132
Lynn, Fred, 162, 163
Lynn Shoemakers, 60
Lyons, Harry, 6

Mack, Connie, 29, 60, 65, 107, 110, 115
Mack, Gene, 141
Macon, Ga. (team), 24
Madison Square Garden, 118
Maine State League, 59, 73-74
Maine, University of, 58
Mann, Fred, 1, **3-6**, *3-5*, 13-14
Manning, Bob, 154
Mantle, Mickey, 96
Manville, R. W., 94
Marberry, Firpo, 53
Marion, Marty, 146
Marquard, Rube, 64
Martin, Father, 49
Martin, Phoney, 26
Massachusetts Institute of Technology (MIT), 15
Massachusetts, University of, 175-76
Mathews, Bobby, 26
Mathews, Eddie, 138, 151, 154
Mathewson, Christy, 20, 38, 62, 76, 77, 131
Mayforth, Larry, 79
Mays, Carl, 98
Mays, Willie, 161
McAleer, James, 77
McCahan, Bill, 146

Podres, Johnny, 172
Polli, Battista, 128, 139
Polli, Crip (Lou), 98, 123, **128-32**, *128-32*
Polli, Margaret, 130, 132
Polli, Mary Catherine Smith, 129, *129*
Polo Grounds (N.Y.), 25, 91
Pond, Abbott Sequard, 28
Pond, Arlington, 1, 22, *24*, **28-33**, *28-31*, 45, 74
Pond, Elizabeth Gambrill, 32
Pond, Erasmus Arlington, 28
Pond & Dean Navigation Co., 33
PONY League, 121, 180
Porter, Albert, 13
Porter, Henry, 1, **13-14**, *13*
Portland, Me. (team), 37-38, 73, 126
Portland, Ore. (team), 110
Post, Archie, 67
Post, Wally, 137
Powell, Sen., 69
Powers, Mike, 35
Pownal, Vt. *See* North Pownal, Vt.
Pratt, Del, 92
Proctor, Vt., 112
Proctor, Don, 96
Providence, R.I. (team), 47, 110
Providence College, 121, 133-34
Provincial League, 148
Purcell, Bill, 12
Purtell, Billy, 48
Putnam, Marguerite Burrell, 165
Putnam, Pat, 19-20, 123, **165-67**, *165-67*

Quebec Braves, 148
Quebec Senior League, 181
Queen City Blues, 94

Radbourn, Hoss, 12
Randolph, Vt. (team), 59
Reading, Pa. (team), 109, 113
Reed, Scott, 181
Reese, Pee Wee, 118
Reinsdorf, Jerry, 163
Reiser, Pete, 142
Reulbach, Ed, 39, 42, 73, 74
Reulbach, Nellie Whalen, 42
Reynolds, Michael, 53
Rhode Island Reds, 54
Rhodes, Vadis, 62
Rice, Jim, 163, 177
Richards, Paul, 155
Richbourg, Lance, 119
Richbourg, Lance Jr., 119
Richford Chinese Spies, 57
Richmond, Va. (team), 49
Richmond, Vt., 111
Rickey, Branch, *94*, 134
Rickey, Branch III, 168
Ripken, Cal, 177
Ripley's Believe It or Not, 128
Roberts, Robin, 94
Robertson, Charlie, 120
Robinson, Frank, *137*
Robinson, Jackie, 8, 134, 142, 146
Robinson, Wilbert, *4*, 29, *30*, 106
Rochester Red Wings, 146
Rochester, N.Y. (team), 41, 47, 100, 119, 146, 176, 178

Rochford, Mike, 179, **182**, *182*
Rockefeller Foundation, 32
Rolfe, Red, 180
Rookie of the Year, 161, 165, 167
Rosar, Buddy, 111
Ross, Charlie, 95, *95*
Ross, Charlotte, 95
Ross, Russell, 131
Roth, Braggo, 65
Roth, Frank, 52
Roush, Edd, 92
Royce, Betty, 26
Rusie, Amos, 34
Ruth, Babe, *78*, 79, 104, 109, 126, 130, 155
Rutland, Vt., 1, 28, 115-17
Rutland, Vt. (team), 47, 112, 182
Ryan, Tim, 158-59

Sacco, Nicola, 130
Sacramento, Cal. (team), 110
Sain, Johnny, 142
St. Albans, Vt., 118
St. Albans, Vt. (team), 34-35, 118
St. Albans Railroaders, 57
St. John Cardinals, 148
St. Johnsbury, Vt., 50, 53
St. Johnsbury Academy, 127
St. Johnsbury Senators, 145
St. Joseph's (team), 22
St. Louis Browns, 6, 13, 19, 23, 102, 130, 165
St. Louis Cardinals, 40, 41, *94*, 102, 126, 146
St. Michael's College, 50-51, *51*, 173
St. Paul, Minn. (team), 15, 129-30
St. Peter's Athletic Association, 115
St. Peter's Field (Rutland, Vt.), 117
Salem, N.H., 182
Salt Lake City, Utah (team), 114
San Francisco, Cal. (team), 129
Sanders, Deion, 164
Santa Fe Community College, 182
Saranac Lake, N.Y. (team), 103, *104*, 115
Savage, John, 181
Savage, Stewart, 181
Saxton's River, Vt., 21
Saxton's River Pirates, 175-76, *176*
Scanlan, Frank, 51
Schlafly, Larry, 99
Schmelz, Gus, 15
Schneider, Pete, 91
Schoendienst, Red, 146
Schoppmyer, Leo, 49
Schott, Marge, 34
Schultz, Joe, 136
Schwall, Don, 82
Scranton (Pa.) Miners, 180
Seattle, Wash. (team), 114
Seattle Mariners, 167
Seitzer, Kevin, 178
Selee, Frank, 42
Senior Professional Baseball Association, 167
Sewell, Joe, 65, 96-97
Seymour, Cy, 37
Shea, Spec, 135
Shedd, Harry, 112
Sheib, Carl, 135
Shelburne, Vt., 26
Shelburne (Vt.) Little League, 165
Shibe Park, 77, 106, 110

Shires, Art, 140
Shoeless Joe (book), 103
Shore, Ernie, 79
Silva, Ralph, 157-59, 162
Simmons, Al, 110
Simon, Tom, *68*
Singleton, Ken, 173
Sisler, Dick, 146
Skiing, 123
Slattery, Jack, 105
Slayton, David, 126
Slayton, Grace Lockwood, 126
Slayton, Steve, 123, **125-27**, *125-27*, 139
Slayton, Steve (grandson), 127
Smith, Bob, **98-99**, *98*, 102
Smith, Elmer, 16
Smith, Francis, 66
Smith, Frank, 48
Smith, Harry, 84
Smith, Millie, 99
Snodgrass, Fred, 62
Soccer, 158-59
Society for American Baseball Research (SABR), 68, 99, 133
South Alabama, University of, 165
South Burlington, Vt., 182
South Burlington (Vt.) High School, 182
South Portland (Me.) Shipbuilding Corp., 145
Southern Association, 102
Southern California, University of, 181
Southern League, 6, 11, 24, 49, 114
Southworth, Billy, 153
Spahn, Warren, 138, 141, 154
Spanish-American War, 31-32
Spaulding High School (Barre, Vt.), 125, 127, *127*, 128, 139
Speaker, Tris, 48, 62-66, 69, 77, *78*, 113
Springfield, Mass., 4, 6
Springfield, Mass. (team), 99
Springfield (Vt.) High School, 152
Stackpole, Cy, 86-87
Stafford, Gladys Durkee, 108
Stafford, Harriet, 107-108
Stafford, Heinie, 45, **103-108**, *103-108*
Stafford, Leila Cushing, 103, 106
Stafford, Robert, 108
Stagg, Alonzo, 22, 28
Stahl, Jake, 77-78
Stallings, George, 88
Stanky, Eddie, 165
State Intercollegiate League (N.Y.), 7
Steinbrenner, George, 34
Stengel, Casey, *67*, 95, 153
Stephens, Vern, 135
Sterling, Ford, 114
Stirnweiss, Snuffy, 135
Stolte Field (Brattleboro, Vt.), 176
Storti, Lin, *131*
Strafford, Vt., 1, 39
Strunk, Amos, 64
Suburban League, 135
Such, Dick, 169
Sukeforth, Clyde, 134
Sullivan, Haywood, 163
Sutton, Vt., 3
Swanson, Karl, 132
Swanton (Vt.) Fish Hatchers, 57

About The Editor

Founder and former president of the Larry Gardner Chapter of SABR, Tom Simon is currently working on a history of Vermont's Northern League. As president of Preservation Burlington, Tom is leading the fight for historic preservation and quality of life in downtown Burlington. In his spare time he's a partner in the Burlington law firm of McCormick, Fitzpatrick, Kasper & Burchard, P.C.

About The Contributors

Bob Bennett: At age eleven Bob Bennett wrote an article on Vermont-born major leaguers that was published in the *Rutland Herald.* Now a New York City attorney, Bob is a wine connoisseur who has authored books on autograph collecting and cartoon art.

John Bennett: Trivia buff John Bennett teaches social studies at Mount Anthony Union High School in Bennington, where he lectures to his students about local baseball legend Amby McConnell. He also spent part of his childhood at his grandparents' home in Center Rutland, just a fly ball away from the home of Harry Hulihan.

Bruce Bosley: A resident of South Burlington, Bruce Bosley is the Assistant Sports Information Director at the University of Vermont. During summer he serves as color analyst for the Vermont Expos radio network. One of the highlights of Bruce's baseball career was playing against Len Whitehouse in Babe Ruth League.

Yves Chartrand: A native of suburban Montreal currently working as a reporter in Ottawa, Yves Chartrand is living proof that Expos fans do exist. Yves is writing a collection of stories about French-Canadian major leaguers.

Merritt Clifton: An award-winning muckrake who covered the Vermont/Quebec eco beat for thirteen years, Merritt Clifton is the author of *Disorganized Baseball,* a three-volume history of outlaw professional baseball in Quebec and Vermont. He currently lives in Clinton, Washington, where he is editor of *Animal People*, an independent newspaper about animal protection.

Dominick Denaro: A photographer who produced the late, lamented television show "Vermont Expos Weekly," Dominick Denaro became a Centennial Field icon by leading the fans behind home plate in various cheers. Since then he has moved from South Burlington to Cleveland Heights, Ohio, where he is working in a photo lab.

Mark Dobson: A produce associate at Hannaford Food & Drug in South Burlington, Mark Dobson is internet coordinator for the Vermont Expos. Mark is a Detroit fan whose wedding was attended by former Tiger Lenny Green.

Stan Hamlet: An Underhill Center architect who serves as secretary of the Larry Gardner Chapter, Stan Hamlet is an avid skier, bicyclist, railroad enthusiast, and Red Sox fan. He remembers seeing Walt Lanfranconi pitch at Braves Field.

Chip Hart: An alumnus of Middlebury College, Chip Hart brought glory to the Larry Gardner Chapter by co-managing the runner-up team in SABR's Bill James Fantasy Baseball League. Chip lives in Burlington and works for a medical software company in Winooski.

Seamus Kearney: A regular at the monthly gatherings of the Boston Hot Stove League, a group of Boston-area SABR members whose motto is "Come as you are, when you can; no advance reservation. Look for baseball caps; listen for baseball talk," Seamus Kearney has written extensively on Brattleboro's Island Park.

Dick Leyden: An artist, fly fisherman, and organic gardener who resides in South Hero, Dick Leyden has collected nearly all of the baseball cards of Green Mountain Boys of Summer that are known to exist. Dick is currently painting portraits of all thirty-four Green Mountain Boys of Summer.

Karl Lindholm: Dean of advising and assistant professor of American literature and civilization at Middlebury College, Karl Lindholm is writing a biography of William Clarence Matthews, a Harvard-educated, African-American shortstop who played for Burlington in the 1905 Northern League and whom the Boston Nationals wanted to break the color barrier some forty years before Jackie Robinson.

Jim Mackay: A proud alumnus of the University of Virginia, Jim Mackay joined the Larry Gardner Chapter on its first trip to Cooperstown and has been a loyal member ever since. Jim is founder and co-owner of two motels in Vermont. Since 1946 he has served as self-appointed "High Commissioner" of the Atlantic Coast League, using a card baseball game of his own invention.

Walt Nelson: A retired schoolteacher from Long Island who follows the New York Mets from his home in Middlebury, Walt Nelson spends much of his free time at Vermont Expos games.

Francis Joseph O'Boyle: A resident of "Beautiful Burlington" (as it says on his checks), Francis Joseph O'Boyle is a retired banker who serves as treasurer of the Larry Gardner Chapter. A fan of the St. Louis Browns, Theodore Roosevelt, and corny jokes, Francis spends much of his time these days caring for his grandchildren.

Pat O'Connor: An Anaheim Angels fan and IBM manager who is president of the Larry Gardner Chapter, Pat O'Connor is building a scaled-down version of Fenway Park for wiffle ball in his yard in Essex.

Jeff Purtell: Formerly at The Quechee Club in Quechee, Vermont, Jeff Purtell is currently working as assistant golf professional at Saucon Valley Country Club in Bethlehem, Pennsylvania. Despite his occupation, he prefers baseball history to golf history.

Jeremy Rosenberg: A journalist who works for the *Los Angeles Times*, former South Burlington resident Jeremy Rosenberg has written a manuscript for a novel set in the neighborhood around Fenway Park. Jeremy also serves as executive editor of *Art Connoisseur* magazine.

Lance Richbourg: The son of a lifetime .306 hitter who played for the Boston Braves and Chicago Cubs, fifty-nine-year-young Lance Richbourg still swings a pretty mean stick himself in the Burlington Twilight League. Lance, who has been called "America's foremost baseball artist," lives in Burlington and works as an art professor at St. Michael's College.

Dana Sprague: The president of North Country Natural, Inc., a natural-foods distributorship, Dana Sprague may own Vermont's finest collection of baseball memorabilia. Born and raised in Brattleboro, Dana is one of only three Vermont-born contributors to *Green Mountain Boys of Summer*.

Brian Stevens: Chief Financial Officer of Smugglers' Notch Resort and vice-president of the Larry Gardner Chapter, Brian Stevens loves skiing, snowboarding, golf, sneaker hockey, and the Red Sox, but spends most of his time with his wife, Catherine, doing repairs on his Jericho farmhouse.

Dick Thompson: A registered nurse who resides in Bridgewater, Massachusetts, Dick Thompson is a member of SABR's biographical committee whose passion is obscure players born in New England. Dick is the world's foremost authority on the now-defunct New England League.

Guy Waterman: A retired speech writer who lives as a homesteader in the hills outside East Corinth, Guy Waterman has written extensively on mountain climbing, environmental ethics, and baseball. He is a past vice-president and secretary of the Larry Gardner Chapter.

Praise for *Dimensions of Human Behavior: Person and Environment* and *The Changing Life Course*

"This is the most thorough and comprehensive text on human behavior that I have seen. It brings together the preeminent sociological, psychological, and anthropological theories on human behavior and the social environment. It covers every possible scenario related to the practice of social work one could imagine. Nothing is sacrificed. The case studies reflected the diversity of the range of consumers of social work services and were utilized well as instruments for understanding and applying concepts."

—Gretchen Heidemann, Whittier College, CA

"I like these books a great deal. I will continue to use the texts in my course. I like the way in which it exposes students to various theories. The dimensions for assessing human development and behavior are clear. Because I use both texts together, I feel that students gained an understanding on human development that is grounded in an environmental context."

—Glenda Dewberry, Augsbury College, MN

"Overall, I think the volume-set is excellent. I love the 'big idea' focus, and the attention to environmental contexts."

—Jim Vanderwoerd, Dordt College, IA

"The three greatest strengths of the book are the inclusion of item/topics of spirituality, case studies, and active learning tasks. The chapters dealing with the lifespan (mainly young adulthood and beyond) and the opening chapters of both books (are also great strengths)."

—Annalisa Enrile, University of Southern California

"I am greatly pleased with the text. It emphasizes diversity. There are good illustrations that bring the concepts to life throughout. It is well organized. I teach in an urban context where students tend to practice with the poor. I like the questions that encourage critical thinking."

—Kimberly Mann, Chicago State University

"Our faculty is quite satisfied with the textbooks, *Dimensions of Human Behavior.* The strengths of both volumes include the use of case studies, vignettes and side-bars to help students understand materials contained in the chapter; the use of tables, figures and illustration; and the horizontal and vertical integration of materials connecting themes and models used in the textbooks."

—Parris Baker, Gannon University, PA

"The content of the two books is solid, strong and comprehensive. It is also presented in a way that our students could make good use of it."

—Elisabeth Reichert, Southern Illinois University

"I really liked this book. It is well written, informative, comprehensive, interesting. The greatest strengths are the uniformity in writing style, cohesion among chapters, strong case examples, integration of learning within chapters, and an amazing ability to be comprehensive without the reader getting lost in the details."

—David Spruill, Louisiana State University